The Child Savers

The Child
Savers / *The*

Invention of Delinquency /

by Anthony M. Platt

The University of Chicago Press

CHICAGO AND LONDON

This study is an outgrowth of the research program
of the Center for the Study of Law and Society,
The University of California, Berkeley

The University of Chicago Press, Chicago 60637
The University of Chicago Press, Ltd., London

© 1969 by The University of Chicago
All rights reserved
Published 1969
Second Impression 1972
Printed in the United States of America

International Standard Book Number: 0–226–67070–8 (clothbound)
Library of Congress Catalog Card Number: 69–14827

To Hazel, Daniel, and Rebecca

It is a maxim, trite but true, that the prevention of evil is easier and better than its cure; and in nothing is this maxim more true than in relation to crime. To destroy the seeds of crime, to dry up its sources, to kill it in the egg, is better than repression,—better even than reformation of the criminal. But after all that the best organized and best administered system of public instruction can accomplish, there will remain a considerable residuum of children (it cannot be, to-day, in the United States, less than half a million) whom these systems will not reach. Their destitution, their vagrant life, their depraved habits, their ragged and filthy condition forbid their reception into the ordinary schools of the people. It is from this class that the ranks of crime are continually recruited, and will be so long as it is permitted to exist. They are born to crime, brought up for it. They must be saved.

Enoch Wines (1880)

Contents

Preface

This study was originally supported by the Center for the Study of Law and Society, University of California, with a grant from the Office of Juvenile Delinquency and Youth Development, United States Department of Health, Education and Welfare. Later revisions of the manuscript were completed under the auspices of the Center for Studies in Criminal Justice, University of Chicago.

My interest in the child-saving movement was stimulated during my graduate work at the University of California. My colleagues and teachers played an important part in influencing the character and development of my research. I am especially grateful for the help and encouragement of James Carey, Aaron Cicourel, Bernard Diamond, Joel Goldfarb, Sanford Kadish, Richard Korn, the late Joseph Lohman, David Matza, Neil Ross, Philip Selznick, Mimi Silbert and Alan Sutter. Norval Morris and Hans Mattick encouraged me to revise and publish the study during my stay at the University of Chicago.

Howard Becker and Sheldon Messinger spent many hours reading, discussing, criticizing, editing, and improving earlier versions of the book. Many of their suggestions prompted considerable substantive and stylistic revisions. To both I owe special thanks for their support, patience, and remarkable editorial skills.

The manuscript was revised and retyped several times. Of those who laboriously provided editorial and secretarial services, I am especially grateful to Gloria Neal, Eddie Spinks, Paula Marshall, and Anne Plusser.

My wife is to be commended for sharing me with the child savers for over three years as well as for her editorial and secretarial assistance.

The Child
Savers

Chapter 1: *Introduction*

Contemporary programs of delinquency control can be traced to the enterprising reforms of the child savers who, at the end of the nineteenth century, helped to create special judicial and correctional institutions for the labeling, processing, and management of "troublesome" youth. The origins of "delinquency" are to be found in the programs and ideas of those social reformers who recognized the existence and carriers of delinquent norms. The term "child savers" is used to characterize a group of "disinterested"[1] reformers who regarded their cause as a matter of conscience and morality, serving no particular class or political interests. The child savers viewed themselves as altruists and humanitarians dedicated to rescuing those who were less fortunately placed in the social order. Their concern for "purity," "salvation," "innocence," "corruption," and "protection" reflected a resolute belief in the righteousness of their mission.

This study addresses the origins, composition, and achievements of the child-saving movement in the United States. The child savers went beyond mere humanitarian reforms of existing institutions. They brought attention to—and, in doing so, invented—new categories of youthful misbehavior which had been hitherto unappre-

1. On the concept of "disinterested" reform, see Svend Ranulf, *Moral Indignation and Middle Class Psychology.*

ciated. It is with this recognition and discovery of youthful crime that this study is specifically concerned.

Granted the benign motives of the child savers, the programs they enthusiastically supported diminished the civil liberties and privacy of youth. Adolescents were treated as though they were naturally dependent, requiring constant and pervasive supervision. Although the child savers were rhetorically concerned with protecting children from the physical and moral dangers of an increasingly industrialized and urban society, their remedies seemed to aggravate the problem. This study consequently attempts to locate the social basis of humanitarian ideals and to reconcile the intentions of the child savers with the institutions that they helped to create. Particular attention will be paid to understanding (1) the relationship between social reforms and related changes in the administration of criminal justice, (2) the motives, class interests, aspirations, and purposes of child-saving organizations, (3) the methods by which communities establish the formal machinery for regulating crime, and (4) the distinctions between idealized goals and enforced conditions in the implementation of moral crusades.

PERSPECTIVES ON THE ORIGINS OF DELINQUENCY

Studies of crime and delinquency have for the most part focused on their psychological and environmental origins. The classical approach to social problems, typified by the work of Clifford Shaw, Frederick Thrasher, Henry McKay, Jane Addams and Sophonisba Breckenridge, stressed as causes of delinquency the disorganized features of slum life and the grinding impact of urban industrialism on migrant and immigrant cultures.[2] Shaw and his colleagues depicted delinquency as an inevitable and frustrating reaction to impelling environmental forces. Delinquency was often regarded by

2. See, for example, Clifford R. Shaw and Henry D. McKay, *Juvenile Delinquency and Urban Areas.*

the earlier sociologists as a cultural opiate which drained away the constructive energies of youth.

Other writers have attributed the "delinquency problem" to more specific factors, such as parent-youth conflict, the modern conditions of family life and the lack of sustained primary relationships, the lure of the peer group in subcultures characterized by female-centered households, the increased professionalism of the police, and a growing acceptance of middle-class definitions of normality.[3] In recent years, there has been significant theoretical interest in the nature and origins of delinquent subcultures. Albert Cohen suggests that lower-class boys are driven into delinquent behavior through a process of reaction formation whereby "the delinquent subculture takes its norms from the larger culture but turns them upside down." Cohen found that by standards of the middle-class ethic, a great deal of delinquent behavior is malicious, nonutilitarian, negativistic, hedonistic, versatile, and free from adult restraint.[4] Walter Miller, on the other hand, suggests that the characteristic patterns and focal concerns of delinquency are so deeply embedded in lower-class culture that they are immune to the impact of such middle-class institutions as schools, welfare agencies, the police, and courts.[5]

Another group of theorists, particularly Robert Merton, Richard Cloward, and Lloyd Ohlin, have explored how social structures exert pressure on youth to engage in nonconforming behavior. According to these writers, delinquency may be regarded as a symptom of strain caused by the gap between culturally prescribed aspirations (e.g., monetary success) and socially structured avenues of achieving these goals in a legitimate fashion. Everybody wants to be a success in American culture, but social differentials decide whether

3. Herbert Bloch, "Juvenile Delinquency: Myth or Threat?" *Journal of Criminal Law, Criminology and Police Science* 49 (1958): 303–9. The literature concerning the sociology of crime is too vast to be cited here, but short abstracts of the leading studies can be conveniently found in Marvin E. Wolfgang, Leonard Savitz, and Norman Johnston, eds., *The Sociology of Crime and Delinquency.*

4. Albert K. Cohen, *Delinquent Boys.*

5. Walter B. Miller, "Lower Class Culture as a Generating Milieu of Gang Delinquency," *Journal of Social Issues* 14 (1958): 5–19.

success can be achieved by legal or illegal means.[6] Similarly, Talcott
Parsons suggests that delinquency is a symptom of youth's economic
and political powerlessness in a culture which derogates stupidity
and attaches great significance to educational credentials.[7] Children,
says Parsons, tend to suffer from

> the fact that the major agents for initiating processes of change lie in
> other sectors of the society, above all, in large-scale organization, in the
> developments of science and technology, in the higher political processes,
> and in the higher ranges of culture. . . . This would suggest that . . . the
> adult agencies on which the youth most depends tend to some extent to
> be "out of tune" with what he senses to be the most advanced develop-
> ment of the time. He senses that he is put in an unfair dilemma by having
> to be so subject to their control.[8]

Parsons seems relatively satisfied, however, that during the last
thirty years youth has become less rebellious, more moderate in its
pleasures, and better integrated into the general culture.[9]

A considerably different approach, growing out of a disenchantment with theories stressing the alien and abnormal features of
delinquency, has been suggested by David Matza. He proposes
that delinquency, along with radicalism and bohemianism, is merely
a subterranean extension of perspectives held in less extreme forms
by "conventional" members of society. Thus, delinquency is a version of teenage culture, radical politics is a caricature of traditional
liberalism, and bohemianism combines the frivolity of fraternity
life with the seriousness of college intellectualism.[10] In a paper written with Gresham Sykes, he further argues that delinquents recog-

6. Robert K. Merton, *Social Theory and Social Structure*, pp. 121–94;
Richard A. Cloward and Lloyd E. Ohlin, *Delinquency and Opportunity*.
7. See, especially on this point, Lewis A. Dexter, "On the Politics and
Sociology of Stupidity in Our Society," in Howard S. Becker, ed., *The Other
Side: Perspectives on Deviance*, pp. 37–49.
8. Talcott Parsons, *Social Structure and Personality*, pp. 171–72.
9. *Ibid.*, 175–76.
10. "Subterranean Traditions of Youth," *Annals of the American Academy of Political and Social Science* 338 (1961): 116–18, and "Positions and
Behavior Patterns of Youth," in Robert E. L. Faris, ed., *Handbook of Modern
Sociology*, pp. 191–216.

nize and circumvent the moral bind of laws by "techniques of neutralization." Much delinquency is "based on what is essentially an unrecognized extension of defenses to crimes, in the form of justifications for deviance that are seen as valid by the delinquent but not by the legal system or society at large."[11]

Sociologists have had a tendency to base theoretical findings on official delinquency rates without a concern for how the label of "delinquency" gets applied to "troublesome" youth. Paul Tappan recognized this deficiency when he recommended for analytical purposes that criminals are "a sociologically distinct group of violators of specific legal norms, subjected to official state treatment. . . . The norms, their violation, the mechanics of dealing with breach constitute major provinces of legal sociology."[12] Recently, other writers have drawn attention to the limitations and narrow vision of the criminological imagination.[13] According to John Kitsuse and Aaron Cicourel:

. . . rates of deviant behavior are produced by the actions taken by persons in the social system which define, classify and record certain behaviors as deviant. If a given form of behavior is not interpreted as deviant by such persons it would not appear as a unit in whatever set of rates we may attempt to explain (e.g., the statistics of local social welfare agencies • "crimes known to the police," Uniform Crime Reports, court records, etc.). The persons who define and activate the rate-producing processes may range from the neighborhood "busybody" to officials of law enforcement agencies. From this point of view, deviant behavior is behavior which is organizationally defined, processed, and treated as "strange," "abnormal," "theft," "delinquent," etc., by the personnel in the social system which has produced the rate. By these definitions, sociological theory of deviance would focus on three interrelated problems of explanation: (1) How different forms of behavior come to be defined as

11. Gresham M. Sykes and David Matza, "Techniques of Neutralization: A Theory of Delinquency," *American Sociological Review* 22 (1957): 664–70. See, also, David Matza, *Delinquency and Drift*.

12. Paul W. Tappan, "Who Is the Criminal," *American Sociological Review* 12 (1947): 96–102.

13. See, particularly, the writings of Edwin Lemert, David Matza, Erving Goffman, Kai Erikson, Howard Becker, and John Kitsuse.

deviant by various groups or organizations in the society, (2) How individuals manifesting such behaviors are organizationally processed to produce rates of deviant behavior among various segments of the population, and (3) How acts which are officially or unofficially defined as deviant are generated by such conditions as family organization, role inconsistencies or situational "pressures."[14]

Studies of official screening of deviants and of legislative crusades on their behalf, suggest a growing theoretical interest in the origins of rules and their enforcement.[15] This book, though recognizing the important contributions that have been made to the study of deviant actors, focuses on rule-makers and rule-making rather than on persons upon whom rules are conferred. Sociologists have provided significant information about the social context of delinquency, the economic inequalities which facilitate illegal behavior, and subcultural behavior; but we know very little about the social processes by which formal organizations define persons as "delinquent." As Howard Becker has observed, delinquency and deviance are not inherent in human behavior but are ascriptive labels which are conferred upon actors in particular social situations:

Social groups create deviance by making the rules whose infraction constitutes deviance, and by applying those rules to particular people and labeling them as outsiders. From this point of view, deviance is not a quality of the act the person commits, but rather a consequence of the application by others of rules and sanctions to an "offender." The deviant is one to whom that label has successfully been applied; deviant behavior is behavior that people so label. . . . It is an interesting fact that most scientific research and speculation on deviance concerns itself with the people who break rules rather than with those who make and enforce them. If we are to achieve a full understanding of deviant behavior, we must get two possible foci of inquiry into balance. We must see deviance, and the outsiders who personify the abstract conception, as a consequence of a process of interaction between people, some of whom in the service

14. John I. Kitsuse and Aaron V. Cicourel, "A Note on the Uses of Official Statistics," *Social Problems* 11 (1963): 135.

15. See, especially, Joseph R. Gusfield, *Symbolic Crusade: Status Politics and the American Temperance Movement;* Kai T. Erikson, *Wayward Puritans: A Study in the Sociology of Deviance;* and Roger Smith, "Status Politics and the Image of the Addict," *Issues in Criminology* 2 (1966): 157–75.

of their own interests make and enforce rules which catch others who, in the service of their own interests, have committed acts which are labeled deviant.[16]

Becker's proposition points to a serious gap in criminological literature. "Pathological" approaches to delinquency and crime neglect the possibility that deviance may play an important part in preserving social stability and reinforcing the status and prestige of the ruling classes.[17] If we know little about the routine activities, customs and self-images of "delinquents," we know even less about the ways in which certain types of youthful behavior come to be registered as "delinquent."[18]

RE-VIEWING JUVENILE JUSTICE

I have chosen to focus specifically on the child-saving movement in Chicago, since the first official juvenile court originated in Illinois in 1899. Many of the social reformers concerned with child welfare in Chicago enjoyed a national reputation and were instrumental in determining the policies of other states. There is some dispute whether or not Illinois was the first state to create a special tribunal for children. Massachusetts and New York passed laws, in 1874 and 1892 respectively, providing for the trials of minors apart from adults charged with crimes. Ben Lindsey, a renowned judge and reformer, also claimed this distinction for Colorado where a juvenile court was, in effect, established through an educational law of 1899. However,

16. Howard S. Becker, *Outsiders: Studies in the Sociology of Deviance,* pp. 9, 163.
17. ". . . deviant behavior is not a simple kind of leakage which occurs when the machinery of society is in poor working order, but may be, in controlled quantities, an important condition for preserving the stability of social life." Erikson, *Wayward Puritans,* p. 13. See, also, for the original statement on this issue, Emile Durkheim, *Rules of Sociological Method,* pp. 65–73.
18. For all that has been written, we still know very little about the subjective experience of delinquency, and most modern theories are built on outdated or fragmentary data. The success of Claude Brown's autobiographical *Manchild in the Promised Land* is a testimony to this ignorance.

it is generally accepted that the Juvenile Court Act, passed by the Illinois legislature in the same year, was the first official such enactment to be acknowledged as a model statute by other states and countries.[19] By 1917 juvenile court legislation had been passed in all but three states and by 1932 there were over 600 independent juvenile courts throughout the United States.[20]

The juvenile court system was part of a general movement directed toward removing adolescents from the criminal law process and creating special programs for delinquent, dependent, and neglected children. Regarded as "one of the greatest advances in child welfare that has ever occurred," the juvenile court was considered "an integral part of total welfare planning."[21] Charles Chute, an enthusiastic supporter of the child-saving movement, claimed that "no single event has contributed more to the welfare of children and their families. It revolutionized the treatment of delinquent and neglected children and led to the passage of similar laws throughout the world."[22]

Although much has been written about the humanitarian philosophy of the juvenile court system and its critical development during the last sixty years, little attention has been paid to its organizational origins. Traditional explanations of the child-saving movement in the nineteenth century emphasize the noble sentiments and tireless energy of middle-class philanthropists. It is widely implied in the literature that the juvenile court and parallel reforms in penology represented a progressive effort by concerned reformers to alleviate the miseries of urban life and to solve social problems by rational, enlightened and scientific methods. With few exceptions, studies of delinquency have been parochial, inadequately descriptive, and show

19. Helen Page Bates, "Digest of Statutes Relating to Juvenile Courts and Probation Systems," *Charities* 13 (January, 1905): 329–36.

20. Joel F. Handler, "The Juvenile Court and the Adversary System: Problems of Function and Form," 1965 *Wisconsin Law Review*, pp. 7–51.

21. Charles L. Chute, "The Juvenile Court in Retrospect," *Federal Probation* 13 (September, 1949): 7; Harrison A. Dobbs, "In Defense of Juvenile Courts," *ibid.*, p. 29.

22. Charles L. Chute, "Fifty Years of the Juvenile Court," 1949 *National Probation and Parole Association Yearbook*, p. 1.

little appreciation of underlying political and cultural conditions.[23] Historical studies, particularly of the juvenile court, are for the most part self-confirming and support an evolutionary view of human progress.[24]

The positivist heritage in the study of social problems has directed attention to (1) the "abnormal" aspects of deviant behavior, (2) a rigidly deterministic view of human behavior, and (3) the primacy of the criminal act rather than the criminal law as the major point of departure in the construction of etiological theory.[25] The lack of rigorous concern for the historical, legislative and political aspects of the administration of juvenile justice may be attributed to the modern criminologist's interest in the criminal actor and neglect of the criminal law.[26] During this century, there have been only sporadic efforts in criminological research to tackle socio-legal problems resulting from governmental invasion of personal liberties. The historical development and positivist bias of academic criminology, suggests Francis Allen, account for this trend:

It is not too much to say that a great part of the criminological labors of the last half-century proceeded with little consideration of the political and ethical values which are inevitably involved. Mistaken or malevolent uses of state power have rarely been considered as possibilities demanding measures or concern. Unfortunately, the history of recent years has demonstrated all too clearly that the criminal law and its sanctions are capable of use as instruments for the destruction of basic political values and, in the world as a whole, the malevolent use of state power has become rather

23. See, for example, Ola Nyquist, *Juvenile Justice*. This "comparative" study is extremely formal and is restricted to interpreting official legislative documents in California and Sweden, with little concern for their behavioral context.

24. See, for example, Herbert H. Lou, *Juvenile Courts in the United States;* Negley K. Teeters and John Otto Reinneman, *The Challenge of Delinquency;* and Katherine L. Boole, *The Juvenile Court: Its Origin, History and Procedure.* One notable exception is Paul W. Tappan, *Delinquent Girls in Court.*

25. Matza, *Delinquency and Drift, passim.*

26. For a more lengthy analysis of this point, see Clarence Ray Jeffrey, "The Historical Development of Criminology," in Hermann Mannheim, ed., *Pioneers in Criminology,* pp. 364–94.

the rule than the exception. Accordingly, the realization has grown steadily that the values of legality and equality at the hands of the state are the essence of a free community and that the substantive criminal law has a major contribution to make in their preservation.[27]

The "rehabilitative ideal" has so dominated American criminology that research is generally undertaken in order to fix the origins of criminal and delinquent behavior within particular individuals or environments rather than in the officially constituted agencies of the criminal law. But, as Allen has observed, "even if one's interests lie primarily in the problems of treatment of offenders, it should be recognized that the existence of the criminal presupposes a crime and that the problems of treatment are derivative in the sense that they depend upon the determination by law-giving agencies that certain sorts of behavior are crimes."[28]

The conservatism and "diluted liberalism" of much research on delinquency results from the fact that researchers are generally prepared to accept prevailing definitions of crime, to work within the premises of the criminal law, and to concur at least implicitly with those who make laws as to the nature and distribution of a "criminal" population.[29] Thus, most theories of delinquency are based on studies of convicted or imprisoned delinquents. As John Seeley has observed in another context, professional caution requires us "to take our problems rather than make our problems, to accept as constitutive of our

27. *The Borderland of Criminal Justice,* pp. 126–27.
28. *Ibid.,* p. 125.
29. ". . . diluted liberalism . . . is the political common denominator of most current social study. . . . In considerable part our immediate situation in social study is characterized by plain and fancy retreats from the tasks which classic sociologists confronted so boldly. After all, it is easier and safer to restrict oneself to smaller problems as part of a tacit conspiracy of the mediocre, a tendency that in due course is reinforced by the selection and training of academic personnel. . . . [T]he most precise and best-tested facts of social inquiry today often have to do with a quite narrow sphere of society: with such affairs as the circulation of magazines, the buying habits of suburban wives, the possible effects of advertising in the several media of mass communication. . . . 'Nothing is so poor and melancholy,' Santayana somewhere remarks, 'as an art that is interested in itself and not in its subject' " (C. Wright Mills, ed., *Images of Man,* p. 5).

'intake' what is held to be 'deviant' in a way that concerns enough people in that society enough to give us primary protection."[30] Money, encouragement, cooperation from established institutions, and a market for publications are more easily acquired for studies of the socialization or treatment of delinquents than for studies of how laws, law-makers, and law-enforcers contribute to the "registration" of delinquency.

Much of the literature on youthful deviance has been preoccupied with the prevention of delinquency, statistical evaluations of its distribution, and the programming of treatment strategies. Law and its implementation have been largely dismissed as irrelevant topics for inquiry into the "causes" of delinquency. According to Herbert Packer, it is typical that the National Crime Commission ignored the fundamental question of "What is the criminal sanction good for?"[31] Theories of personality development and socialization into crime have preempted criminological research to the exclusion of classical interests in the development of legal institutions and in the relationship between state power and individual liberty. This book revises popular conceptions about the child-saving movement and analyzes the dynamics of the legislative and popular drive to "criminalize."[32]

Chapter 2 examines the intellectual resources of the child-saving movement, particularly the influence of social Darwinism and European positivism. Special attention is paid to biological and environmental theories of crime as reflected in the concepts of the "natural" and "nurtured" criminal. Chapter 3 discusses the institutional and penal system whereby the child savers attempted to transform delinquent youth into law-abiding citizens. The reformatory to which delinquents were committed was characterized by a rural location and a trend away from congregate housing to the "cottage plan" of im-

30. "The Making and Taking of Problems: Toward an Ethical Stance," *Social Problems* 14 (1967): 384–85.
31. "Copping Out," *New York Review of Books* 9, October 12, 1962, pp. 17–20.
32. Sanford H. Kadish, "The Crisis of Overcriminalization," *The Annals* 374 (November, 1967): 157–70.

prisonment. These developments in the "new penology" are related to ideological images of crime and to the rising professional interests of correctional workers. Chapter 4 suggests that the child-saving movement was heavily influenced by maternal values and especially by middle-class women who extended their housewifely role into .public service and used their political and economic contacts to advance their cause. Child saving also provided professional women with legitimate career openings and served the expressive needs of middle-class reformers in a rapidly changing society. Chapter 5 is a case study of the child-saving movement in Illinois, where the juvenile court system originated. This chapter investigates the nature of the times and social conditions in which the juvenile court was created, the practical problems it was designed to remedy, the persons who had a vested interest in its success, and the political context in which it was engineered through the legislature. Chapter 6 reflects upon the impact and ideology of the juvenile court system, and its development over the past sixty years. Two major ideological attacks on the juvenile court are analyzed and consequent constitutional reforms evaluated.

Chapter 2: *Images of Delinquency, 1870-1900*

THE VALUE OF PUNISHMENT

The modern defense of punishment has been built on the concepts of deterrence and reformation; the former encompasses the scientific control of criminal behavior, the latter refers to the means for achieving control.[1] It is usually suggested that the philosophy of reformation—or its modern counterpart, "rehabilitation"—embodies a humanistic respect for the integrity of the individual offender, though this polemical sentiment has not been empirically corroborated. Punishment which is designed to fit the offender rather than the offense may be more coercive and intrusive than traditional penalties.

The eighteenth- and nineteenth-century theorists who endorsed punishment on considerations of its deterrent effect refuted the argument that "punishment, in short, is an effort of man to find a more exact relation between sin and suffering than the world affords us."[2] To them, right and wrong cannot be defined in terms of moral absolutes. The fundamental source of the distinction must be found in

---

1. The following discussion is treated more fully by Egon Bittner and Anthony Platt, "The Meaning of Punishment," *Issues in Criminology* 2 (1966): 83–93.
2. Sir Edward Fry quoted by Charles Mercier, *Criminal Responsibility*, pp. 37–38.

human nature and in the structure of social life. All that man experiences as painful and understandable he defines as evil, and all that pleases him he defines as good. Since this hedonistic outlook is apt to bring people in frequent conflict with each other, the greatest good is found in those patterns of conduct which provide the maximum happiness for the greatest number of people. Thus, as Jeremy Bentham taught, "all punishment is mischief; all punishment is in itself evil. . . . [I]f it ought at all to be admitted, it ought only to be admitted in as far as it promises to exclude some greater evil."[3] The use of punishment is a matter of moral economy. It is imposed with misgivings, and only because it is held to be an effective means for securing happiness and tranquility for the majority.

The imposition and measure of punishment requires calculating the value of social protection that derives from it. Indeed, social value may be the sole guideline for measuring the relationship between the crime and its punishment. According to Francis Hutcheson, "since the end of punishment is the general safety, the precise measure of human punishment is the necessity of preventing certain crimes for the public safety, and not always the moral turpitude of actions. . . . Severe punishments are necessary too for small guilt whensoever there is danger of such frequent transgressions as might be destructive to a state in certain exigencies.[4]

Initially, the utilitarian approach to deterrence took only a minimal interest in the offender. Though its advocates, by and large, proposed relatively mild forms of physical punishment, this was only partly based on humane considerations for the punished. Their attitude toward the offender was well expressed by Sidney Smith:

When we recommend severity, we recommend, of course, that degree of severity which will not excite compassion for the sufferer, and lessen the horror of the crime. That is why we do not recommend torture and amputation of limbs. When a man has been proven to have committed a crime, it is expedient that society should make use of that man for the diminution of crime; he belongs to them for that purpose. Our primary duty, in such a case, is to treat the culprit that many other persons may be

3. Cited by James Heath, ed., *Eighteenth Century Penal Theory*, p. 219.
4. *Ibid.*, p. 84.

rendered better, or prevented from being worse, by dread of the same treatment; and making this the principal object, to combine with it as much as possible the improvement of the individual.[5]

It was under the banner of utilitarianism that the campaigns for penal reform were mobilized. The idea of deterrence easily lent itself to proposals that the offender himself should learn the lesson of his crime. That is, one of the first tests of deterrence was whether the punishment deterred the offender from repeating his crime. For this goal it was necessary to have programs of punishment that would be severe enough to have sufficient impact to accomplish a change in the disposition of offenders, but not so severe as to make it impossible for the reformed criminals to resume or initiate a decent life. If punishment is to be a lesson, it must not destroy. Thus, the argument of deterrence, in its modern utilitarian form, came to encompass a strong interest in the offender, and the justification of punishment came to rest, at least in part, on the notion that it is good for the punished person. Though this interpretation of the philosophy of deterrence absolves punishment of its "mischievous" aspects and provides some limits to its administration, it is essentially based on a weak and vulnerable argument. In the first place, the argument implies that the effects of punishment can be demonstrated; but the required evidence was and is today notoriously difficult to obtain. Second, punishment on the basis of deterrence is inherently unjust. For if an example is made of a person to induce others to avoid criminal actions, then he suffers not for what he has done but on account of other people's tendency to do likewise. Finally, the public interest that punishment is meant to serve is an ambiguous notion and could be defined, as some critics have suggested, to be the particular interests of the governing elite. Despite such weaknesses, the utilitarian-deterrence argument furnished the official rhetoric of justification of punishment throughout the nineteenth century. Conservatives and reformists alike sought to base their recommendations mainly on considerations of the expediency value of punishment. The idea that punishment

5. Quoted by Leon Radzinowicz and J. C. W. Turner, "A Study of Punishment," *Canadian Bar Review* 21 (1943): 91–97.

simply executes some norms implied in the ideal of justice did not disappear from penological polemics, but it carried relatively little weight.

THE NATURAL CRIMINAL

The child-saving movement, like all moral crusades, reaffirmed ideal values and stressed the positive capacities of traditional institutions. The child savers' ideology was an amalgam of convictions and aspirations. From the medical profession, they borrowed the imagery of pathology, infection, immunization, and treatment; from the tenets of social Darwinism, they derived their pessimistic views about the intractability of human nature and the innate moral defects of the lower classes; finally, their ideas about the biological and environmental origins of crime can be attributed to the positivist tradition in European criminology and anti-urban sentiments associated with the Protestant, rural ethic.

American criminology in the last century was essentially a practical affair—a curious conglomeration of pseudo-scientific theory, Old World ideas, and religious humanitarianism. Theories of crime were imported from Europe and an indiscriminating eclecticism dominated the literature. Educated amateurs, physicians, clergymen, and scholar-technicians became the experts on crime. Before 1870, there were only a few American textbooks on crime, and even the various penal and philanthropic organizations lacked specialized journals. Departments of law and sociology in the universities were rarely concerned with more than the formal description and classification of crimes.[6]

6. Arthur E. Fink, *Causes of Crime: Biological Theories in the United States, 1800–1915.* Needless to say, histories of American criminological thought are hard to find. Fink's study makes a useful bibliographical contribution to the literature by assembling and condensing a vast amount of interesting primary sources. But he rarely attempts to interpret his data other than to make the occasional bow to the evolutionary perspective. There are of

American pioneers in criminology were either physicians, like Benjamin Rush or Isaac Ray, or at least guided by medical ideology. Their training was often based on European methods and some, like Rush, actually attended European universities. With the notable exception of Ray's work, the authoritative literature on medical jurisprudence was of English origin.[7] The social sciences were similarly imported from Europe, and American criminologists fitted their data within the theoretical framework of criminal anthropology. Herbert Spencer's writings had an enormous impact on American intellectuals and made him even more popular in the United States than he was in his own country.[8] Cesare Lombroso, perhaps the most significant figure in nineteenth-century criminology, also sought recognition in the United States when he felt that his experiments had been neglected in Italy.[9]

Spencer and Lombroso, with their emphasis on Darwinist and biological images of human behavior, provided the ideological premise for crime workers and reformers. Anthropological explanations of crime complemented social Darwinism, which, in its most simple form, suggested that life is a competitive struggle for existence whereby the fittest survive and thus elevate the whole human race. The doctrine of "natural selection" also refuted revolutionary change and characterized human progress as a slow, natural, and

course numerous modern textbooks on the history of penology—such as H. E. Barnes and N. K. Teeters, *New Horizons in Criminology* (1943), Max Grünhut, *Penal Reform* (1948), and George B. Vold, *Theoretical Criminology* (1958)—but these are essentially compiled for undergraduate reading.

7. Isaac Ray, *A Treatise on the Medical Jurisprudence of Insanity.* The influence of English medical jurisprudence on American physicians is cursorily examined by Anthony M. Platt and Bernard L. Diamond, "The Origins of the 'Right and Wrong' Test of Criminal Responsibility and its Subsequent Development in the United States," *California Law Review* 54 (1966): 1227–60. See, also, Seymour Halleck, "American Psychiatry and the Criminal: A Historical Review," *American Journal of Psychiatry* 121, no. 9 (March, 1965): i–xxi.

8. Richard Hofstadter, *Social Darwinism in American Thought,* pp. 31–50.

9. See Lombroso's introduction to Arthur MacDonald, *Criminology.*

inevitable process of evolution.[10] As Richard Hofstadter has observed, this view of social life was "seized upon as a welcome addition, perhaps the most powerful of all, to the store of ideas to which solid and conservative men appealed when they wished to reconcile their fellows to some of the hardships of life and to prevail upon them not to support hasty and ill-considered reforms."[11]

Spokesmen for conservative Darwinism opposed welfare legislation and organized state care of the "dependent classes" on the grounds that all men, whatever their ability and resources, should engage in the competition for survival. The care and support of criminals, idiots, cripples, and the like, merely prolongs suffering, impedes human progress, and contradicts the laws of nature. The Darwinists, however, did not approve class warfare or the total elimination of the "unfit" through eugenic techniques. Hofstadter has pointed out that Spencer, accused of inhumanity in his application of biological principles to social life, "was compelled to insist over and over again that he was not opposed to voluntary private charity to the unfit, since it had an elevating effect on the character of the donors and hastened the development of altruism. . . ."[12]

Although Lombroso's theoretical and experimental studies were not translated into English until 1911, his findings were known by American academics in the early 1890's, and their popularity, as that of Spencer's, was based on the fact that they confirmed popular assumptions about the character and existence of a "criminal class." Lombroso's original theory suggested the existence of a criminal type distinguishable from non-criminals by observable physical anomalies of a degenerative or atavistic nature. He proposed that

10. As Charles Cooley remarked, "most of the writers on eugenics have been biologists or physicians who have never acquired the point of view which sees in society a psychological organism with a life process of its own. They have thought of human heredity as a tendency to definite modes of conduct, and of environment as something that may aid or hinder, not remembering what they might have learned even from Darwin, that heredity takes on a distinctively human character only by renouncing, as it were, the function of predetermined adaptation and becoming plastic to the environment" (*Social Process*, p. 206).

11. Hofstadter, *Social Darwinism*, p. 5.

12. *Ibid.*, p. 41.

the criminal was a morally inferior human species, one characterized by physical traits reminiscent of apes, lower primates, and savage tribes. The criminal was thought to be morally retarded and, like a small child, instinctively aggressive and precocious unless restrained.[13] It is not difficult to see the connection between biological determinism in criminological literature and the principles of "natural selection"; both of these theoretical positions, according to Leon Radzinowicz, automatically justified the "eradication of elements that constituted a permanent and serious danger."[14]

Lombroso and his colleagues recognized other types of criminal behavior and even acknowledged the influence of social as well as biological factors on criminals.[15] Before 1900, however, American writers were only familiar with his general propositions and had only the briefest knowledge of his research techniques. Arthur Mac-Donald, in his authoritative treatise on *Abnormal Man* (1893), gave American readers the following abstract of Lombroso's *L'Homme Criminel:*

To-day there is a vague feeling, an echo of an ancient retaliation in our punishments. If punishment rests on free will, the worse men, the criminals by nature, should have a very light punishment or none. Penal repressions should be based on social utility scientifically demonstrated; instead of studying law texts, we need to study the criminal. The criminal by nature has a feeble cranial capacity, a heavy and developed jaw, a large orbital capacity, projecting superciliary ridges, an abnormal and symmetrical cranium, a scanty beard or none, but abundant hair, projecting ears, frequently a crooked or flat nose. Criminals are subject to Daltonism; left-handedness is common; their muscular force is feeble. Alcoholic and epileptical degeneration exists in a large number. Their nerve centers are frequently pigmented. They blush with difficulty. Their moral degen-

13. An excellent critique of Lombroso's theories, findings and intellectual traditions is provided by Marvin E. Wolfgang, "Cesare Lombroso," in Hermann Mannheim, ed., *Pioneers in Criminology,* pp. 168–227.

14. *Ideology and Crime,* p. 55.

15. This study is not the place to debate Lombroso's contributions to criminology or to measure his effect on European ideas; what I am concerned with here is how Lombroso was interpreted and simplified in the United States before 1900. It is well recognized that his later writings were more cautious and emphasized a multifactor approach.

eration corresponds with their physical, their criminal tendencies are manifested in infancy by onanism, cruelty, inclination to steal, excessive vanity, impulsive character. The criminal by nature is lazy, debauched, cowardly, not susceptible to remorse, without foresight; fond of tatooing; his handwriting is peculiar, signature complicated and adorned with flourishes; his slang is widely diffused, abbreviated, and full of archaisms. In their associations they return to primitive social forms. The general cause of the persistence of an inferior race type is atavistic. As the born criminal is without remedy, he must be continually confined, and allowed no provisional liberty or mercy; the ancient tradition of vigorous initiatives should be upheld the more we increase that of society, which is still more severe. Nature is responsible for the born criminal, society (in a great measure) for the criminal by occasion.[16]

MacDonald eulogized Lombroso, found him to be sincere and patient, "an expert experimenter and a person of philosophical acuteness." He welcomed the work as comprehensive and factual but did not endorse Lombroso's findings concerning the "incorrigibility" and "incurability" of most criminals. "Neither of these positions," he wrote in his capacity as a representative of the Federal Bureau of Education, "is supported by a sufficient number of scientific facts." MacDonald, like many of his professional colleagues, could not accept the ultimate logic of biological theories that criminals are irrevocably constrained and committed to crime. "The inmates of institutions for the delinquent and dependent differ little or none at all from individuals outside. . . . One of the main objects of education," he wrote, "is to eradicate or modify undesirable tendencies and to develop the favorable ones. Here is an opportunity for the rational method of treatment, which is, first, to study the unfavorable characteristics, and, second, to investigate their causes as far as possible."[17]

16. *Abnormal Man,* pp. 44-45.

17. *Ibid.,* pp. 12, 44-45. In reviewing Garofolo's *La Criminologie* (1888), MacDonald commented that Garofolo's "insistence on the absolute elimination of the born criminal is extreme; first, because it assumes the criminal's utter want of adaptation to society, which is not warranted by a sufficient number of facts; second, admitting his want of adaptation, we fail to see why a society in which the public conscience is highly sensitive might not substitute perpetual detention; for it is a question of social utility whether the hardening of the public conscience is not morally injurious" (*ibid.,* p. 46).

In England, the ideas and data of the so-called Italian School of criminology had already been summarized and publicized by Havelock Ellis.[18] A similar, though much more superficial and less endurable, service was provided by Robert Fletcher in an address before the Anthropological Society of Washington, D.C., in 1891. Fletcher told his audience that criminal anthropology consisted of the study of individuals who are compelled to commit crimes as a consequence of "physical conformation, hereditary taint, or surroundings of vice, poverty, and ill example." The modern view of the criminal depicts him as a "variety of human species who had degenerated physically and morally." There is some dispute, said Fletcher, as to whether the criminal is a distinct anatomical type, but most experts agree that certain abnormalities are more frequently observed among criminals than among the "supposed honest class." Fletcher, like MacDonald, was optimistic about the implications of Lombrosian data:

While the opinions of experienced observers in almost all parts of the world, based on statistical results, show the uselessness of attempts to reform the instinctive criminal, it is gratifying to know that in one institution (the New York State Reformatory at Elmira) a more hopeful result has been attained.[19]

Although the philosophy of preventive criminology and social defense implied human malleability, the majority of American criminologists were preoccupied with the intractability of the "criminal class." Hamilton Wey, an influential physician at Elmira reformatory, argued before the National Prison Association in 1881 that criminals were "a distinct type of human species." Influenced by Galton's *Inquiry Into Human Faculty* (1881), Benedikt's *Anatomical Studies Upon Brains of Criminals* (1886), and Mills' *Study of the Brains of Paranoiacs, Criminals, Idiots and Negroes* (1886), Wey later argued that incorrigible criminals would always be "criminal in instinct and act." The criminal, he said, is usually "undersized, his weight being disproportionate to his height, with a

18. Havelock Ellis, *The Criminal*.
19. Robert Fletcher, *The New School of Criminal Anthropology*, pp. 6, 8, 33.

tendency to flat-footedness. He is coarse in fiber and heavy in his
movements, lacking anatomical symmetry and beauty. The head is
markedly asymmetrical, . . . characteristic of a degenerative physi-
ognimy." To correct these deficiencies, or at least to contain them,
Wey advocated physical training and military drills.[20]

Charles Reeve, at another meeting of the National Prison Association, attributed the weaknesses and deformities of the "dependent classes" to "erroneous and perverted" marriages in which
many a "viciously diseased man or woman was being permitted to
procreate. Both the statutes and the church, as well as social usages,
have been and are indolent ulcers, the discharges from which breed
festers all over the bodies political, social and ecclesiastical." Reeve
argued that "no viciously or hereditarily diseased or deformed men-
tality" could improve in a marriage lacking "conjugal love" and a
"complete union of minds." The only solution to the problem,
claimed Reeve, was to gather up all the dependent classes into large
rural institutions where they could be disciplined, have companionship with their own kind, and somehow develop "feelings of
affection."[21]

American penologists supported this derogatory image of criminals and enthusiastically welcomed pseudo-scientific proposals for
their containment.[22] A typical medical view was expressed by
Nathan Allen at the National Conference of Charities and Correction, where he observed that criminals are usually incapable of
overcoming their biological fate:

All history proves that the criminal class as a body originates from a
peculiar stratum or type in society—sometimes from the middle or common walks of life, but more generally from the lowest orders, especially
from the ignorant, the shiftless, the indolent and dissipated. . . . If our

20. Hamilton D. Wey, "A Plea for Physical Training of Youthful Criminals," *Proceedings of the Annual Congress of the National Prison Association, Boston, 1888,* pp. 181–93. Wey's work is also discussed by Fink, *Causes
of Crime, passim,* and Vold, *Theoretical Criminology,* p. 58.

21. Charles H. Reeve, "Dependent Children," *Proceedings of the Annual
Congress of the National Prison Association, Boston, 1888,* pp. 101–13.

22. See, for example, Fink, *Causes of Crime,* pp. 188–210, on criminological attitudes toward sterilization.

object, then, is to prevent crime in a large scale, we must direct attention to its main sources—to the materials that make criminals; the springs must be dried up; the supplies must be cut off.

Allen further proposed that crime would be reduced if "certain classes of vicious persons could be hindered from propagation. What right have such individuals to bring upon the public so much misery, shame, and cost?"[23]

Literature on "social degradation" was extremely popular during the 1870's and 1880's, though most such "studies" were little more than crude polemics, padded with moralistic epithets and preconceived value judgments.[24] Richard Dugdale's series of papers on the Jukes family, which became a model for the case-study approach, was distorted almost beyond recognition by anti-intellectual supporters of hereditary theories of crime.[25] Although Dugdale attempted to demonstrate a relationship between crime and heredity, and often referred to the "stock" and "breeding" of criminals as though they were a herd of poorly developed cattle, he was also "profoundly convinced that 'environment' could be relied upon to modify, and ultimately to eradicate even such deep-rooted and widespreading growths of vice and crime as the 'Jukes' group exemplified."[26] Dugdale warned his readers that his findings were tentative and inconclusive. But Robert Fletcher, in his lecture on criminal

23. Nathan Allen, "Prevention of Crime and Pauperism," *Proceedings of the Annual Conference of Charities (PACC), 1878,* pp. 111–24.

24. Roy Lubove, *The Professional Altruist: The Emergence of Social Work as a Career, 1880–1930,* pp. 1–21; Robert Bremner, "The Historical Background of Modern Welfare: Shifting Attitudes," in Mayer N. Zald, ed., *Social Welfare Institutions: A Sociological Reader,* pp. 21–37.

25. Richard L. Dugdale, "Heredity Pauperism, as Illustrated in the 'Juke' Family," *PACC, 1877,* pp. 81–99; *The Jukes: A Study in Crime, Pauperism, Disease, and Heredity.*

26. Introduction by Franklin H. Giddings to Richard L. Dugdale, *The Jukes: A Study in Crime, Pauperism, Disease, and Heredity,* p. iv, 4th ed. (New York: G. P. Putnam's Sons, 1910). According to Dugdale, "Those who comprehend the specific process of moral education, that it begins with certain concrete acts which, by repetition and variation, organize in the mind definite and permanent abstract conceptions of right and wrong, will see at once that the foundations of the moral character must be laid in the earliest infancy and must begin by the education of the senses" (*ibid.,* p. 118).

anthropology, noted that evidence from *The Jukes* was "so striking" that "it seems impossible to doubt that criminal propensities can be and are transmitted by descent."[27] Nathan Oppenheim, writing in 1896, declared the Jukes family to be a clear example of transmitted crime, and George E. Dawson also believed that the statistical study of criminal heredity used with the Jukes tended to establish the fact of youthful degeneracy.[28] Franklin Giddings, in his introduction to the 1910 edition of *The Jukes,* commented that "an impression quite generally prevails that 'The Jukes' is a thorough-going demonstration of 'hereditary criminality,' 'hereditary pauperism,' 'hereditary degeneracy,' and so on. It is nothing of the kind, and its author never made such a claim for it."[29]

Nevertheless, *The Jukes* easily lent itself to all kinds of misinterpretation and wishful thinking. Obviously influenced by Dugdale, Oscar McCulloch traced the records of a family of paupers, illegitimates, gypsies, and criminals in Indiana and presented his findings to the National Conference of Charities and Correction in 1888. "The individuals already traced are over five thousand," he said, "interwoven by descent and marriage. They underrun society like devilgrass. Pick up one, and the whole five thousand would be drawn up." McCulloch traced the "parasitism" and "social degradation" of the "tribe of Ishmael," as he called them, to the "old convict stock" which had originally been transported from England. He described his subjects as licentious, unchaste, idle, and incestuous—qualities which he characterized as a form of "animal reversion." His proposed solutions for the social problems caused by these people are reminiscent of Ernest Hooton's "criminal colonies" and the "relocation camps" for Japanese Americans during the Second World War. "First," said McCulloch, "we must close up official outdoor relief. Second, we must check private and indiscriminate benevolence, or charity, falsely so-called. Third, we must get hold of the children."[30]

27. Fletcher, *The New School,* p. 9.
28. Cited by Fink, *Causes of Crime,* p. 182.
29. Giddings, intro. to *The Jukes,* pp. iii, iv.
30. Oscar C. McCulloch, "The Tribe of Ishmael: A Study in Social Degradation," *Proceedings of the National Conference of Charities and Correction (PNCCC), 1888,* pp. 154–59. Compare this with Ernest Hooton's

Confronted by the evidence of Darwin, Galton, Dugdale, Caldwell, and many other disciples of the biological image of man, correctional professionals were compelled to admit that "a large proportion of the unfortunate children that go to make up the great army of criminals are not born right." According to Sarah Cooper, who pioneered the kindergarten system in California, many criminal children "come into the world freighted down with evil propensities and vicious tendencies. They start out handicapped in the race of life."[31] Penal reformers adopted the rhetoric and imagery of Darwinism in order to emphasize the urgent need for confronting the problem of crime before it got out of hand. Louise Wardner, of the Illinois Industrial School for Girls, was convinced that Galton's work demonstrated conclusively that "original constitution is a much more important factor than either education or surrounding" in the determination of character. It was "self-evident" to Mrs. Wardner that "each unprincipled, impure girl left to grow up, and become a mother, is likely to increase her kind three to five fold."[32]

By 1890, the findings of such European criminologists as Lombroso, Lacassagne, Garofolo, and Ferri, which were widely circulated in the United States, were often cited to justify the argument that crime was partially determined by "congenital and hereditary evil propensities." Dr. I. N. Kerlin, of the Pennsylvania Institute of Feeble-Minded Children, concluded from the evidence of European studies that

if there existed a class of little children whose heredity and aberrations are such as to make them the predestined inmates of our insane hospitals

---

contention that "crime prevention is centered upon the treatment of juveniles and when it gets to be really scientific, it will have to start earlier still and concern itself with familial heredity. . . . We can direct and control the progress of human evolution by breeding better types and by the ruthless elimination of inferior types, if only we are willing to found and to practice a science of human genetics" (*Crime and The Man*, pp. 391, 396). See also Thomas Szasz's polemical discussion of "relocation camps" for Japanese Americans during the Second World War in *Psychiatric Justice*, pp. 61–65.

31. "The Kindergarten as Child-Saving Work," *PNCCC*, *1883*, pp. 130–38.

32. Mrs. Louise Rockford Wardner, "'Girls in Reformatories," *PACC*, *1879*, p. 188.

and jails, what an advance we would make in the diminution of crime and lunacy by a methodized registration and training of such children, or these failing, by their early and entire withdrawal from the community! . . . Let us accept this moral imbecility as the incurable infirmity of an irresponsible victim, to whom, as the piteous cross-bearers of the sins of society, we owe kindly nursing and protection against himself by a grateful and total withdrawal from the community, which, in turn, has a right to demand that he shall not scathe our common stock with permanent taint in blood and morale.[33]

In summary, a basic thrust of nineteenth-century criminological thought in the United States was an emphasis on the non-human qualities of criminals. Darwinist and Lombrosian rhetoric suggested that criminals were a "dangerous"[34] and discredited class who stood outside the boundaries of morally regulated and reciprocal relationships. According to Erving Goffman,

we believe the person with a stigma is not quite human. On this assumption, we exercise varieties of discrimination, through which we effectively, if often unthinkingly, reduce his life chances. We construct a stigma-theory, and ideology to explain his inferiority and account for the danger he represents, sometimes rationalizing an animosity based on other differences. . . .[35]

The traditional forms of punishment and redemption were not appropriate for persons who were not deserving of moral recognition. Criminals were regarded as the "disreputable" poor,[36] requiring special precautions and extraordinary strategies of intervention.

NATURE VERSUS NURTURE

American criminology in the nineteenth century was pragmatic, cau-

33. "The Moral Imbecile," *PNCCC, 1890*, pp. 244–50.
34. Theodore R. Sarbin, "The Dangerous Individual: An Outcome of Social Identity Transformations," *British Journal of Criminology* 7 (1967): 285–95.
35. Erving Goffman, *Stigma: Notes on the Management of Spoiled Identity*, p. 5.
36. David Matza, "Poverty and Disrepute," in Robert K. Merton and Robert A. Nisbet, eds., *Contemporary Social Problems*, pp. 619–69.

tious and somewhat distrustful of theoretical schemes. The most influential organizations concerning penology and the administration of criminal justice were the National Prison Association and the Congress of Charities and Correction. The delegates to these organizations were for the most part practitioners and technicians who worked from day to day with the "dependent classes." Their annual conferences were generally devoted to practical affairs, and they were not particularly concerned with intellectual creeds or philosophical justifications for their work.

The organization of correctional workers—through their national representatives and their identification with the established professions, such as law and medicine—operated to neutralize the pessimistic implications of social Darwinism, because hereditary and fatalistic theories of crime inevitably frustrated the professional aspirations of correctional functionaries. At the same time, even though the job of guard requires minimal training, skill, or intelligence, crime workers did not wish to regard themselves as merely the custodians of a pariah class.[37]

The self-image of penal reformers as doctors rather than guards and the domination of criminological research in the United States by physicians, helped to encourage the acceptance of "therapeutic" strategies in prisons and reformatories. As Arthur Fink has observed, "the role of the physician in this ferment is unmistakable. Indeed, he was the dynamic agent. . . . Not only did he preserve and add to existing knowledge—for his field touched all borders of science—but he helped to maintain and extend the methodology of science."[38] Perhaps what is more significant is that physicians furnished the official rhetoric of penal reform. Admittedly, the criminal was "pathological" and "diseased," but medical science offered the possibility of miraculous cures. It was, therefore, the task of correctional agencies to make every individual self-supporting and independent by restraining "prodigality and extravagance of expenditure of human force and substance."[39] Although there was

37. Analogous developments in the emergence of social work as a professional career are treated by Lubove in *The Professional Altruist*.
38. Fink, *Causes of Crime*, p. 247.
39. *First Biennial Report of the Board of State Commissioners of Public*

widespread belief in the existence of a "criminal class" separated from the rest of mankind by a "vague boundary line," there was no good reason why this class could not be identified, diagnosed, segregated, changed, and controlled. Crime, like disease, was revealed "in the face, the voice, the person and the carriage," so that a skillful and properly trained diagnostician could arrest criminal tendencies. According to one state board of public charities:

The impress of criminal dispositions and pursuits is stamped upon every feature and movement of the body—the dress, the walk, the skin, the eye, the shape of the hands and feet, the size and contour of the skull, the voice, the hair; all reveal it—not, perhaps with certainty, but with sufficient clearness to awaken suspicion and afford a clue. The improvement or deterioration of a criminal is as palpable as that of a lunatic. If prison-keepers, as a class, had the education, the devotion, and the ability of medical superintendents, the principles which lie at the foundation of all rational treatment of crime, would be as well known and as certainly demonstrated, as those which underlie the treatment of insanity.[40]

Despite the wide acceptance of biological imagery, penal reformers stressed the possibility of redemption through religious and medical intervention. The desire to promote the "welfare of the community and future of the race," the stress on pseudo-scientific methods of eliminating criminality, and the ruthless, mechanistic classification of criminals had to be weighed against traditional Christian benevolence, the indulgence of the unfit, and the "optimism of Religion" (as compared with the "pessimism of Science").[41] Charles Henderson, professor of sociology at the University of Chicago and President of the National Conference of Charities and Correction for 1899, resolved this dilemma by observing that the laws of "natural selection" and the principles of educative reform

Charities of the State of Illinois, p. 18 (Springfield, Illinois: Illinois Journal Printing Office, 1871).

40. Ibid., Second Biennial Report, pp. 195–96 (Springfield: State Journal Steam Print, 1873).

41. Charles Henderson, "Relation of Philanthropy to Social Order and Progress," PNCCC, 1899, pp. 1–15. Cf. Charles E. Faulkner, "Twentieth Century Alignments For the Promotion of Social Order," with Frederick H. Wines, "The Healing Touch," PNCCC, 1900, pp. 1–9, 10–26.

were not antagonistic. To hurt the "defective classes," said Henderson, would be to hurt the social order itself; social progress must rest on the capacity of those persons who deal with this class to develop altruistic sentiments. Crime, however, cannot be reduced by sudden social reforms, by changes of government, by introducing a new industrial system, by socialism or redistribution of wealth. "The causes of defect are not all in industry and in government. They exist under all modes of industry and government. They are largely biological, deep in our relations to nature. A swift and superficial change in law or modes of employing labor would not touch these causes. They would remain and be as active as before." Henderson's support for the existing social order rested on the belief that the "rising tide of pauperism, insanity, and crime" was about to "overwhelm and engulf" American civilization. "We must resist," he exhorted the delegates,

by all available means, the deterioration of the common stock, the corruption of blood, the curses of heredity. It must be included in our plan that more children will be born with large brains, sound nerves, good digestive organs, and love of independent struggle. We wish the parasitic strain, the neuropathic taint, the compulsive tendency, the foul disease, to die out.[42]

Professional correctional workers and administrators gradually refuted monolithic explanations of crime based on biological imagery. In 1891, W. P. Fishback, chairman of the Indianapolis reception committee at the National Conference of Charities and Correction, welcomed the delegates with the observation that

while you utterly reject the cold and hard laissez-faire philosophy of Mr. Herbert Spencer, you are no less opposed to the equally false and fatalistic pessimism of certain ecclesiastics, who affect to see in the great spectacle of the world's misery a wise scheme for the edification of a few select saints who are to be caught up some day and whisked away from their cushioned pews to paradise. . . . Disease, vice, poverty are not preordained.[43]

42. Henderson, "Relation of Philanthropy," pp. 1–15.
43. Fishback, "A Welcome Address," *PNCCC, 1891*, p. 5.

Most delegates, however, preferred to accept a modified and cautious version of biological determinism which admitted the existence of "degenerate classes" but also allowed the possibility of change and redemption. Typical of this pragmatic approach was J. D. Scouller, superintendent of the Illinois Reform School, who believed that he could reform two-thirds of the boys in his institution. The remaining third constituted the future criminals, the boys who "love the world, the flesh and the devil." This class of delinquents was "almost past redemption" but could possibly be reformed if they were reached while still "susceptible to moral lessons." The state, said Scouller, has a natural right of self-defense to control all persons who might weaken its powers. Since it was the aim of the criminal class to "undermine the confidence of the community and to weaken the strength of the Commonwealth," crime could only be reduced by "stopping production" of criminals and by regulating the upbringing of children who had criminal propensities.[44] It was not made clear by penal administrators like Scouller how these future criminals were to be identified with any degree of certainty or who was to be entrusted with the discretionary job of determining which children were redeemable and which were expendable.

Scouller's simplistic, workmanlike typology was confirmed by the experiences of other penal administrators. Franklin Giddings, professor of sociology at Columbia University, tried to refine these subjective schemes by constructing a typology of social classes from a Darwinist perspective. He objected to the arbitrary use of the term "social classes" to denote social superiority or inferiority, differences in wealth or economic status, and different interpretations of the "phenomena of progress, social unrest, degeneration, pauperism and crime." A "true class," he suggested, exists when "objects or individuals are grouped with reference to some characteristic that has been produced by evolutionary differentiation." The genesis of crime is a proper interest of sociologists because it is

an integral part of the general process of social differentiation. . . . The moment that associations begin to act upon unequally endowed indi-

44. Dr. J. D. Scouller, "Can We Save the Boys," *PNCCC, 1884,* pp. 102–14.

viduals, strengthening and enriching the social nature of some, while hardening the unsocial or anti-social nature of others, society begins to realize that it has to deal henceforth with the pauper and the criminal classes.

Although Giddings was unhappy with the lack of scientific rigor in the analyses of correctional administrators, his own typology revealed a similar judgmental bias and conservative distrust of the "criminal class." His typology ranked four classes according to wealth and prestige. The "social class," he said, is "sympathetic" and cooperative, "the natural aristocracy among men," whose "dispositions and abilities enable them and impel them to make positive contributions to that sum of helpful relations and activities which we call society."[45] The second class is "non-social," waiting to be "reached and impelled upward and downward by the resistless currents of social life," and the third class is a residual category consisting of "pseudo-social" paupers. The fourth class is composed of "anti-social" criminals for whom Giddings had little sympathy. "The criminal," he said, "makes no pretense of social virtue, for he frankly despises society and all its ways. Why a man should beg so long as there is anything to steal, why he should go to law if he is able to avenge himself, are the things that the true criminal cares not to understand."[46]

Although Giddings' "scientific" typology confirmed the private fears and prejudices of many correctional administrators, the mood of correctional work was slowly changing and environmental determinism was not as rigid and esoteric as its biological counterpart. The superintendent of the Kentucky Industrial School of Reform, for example, was convinced by 1898 that hereditary theories of crime were over-fatalistic. "While I believe heredity, of both moral and physical traits, to be a fact," he told delegates to a national conference, "I think it is unjustifiably made a bugaboo to discourage

45. Compare this with MacDonald's "normal class of individuals, who greatly exceed all other classes in number; these in every community constitute the conservative and trustworthy element and may be said to be the backbone of the race" (*Abnormal Man*, p. 9).

46. Franklin H. Giddings, "Is the Term 'Social Classes' a Scientific Category?" *PNCCC, 1895*, pp. 110–16.

efforts at rescue. We know that physical heredity tendencies can be neutralized and often nullified by proper counteracting precautions."[47] E. R. L. Gould, a sociologist at the University of Chicago, similarly objected to hereditary theories of crime, on the grounds that the empirical data was unconvincing. He criticized many so-called scientific studies for being unclear, morbid, and sentimental:

There is great danger in emphasizing heredity, and by contrast minimizing the influence of environment and individual responsibility. Consequences doubly unfortunate must ensue. Individual stamina will be weakened, and society made to feel less keenly the duty of reforming environment. Is it not better to postulate freedom of choice than to preach the doctrine of the unfettered will, and so elevate criminality into a propitiary sacrifice?[48]

The problem confronting criminologists of "whether the man makes the circumstances or the circumstances make the man" was skillfully clarified by Charles Cooley in an address before the National Conference of Charities and Correction in 1896. He considered it unnecessary and pointless to create a dichotomy between "nature" and "nurture," inferring that there is a choice of alternatives.[49] "Like male and female, each is sterile without the other." Cooley took a dynamic and flexible position regarding the way in which social character is formed:

The union of nature and nurture is not one of addition or mixture, but of growth, whereby the elements are altogether transformed into a new organic whole. One's nature acts selectively upon the environment, assimi-

47. Peter Caldwell, "The Duty of the State to Delinquent Children," *PNCCC, 1898*, pp. 404–10.
48. E. R. L. Gould, "The Statistical Study of Hereditary Criminality," *PNCCC, 1895*, pp. 134–43.
49. According to Hofstadter, "The new psychology . . . was a truly social psychology. . . . [I]nsistence upon the unreality of a personal psyche isolated from the social surroundings was a central tenet in the social theory of Charles H. Cooley. . . . The older psychology had been atomistic. . . . The new psychology, prepared to see the interdependence of the individual personality with the institutional structure of society, was destroying this one-way notion of social causation and criticizing its underlying individualism" (*Social Darwinism*, p. 150).

lating materials proper to itself; while at the same time the environment moulds the nature, and habits are formed which make the individual independent, in some degree, of changes in either.

As an example of the imperfections of the nature-nurture debate, Cooley, much influenced by the French sociologist Tarde, pointed out that in social life it is emulation and imitation which play a fundamental role in the "unified, communicative and co-operative life." Social institutions and social progress emanate from cooperation and conformity. "We have emulation by nature, but the direction in which emulation will lead us depends entirely upon the ideals suggested to us by our social experience." In proposing a crude theory of differential association, Cooley observed that the

well-nurtured boy emulates his own father and George Washington; but the child of the criminal, for precisely similar reasons, emulates *his* father ... or some other illustrious rascal. The very faculties that serve to elevate and ennoble a child who lives among good associations may make a criminal of one who lives among bad ones. We rise or fall with equal facility through our associative instincts.

Cooley made the important observation that criminal behavior depended as much upon social experiences and economic circumstances as it did upon the inheritance of biological traits. The delinquent child is constrained by social rather than biological forces; in essence, however, he is normally constituted and the "criminal class is largely the result of society's bad workmanship upon fairly good material." Cooley criticized theories of crime based on physical peculiarities, noting that there was a "large and fairly trustworthy body of evidence" to support the fact that many so-called degenerates could be made "useful citizens by rational treatment."[50]

In summary, the concept of the natural criminal was modified with the rise of a professional class of correctional administrators and social servants who promoted a medical model of deviant behavior and suggested techniques of remedying "natural" imperfections. The pessimism of Darwinism was counterbalanced by the

50. Charles H. Cooley, " 'Nature v. Nurture' in the Making of Social Careers," *PNCCC, 1896*, pp. 399–405.

spirit of philanthropy, religious optimism, and a belief in the dignity
of suffering.

URBAN DISENCHANTMENT

Another important influence on nineteenth-century images of crime
was a disenchantment with urban life. The city was depicted as the
main breeding ground of criminals: the impact of the physical
horrors of urban ghettos on unskilled, poorly educated European
immigrants "created" criminals. Immigrants were regarded as "un-
socialized" and the city's impersonality compounded their isolation
and degradation. "By some cruel alchemy," wrote Julia Lathrop,
"we take the sturdiest of European peasantry and at once destroy in
a large measure its power to rear to decent livelihood the first generation of offspring upon our soil."[51] Children born in the late nineteenth century confronted an increasingly complex and industrial
way of life. "The laborer on the verge of destitution," writes Oscar
Handlin, "was more characteristic than the yeoman farmer."[52]

To some social reformers, children were the innocent victims of
culture conflict and the technological revolution. Charles Loring
Brace felt that most homeless and vagrant children "are often of
very good stock; coming of honest European peasantry who, in a
foreign land, have become unfortunate. They are not links of a chain
of criminal inheritance. A criminal family in a large city, much
sooner than in rural districts, breaks up rapidly."[53] In general, however, criminal immigrants in the 1880's and 1890's were regarded
as an inferior human species who either refused to or were inherently
incapable of adjusting to American traditions.[54] One penologist,
William Douglas Morrison, typically commented that:

51. Julia Lathrop, "The Development of the Probation System in a Large
City," *Charities* 13 (January, 1905): 348.
52. Oscar Handlin, ed., *Children of the Uprooted,* p. 3.
53. "The 'Placing Out' Plan for Homeless and Vagrant Children," *PACC,*
1876, pp. 135–36.
54. John Higham, *Strangers in the Land,* pp. 68–105.

It is notorious that peoples of the type of the Italians and Hungarians exhibit much less respect for human life than is to be found among the northern races. Contact with the humanizing influences of American civilization no doubt has a wholesome effect in modifying the character and temperament of the children of the emigrants from the south. But family and racial characteristics cannot be altogether obliterated by social surroundings, and it is not at all unlikely that juvenile delinquency of the most serious kind in the United States is in some measure to be set down to the boundless hospitality of her shores.[55]

From 1860 to 1900, towns and cities suddenly emerged, grew with ferocious rapidity, and developed throughout the United States. While the rural population almost doubled during the latter half of the nineteenth century, the urban population increased by nearly seven times. Chicago expanded and its population multiplied more rapidly than any other city. Beginning as a trading post at the mouth of the Chicago River, it was organized into a village community by 1833 (with a population of approximately two hundred), granted a city charter in 1837, and in 1840 still had fewer than five thousand residents. But during the next fifty years its population more than doubled in every decade except that of the Great Fire of 1871. By 1890 more than a million people lived in Chicago and, from 1880 to 1910, the population rose by a half-million every ten years.[56]

Chicago at the peak of its population increases was a place of tremendous size, diversity and activity. To Lincoln Steffens it was "first in violence, deepest in dirt; loud, lawless, unlovely, ill-smelling, irreverent, new; an overgrown gawk of a village, the 'tough' among cities, a spectacle for the nation."[57] Many penal and educational reformers considered that human nature operated in a radically different way in the city compared with the country. It was, therefore, the task of reformers to make city existence more like life on the farm, where social relationships were considered wholesome,

---

55. *Juvenile Offenders*, p. 22.
56. Richard Hofstadter, *The Age of Reform*, pp. 174–86; Ray Ginger, *Altgeld's America: The Lincoln Ideal Versus Changing Realities, passim;* Bessie Louise Pierce, *A History of Chicago*, vol. 3, *passim*.
57. *The Shame of the Cities*, p. 234.

honest, and free from depravity and corruption. Jenkin Lloyd Jones, in a speech before the Illinois Conference of Charities in 1898, expressed the hope that redistribution of the population would remedy some of the serious social problems associated with industrialism:

The currents of industrial and commercial life have set in tremendously towards the city. Thither flows with awful precipitancy the best nerve, muscle and brain of the country, and the equilibrium will be permanently destroyed if there cannot be a counter current established, whereby the less competent, the unprotected, the helpless and the innocent can be passed back, to be restored and reinvigorated. And the over-accumulation of capital in the congested parts cannot be better or more normally invested than in restoring the equilibrium, giving to money as well as to life the circuit that passes from urban to rural centers. Here the more dependent wards of the state will find to a large measure the continuous activities necessary to full development, hinted at but not fully realized in the occupations of the kindergarten, activities that will command, if they do not always delight, the energy throughout the live-long day and the round year, occupations that may bring chapped hands, cold fingers and bruised heels; the activities that may be accompanied with hard beds and coarse clothing and crude schooling; activities that may leave the child in that blushing modesty that falls short of the etiquette of the town, but through this activity and through the enforced seclusion will the truer education come. . . . Let no one dismiss this suggestion as impossible or impracticable.[58]

The concentration of the population in the cities, combined with economic instability, was a certain portent of criminal behavior. "A community of this sort," wrote Morrison,

produces a large proportion of weak and ineffective people possessing very inadequate physical equipment for successfully fighting the battle of life. As a result of their physical deficiencies people of this kind are unable to obtain regular employment or to keep in work when they obtain it. Disease and sickness interfere with them and incapacitate them, and

58. "Who Are the Children of the State?" Illinois Conference of Charities (1898), *Fifteenth Biennial Report of the State Board of Commissioners of Public Charities of the State of Illinois,* pp. 286–87 (Springfield: Phillips Brothers, 1899).

they are driven down to the very lowest social stratum if they do not happen to have been born in it.[59]

A child entering such a social world is impelled by circumstance, by temptation, by parental neglect, and by a sense of adventure into a life of crime.

In the city, people live in an "atmosphere of suspicion and distrust," regarding the stranger as an intruder and treating him with open hostility. "These conditions of existence are destructive of social cohesion in its highest forms, and have a tendency to develop selfish instincts till they overstep the borderland which separates selfishness from crime."[60] Children coming from the country to this kind of environment are insufficiently controlled and protected:

The restraining eye of the village community is no longer upon them. In many cases they find themselves in a large city without friends, without family ties, and belonging to no social circle in which their conduct is either scrutinized or observed. In youth the social instincts are keen, and in one way or another be gratified, but the only method in which the solitary dweller in vast cities can do this is at the cheap music-hall and the public house [or bar]. . . . From a moral point of view it is unquestionable that the decentralization of industry is one of the most needed of present-day reforms. . . . It is highly questionable whether the enormous increase of national wealth which this century has witnessed is not being purchased at too high a price. . . . In a world such as ours, where in international matters might is right, it is highly perilous to undermine the vitality of a nation merely in order to make its population somewhat more opulent. . . .[61]

Although Morrison was writing for a European audience, it is understandable why *Juvenile Offenders,* published by Appleton in New York in 1897, was welcomed by American writers and correctional workers. His eclectic, multifactor approach which emphasized the interdependence of social and biological causes, and his basic distrust of urban life appealed to his American contemporaries

59. Morrison, *Juvenile Offenders,* p. 28.
60. *Ibid.,* p. 29.
61. *Ibid.,* pp. 31–33.

and supported the arguments of progressive reformers. Morrison's description of city life corresponded with the feelings of many middle-class reformers who decried the decline of rural life and, with it, the values associated with small agricultural communities.

The city symbolically embodied all the worst features of modern industrial life. The city was no place for the innocence of a young child; it debilitated, corrupted, misled, and tarnished youth. "Children," noted a member of the Massachusetts Board of Charities, "acquire a perverted taste for city life and crowded streets; but if introduced when young to country life, care of animals and plants, and rural pleasures, they are likely to enjoy these, and to be healthier in mind and body for such associations."[62] In order to prevent crime, said another delegate to a national conference, communities should establish schools, kindergartens and other preventive institutions in order to counteract the "foul tenements and the dirty streets and alleys of our great cities" where "the tainted air is sapping the vitality of the children, poisoning their blood, sowing their bodies with the seeds of disease, and educating the helpless hosts who crowd every market place of labor, unfit physically to contend in the struggle for existence."[63]

Children living in the city slums were described as "intellectual dwarfs" and "physical and moral wrecks" whose characters were predominantly shaped by their physical surroundings. Beverley Warner told the National Prison Association in 1898 that philanthropic organizations all over the country were

making efforts to get the children out of the slums, even if only once a week, into the radiance of better lives. Seeing the beauties of a better existence, these children may be led to choose the good rather than the evil. Good has been done by taking these children into places where they see ladies well dressed, and with their hands and faces clean, and it is only by leading the child out of sin and debauchery, in which it has lived, into

62. Mrs. Clara T. Leonard, "Family Homes for Pauper and Dependent Children," *PACC, 1879*, p. 174.
63. R. Heber Newton, "The Bearing of the Kindergarten on the Prevention of Crime," *PNCCC, 1886*, pp. 53–58.

a circle of life that is a repudiation of things that it sees in its daily life, that it can be influenced.[64]

The 1880's and 1890's represented for many middle-class intellectuals and professionals a period of discovery of the "dim attics and damp cellars in poverty-stricken sections of populous towns," and of "innumerable haunts of misery throughout the land."[65] The city was suddenly found to be a place of scarcity, disease, neglect, ignorance, and "dangerous influences." Its slums were the "last resorts of the penniless and the criminal"; here humanity reached the lowest level of degradation and misery.[66] Frederick Wines was one of few nineteenth-century criminologists to appreciate the relationship between urban disorganization and criminal behavior in the larger context of technological and social changes in American life:

In the history of modern times, there are three or four great facts which stand out pre-eminent above all the rest, as characteristic of the social life of today. One of these is the invention of labor-saving machinery, and its general adoption and use. I think that the invention of machinery has changed not only the appearance of the world, but also the relations of man to man. Another is the aggregation of capital in the hands of large and wealthy corporations. A third is the tendency everywhere apparent to the aggregation of population in great centers, in towns and villages, instead of being distributed, as it was formerly, over a great extent of

64. Beverley Warner, "Child Saving," *Proceedings of the Annual Congress of the National Prison Association, Indianapolis, 1898*, pp. 377–78.
65. William P. Letchworth, "Children of the State," *PNCCC, 1886*, p. 138. "Born in homes of comfort," said Letchworth, "and surrounded by the protecting influences of the church and good society, we are slow to appreciate the immense difference between our favored fate and that of the child whose first breath is drawn in an atmosphere of moral impurity and in the midst of privation . . ." (*ibid.,* 139). Urban imagery of social reformers in the late nineteenth century is further examined by Anselm Strauss, *Images of the American City*, pp. 215–45. The idea that intellectuals *discovered* poverty and alienation as a result of their own alienation from the centers of power has been fully treated by Hofstadter, *The Age of Reform*, pp. 148 f., and Christopher Lasch, *The New Radicalism in America, 1889–1963: The Intellectual as a Social Type, passim.*
66. R. W. Hill, " 'The Children of Shinbone Alley,' " *PNCCC, 1887*, p. 231.

rural area. I might possibly add to these a fourth, which is sometimes called—though I do not like the term very much—the emancipation of women. Taking these together, you will see that conditions of our social life today are, and must be, very different from what they were a hundred years ago. Our recent sudden and rapid development in these several directions may account in some degree for the present measure and manifestations of pauperism, insanity, and crime.[67]

The noncommercial and anti-urban sentiments of the urban reformers have been explained as a "sentimental attachment to rural living" and "a series of notions about rural people and rural life." Originally, the "agrarian myth" was a preoccupation of the eighteenth-century landowners, of those who had been classically educated and comprised the learned agricultural gentry. A central theme of the myth was the idea that the city was a parasitical growth on the country, corrupting the tranquillity, independence and moral integrity of the yeoman farmer. The agrarian view of the city was also dominant in the nineteenth century and was especially held by those reformers who feared that a traditional and highly idealized way of life was being denigrated by immigrants and foreigners. Richard Hofstadter suggests that:

One of the keys to the American mind at the end of the old century and the beginning of the new was that American cities were filling up in very considerable part with small-town or rural people. The whole cast of American thinking in this period was deeply affected by the experience of the rural mind confronted with the phenomena of urban life, its crowding, poverty, crime, corruption, impersonality, and ethnic chaos. To the rural migrant, raised in respectable quietude and the high-toned moral imperatives of evangelical Protestantism, the city seemed not merely a new social form or way of life, but a strange threat to civilization itself. . . . The Progressive mind . . . was pre-eminently a Protestant mind; and even though much of its strength was in the cities, it inherited the moral traditions of rural evangelical Protestantism. The Progressives were still freshly horrified by phenomena that we now resignedly consider indigenous to urban existence. However prosperous they were, they lived in

67. Frederick H. Wines, "Report of Committee on Causes of Pauperism and Crime," *PNCCC, 1886,* pp. 207–14.

the midst of all the iniquities that the agrarian myth had taught them to expect of urban life, and they refused to accept them calmly.[68]

Progressive reformers claimed that crime would diminish if children were controlled within their homes, thus restoring the "natural" relationships which the city had destroyed. "So far have we gone astray from the old democratic social relations of the village," noted the Boston Associated Charities,

that we even take pride in our lack of knowledge of each other and each other's welfare. The latest comer from the country, where he had known every family and child in his town, and been wont to regard them all as neighbours whose interests could not be separated from his own, soon falls prey to the vast selfishness which, like a vapor, is exhaled from these unnatural conditions. Subtly and imperceptibly it affects him, transforming him from the warm-hearted provincial to the cautious citizen.[69]

The preoccupation with the "natural" criminal was replaced by a concern for the "nurtured" criminal. Environmental constraint, unlike biological determinism, at least suggested the possibility of preventing crime by manipulating social institutions. Except for a brief period in the 1930's, the idea that criminals are born rather than made disappeared from correctional polemics.

SUMMARY

Important developments in the imagery of crime at the end of the last century were (1) the concept of the criminal as less than a complete human being, whether by nature or nurture, (2) the growth of professionalism in corrections work, and (3) the acceptance of the medical model and the "rehabilitative ideal," particularly with regard to the correction of "delinquent" children and adolescents.

　1. Although there was a wide difference of opinion as to the precipitating causes of crime, it was generally agreed among experts

68. *The Age of Reform,* pp. 24–25, 176, 204.
69. Quoted by Lubove, *The Professional Altruist,* p. 15.

that criminals were *abnormally* conditioned by biological and environmental factors. Early theories stressed the permanent, irreversible, and inherited character of criminal behavior. To the image of natural depravity was added the image of urban corruption. Reformers emphasized the disorganized features of urban life and encouraged remedial programs which embodied rural and primary group concepts. Slum life was regarded as unregulated, vicious and lacking in social rules; its inhabitants were depicted as abnormal and maladjusted, living their lives in conflict and chaos.[70]

2. The element of fatalism in theories of crime was modified with the rise of a professional class of penal administrators and social servants who promoted a developmental view of human behavior. The pessimistic implications of Darwinist creeds were antagonistic not only to the Protestant ethic but also to crime workers who aspired to the professional status of doctors, lawyers, and other human service functionaries. It was fortunate, as John Higham has observed, that Darwinism was flexible enough to suit both philanthropic and misanthropic views of social life.[71]

3. There has been a shift in the last fifty years or so in official policies concerning crime. The warrant has shifted from one emphasizing the criminal nature of delinquency to the "new humanism,"

70. William Foote Whyte, "Social Disorganization in the Slums," *American Sociological Review* 8 (1943): 34–39.

71. ". . . the general climate of opinion in the early Darwinian era inhibited the pessimistic implications of the new naturalism. What stood out in the first instance, as the great social lesson of the theory of natural selection, was not the ravages of the struggle for survival but rather the idea of 'the survival of the fittest.' To a generation of intellectuals steeped in confidence, the laws of evolution seemed to guarantee that the 'fittest' races would most certainly triumph over inferior competitors. . . . Darwinism, therefore, easily ministered to Anglo-Saxon pride, but in the age of confidence it could hardly arouse Anglo-Saxon anxiety.

"Secondly, Darwinism gave the race-thinkers little concrete help in an essential prerequisite of racism—belief in the preponderance of heredity over environment. Certainly the biological vogue of the late nineteenth century stimulated speculation along these lines, but the evolutionary theory by no means disqualified a fudamentally environmentalist outlook. Darwin's species struggled and evolved through adaption to those settings" (Higham, *Strangers in the Land,* pp. 135–36).

which speaks of disease, illness, contagion, and the like. The emergence of the medical warrant is of considerable significance, since it is a powerful rationale for organizing social action in the most diverse behavioral aspects of our society.

The "rehabilitative ideal"[72] presupposed that crime was a symptom of "pathology" and that criminals should be treated like irresponsible, sick patients. The older a criminal, the more chronic was his sickness; similarly, his chances of recovery were less than those of a young person. Adult criminals, particularly recidivists, were often characterized as nonhuman. Children, however, were less likely to be thought of as nonhuman since universalistic ethics, especially the ethic of Christianity, made it almost impossible to think of children as being entirely devoid of moral significance.

Social reformers emphasized the temporary and reversible nature of adolescent crime. As Charles Cooley observed, "when an individual actually enters upon a criminal career, let us try to catch him at a tender age, and subject him to rational social discipline, such as is already successful in enough cases to show that it might be greatly extended."[73] If, as the child savers believed, criminals are conditioned by biological heritage and brutish living conditions, then prophylactic measures must be taken early in life. Delinquent children—the criminals of the next generation—must be prevented from pursuing their criminal careers. "They are born to it," wrote the penologist Enoch Wines in 1880, "brought up for it. They must be saved."[74] Many new developments in penology took place at this time in the reformatory system where, it was hoped, delinquents would be saved and reconstituted.

72. This term is used by Francis A. Allen, *The Borderland of Criminal Justice.*
73. Cooley, " 'Nature v. Nurture,' " p. 405.
74. Enoch C. Wines, *The State of Prisons and of Child-Saving Institutions in the Civilized World,* p. 132.

Chapter 3: *The New Penology*

It was through the reformatory system that the child savers hoped to demonstrate that delinquents were capable of being converted into law-abiding citizens. The reformatory was developed in the United States during the middle of the nineteenth century as a special form of prison discipline for adolescents and young adults. Its underlying principles were formulated in Britain by Matthew Davenport Hill, Alexander Maconochie, Walter Crofton, and Mary Carpenter.[1] "Much more than any European country," wrote Max Grünhut, "the United States was prepared to accept and develop the new ideas of individualization of treatment and a progressive form of prison discipline."[2] If the United States did not have any great penal theorists, it at least had energetic penal administrators who were prepared to experiment with new programs. The most notable

1. This study is not concerned with European penology except to examine its influences on American criminology. A good overview of correctional practices until the middle of the nineteenth century is to be found in W. David Lewis, *From Newgate to Dannemora*, pp. 1–28. A widely cited book on penal practices is Harry Elmer Barnes and Negley K. Teeters, *New Horizons in Criminology*, pp. 322–542. A thoughtful and original study is provided by Hermann Mannheim, *The Dilemma of Penal Reform*.

2. *Penal Reform*, p. 89.

advocates of the reformatory plan in the United States were Enoch Wines, Secretary of the New York Prison Association, Theodore Dwight, the first Dean of Columbia Law School, Zebulon Brockway, Superintendent of Elmira Reformatory in New York, and Frank Sanborn, Secretary of the Massachusetts State Board of Charities.

The reformatory was distinguished from the traditional penitentiary by a policy of indeterminate sentencing, the "mark" system, and "organized persuasion" rather than "coercive restraint."[3] Its administrators assumed that abnormal and troublesome individuals could be trained to become useful and productive citizens.[4] Wines and Dwight, in a report to the New York legislature in 1867, proposed that the ultimate aim of penal policy was reformation of the criminal, which could only be achieved "by placing the prisoner's fate, as far as possible, in his own hand, by enabling him, through industry and good conduct to raise himself, step by step, to a position of less restraint; while idleness and bad conduct, on the other hand, keep him in a state of coercion and restraint."[5]

Brockway told delegates to the first meeting of the celebrated National Prison Congress, held in Cincinnati in 1870, that it was the task of scientific penology to protect society *"by the prevention of crime and reformation of criminals."* But "science" was not to be confused with "sickly sentimentalism": "criminals shall either be cured, or kept under such continued restraint as gives guarantee of safety from further depredations."[6]

Zebulon Brockway was typical of the new breed of penal reformers. Born in Connecticut, the son of a successful merchant who held a number of important civic offices, he entered the prison serv-

3. *Ibid.,* pp. 89–94.
4. James A. Leonard, "Reformatory Methods and Results," in Charles R. Henderson, ed., *Penal and Reformatory Institutions,* pp. 121–28; O. F. Lewis, *The Development of American Prisons and Prison Customs, 1776–1845,* pp. 293–322 (Albany, New York: Prison Association of New York, 1922).
5. Cited by Grünhut, *Penal Reform,* p. 90.
6. This speech is reprinted in Zebulon Reed Brockway, *Fifty Years of Prison Service,* pp. 389–408; emphasis added.

ices soon after his twenty-first birthday and worked his way up as
a guard, clerk, and assistant superintendent of state prisons at
Rochester and Detroit. In 1876, he became superintendent at Elmira
where he remained for nearly twenty-five years. He was a man of
limited education and practical wisdom who had a thorough grasp
of penal administration and was held in high esteem by his professional colleagues. Brockway's other suggestions to the National
Prison Congress included an independent board of guardians
controlling the new reformative institutions, primary and reform
schools for children and juveniles, and a graduated system of reformatories for adults.[7]

The foremost American authority on reformatories and institutions for children prior to the twentieth century was Enoch C.
Wines. Born in Hanover, New Jersey, in 1806, he soon moved to
Vermont with his family, where he worked on his father's farm
until attending college. After graduating from Middlebury College
with doctorate degrees in divinity and law, he taught at various experimental colleges in New Jersey, spent some time as an educational
administrator, and for a short while accepted the position of school-
master on a training frigate, thus traveling and visiting the Medi-
terranean countries where he studiously learned the Romance
languages. In 1832, he married Emma Stansbury who bore him
seven sons, one of whom, Frederick, also became a renowned expert
on crime and penology.

In 1861, he gave up the presidency of the newly founded University of St. Louis and returned to the East coast to take up the job
of secretary of the New York Prison Association. Together with

7. *Ibid.*, pp. 3–22, 161 f., 396–99. By a "graduated series of reformatory
institutions," Brockway meant (1) a House of Reception where "all prisoners should be received and retained, until reliable information is obtained as
to their ancestral history, their constitutional tendencies and propensities,
their early social condition and its probable influence in forming their character . . . upon which basis a plan of treatment may be outlined"; (2) an
Industrial Reformatory where "prisoners coming into this institution with
good physical health will be here so trained in labor as to ensure their productive employment thereafter . . ."; (3) an Intermediate Reformatory,
established as a cooperative settlement, which would serve the same function
as Crofton's intermediate prison, "an outpost on the brink of society" (*ibid.*,
pp. 397–98).

Dwight, Brockway, and Sanborn, he gave wide publicity to the Irish system of prison reform, encouraged the adoption of the reformatory system for youthful offenders, and was a regular delegate to national conferences on philanthropy and corrections. In 1870, he called a meeting in Cincinnati for the purpose of organizing the influential National Prison Association and, in 1872, he was honored with the presidency of the first International Penal Congress which was held in London.[8]

Prior to his death in 1879, at the age of 73, he had been collecting information on prison and reformatory systems around the world. The manuscript was revised and edited by his son, Frederick Wines, and published posthumously in 1880 as *The State of Prisons and of Child-Saving Institutions in the Civilized World*. An immense and comprehensive treatise, it was immediately recognized as a unique and authoritative piece of scholarship. It represented the "best" thought of the day and was widely cited, for it included a chapter on the "ideal system of institutions for the prevention and repression of crime." Wines' book had an appealing blend of conventional wisdom, religious dogma, and reformistic vigor. The book was widely used until the early 1900's and, although it contained no remarkable innovations, it nevertheless solidified and synthesized a large body of theories, opinions, and practical experiences.

Like Mary Carpenter in England and Zebulon Brockway in New York, Enoch Wines was concerned with programming an ideal penal system which, given the proper financial and institutional resources, could be practically implemented. He proposed that state authorities should assume control of children under fourteen years who lack proper care or guardianship; their supervision should be delegated, he said, to private citizens and charity organizations, which should be state subsidized, provided that certain minimal standards were observed.[9] Reformatories for children should develop as far as possible the conditions of home life and they should be built in the country, for "the normal place of education for such children is in the fields."

8. Negley K. Teeters, *Deliberations of the International Penal and Penitentiary Congresses, 1872–1935*, pp. 27–28.
9. Enoch C. Wines, *The State of Prisons and of Child-Saving Institutions in the Civilized World*, p. 608.

They should preferably be modeled on the "cottage plan" with forty children in each institution; institutions for very young children should be managed exclusively by women. "More voluntary effort, more individual interest; more sympathy and zeal will thus be called forth."[10]

Frederick Wines inherited his father's tireless energy and pragmatic philosophy. He was responsible, as Secretary of the Board of Public Charities, for many penal reforms in Illinois and yet he also found time to write articles and books, as well as attending and participating in numerous national conferences. In 1878, he was appointed a Special Commissioner from the United States to the second International Penitentiary Congress, held in Stockholm. He heard a number of influential penal reformers, notably Mary Carpenter and T. B. L. Baker, discuss problems associated with the prevention of juvenile delinquency. He was pleased with the "peculiarly practical turn" of the Congress and made a special note of the resolutions on preventive legislation. The Congress resolved that delinquent children should not be punished but educated so as to enable them to "gain an honest livelihood and to become of use to society instead of an injury to it." Reformatories should educate children by moral training, religion, and labor—similar to the upbringing they would receive in an "honest family." Children should be segregated in reformatories according to religious preference, and "the number of pupils in one institution should be sufficiently small to enable the director at all times to take a personal interest in each pupil." The training program should "correspond to the mode of life of working people; it should include primary instruction, and should be characterized by the greatest simplicity in diet, dress, and surroundings, and above all by labor." Children should be kept in reformatories indeterminately until the age of eighteen but

to the utmost extent possible, the placing of vicious children either in families or in public institutions should take place without the interven-

10. *Ibid.*, pp. 609–10. Wines' "ideal system" owes much to the ideas of Mary Carpenter. See Mary Carpenter, "What Should be Done for the Neglected and Criminal Children of the United States?" *Proceedings of the Annual Conference of Charities (PACC), 1875*, pp. 66–76.

tion of the courts. . . . The Congress approves the efforts in this direction made by some governments to substitute for the action of the judiciary the intervention of a tutelary agency created for this purpose.[11]

Assuming, then, that "nurture" could usually overcome most of nature's defects, reformatory administrators set about the task of establishing programs consistent with the aim of retraining delinquents for law-abiding careers. It was noted at the Fifth International Prison Congress held in Paris in 1895 that reformatories were capable of obliterating hereditary and environmental taints.[12] In a new and special section devoted to delinquency, the Congress proposed that children under twelve years "should always be sent to institutions of preservation" and "unworthy parents must be deprived of the right to rear children. . . . The preponderant place in rational physical training should be given to manual labor, and particularly to agricultural labor in the open air, for both sexes."[13]

"How can we reach the germ and prevent its development into self-perpetuating evil?" was a question occupying the minds of many correctional workers. "Is the hereditary taint too inherent in the constitution to be arrested and healthy development secured? Or are the conditions of their existence such as renders their elevation into respectability or soundness impossible?"[14] Most experts answered this query optimistically, partly as a rationalization for their own endeav-

11. Frederick Wines, "Report on the International Penitentiary Congress, 1878," in Board of State Commissioners of Public Charities of the State of Illinois, *Fifth Biennial Report*, pp. 273–85 (Springfield, Illinois: Weber, Magie & Co., 1879).

12. Frederick Wines had begun to accept this position several years earlier. "We do not claim, and no sensible person will ever claim, that all prisoners can be reformed. The influences of heredity, of early associations and training, and of acquired habits, are in very many instances, too strong to encourage any reasonable expectation that they can be successfully counteracted and overcome in prison. . . . We do contend, however, that the experience of prison officers does not warrant the assertion that efforts for their reformation are hopeless" ("Reformation as an End in Prison Discipline," *Proceedings of the National Conference of Charities and Correction* [*PNCCC*], *1888*, p. 193).

13. Teeters, *Deliberations*, pp. 97–102.

14. Mrs. W. P. Lynde, "Prevention in Some of its Aspects," *PACC*, *1879*, p. 163.

ors and partly as an acknowledgment of the fact that reformatories
appeared to be doing a successful job of regeneration and retraining.
At the National Conference of Charities and Correction in 1898,
Henry D. Chapin observed that

we must first distinguish the deformities of disease from the commonly
accepted stigmata of degeneration. . . . The earlier such proclivities are
discovered, the more may be done by special education and care to correct
them. Environment of the right sort may do much to correct any of the
recognized vices of heredity.[15]

Superintendents of reformatories had to surpass overwhelming
obstacles in order to achieve successful reformation. "We have deep-
seated convictions," wrote Levi S. Fulton, "concerning heredity, constitutional bias, physical and mental limitations."[16] Peter Caldwell,
another reform school superintendent, observed that reformatories
were expected to "remedy the neglect and vice of parents, the failure
of public schools, of mission and Sunday schools, and other moral
agencies in the outside world." It demanded skill and resolution to
"develop the bent sapling into the straight tree, and transform the
embriotic criminal into the excellent citizen." But by proper training
the reformatory could offer a young offender a "fair chance for future
usefulness and respectability." The typical resident of a reformatory,
said Caldwell, has been "cradled in infamy, imbibing with its earliest
natural nourishment the germs of a depraved appetite, and reared in
the midst of people whose lives are an atrocious crime against natural
and divine law and the rights of society." In order to correct and
reform such a person, the reformatory plan was designed to teach the
value of adjustment, private enterprise, thrift and self-reliance. "To
make a good boy out of this bundle of perversities, his entire being
must be revolutionized. He must be taught self-control, industry,
respect for himself and the rights of others."[17]

Penal administrators had great faith in the capacity of reformatories to save children "to virtue and honor." Enoch Wines, for ex-

15. Henry Dwight Chapin, "Anthropological Study in Children's Institutions," *PNCCC, 1898,* pp. 424–25.
16. "Education as a Factor in Reformation," *PNCCC, 1886,* p. 65.
17. Peter Caldwell, "The Reform School Problem," *PNCCC, 1886,* pp.
71–76.

ample, claimed a success rate of 60 per cent—some administrators claimed up to 80 per cent—for the reformatory plan:

Our prisons have heretofore been mainly places of punishment, and have done little comparatively to check crime; our reformatory and preventive institutions have checked crime, and in a large majority of instances have wrought a practical reformation of their inmates. Of course, the material is better in these establishments than in the prison—the inmates are more tender in years, less hardened in crime, more easily moulded, and far less under the slavery of degrading habits. But this is not all. The spirit of our reformatories is that of hope and effort, while listless indifference or despair too often reigns in our prisons. The sentences of young offenders are wisely regulated for their amendment; they are not absurdly shortened as if they signified only so much endurance of vindictive suffering. The whole machinery of the establishment is set in the reformatories for the good training of the child, while in prisons it is too often allowed to chafe and wear upon the moral nature and chill the best aspirations of the adult convict. America has little reason today to be proud of her prisons; but she can justly take pride in her juvenile reformatories; from the very beginning of their work fifty years ago until now.

Reformatories were the answer to the "torrent of criminality that is sweeping the land." Here children would be safe from "a catalogue of exposures, temptations, and perils."[18]

The reformatory system was based on the assumption that proper training can counteract the impositions of poor family life, a corrupt environment and poverty, while at the same time toughening and preparing delinquents for the struggle ahead. "The principle at the root of the educational method of dealing with juvenile crime," wrote William Douglas Morrison,

is an absolutely sound one. It is a principle which recognizes the fact that the juvenile delinquent is in the main a product of adverse individual and social conditions. From this fundamental fact it draws the obvious conclusion that the only effective treatment of juvenile crime must consist in placing the juvenile in the midst of wholesome material and moral surroundings.[19]

18. Enoch Wines, *The State of Prisons*, pp. 80–81, 125, 131–32.
19. William Douglas Morrison, *Juvenile Offenders*, pp. 274–75.

Reformatories, unlike penitentiaries and jails, theoretically repudiated punishments based on intimidation and repression. Restraint and punishment were only the means and not the goals of penal programs. Corporal punishment, suggested the Superintendent of the Connecticut State Reform School, should only be inflicted as a last resort. "All ludicrous and highly artificial punishments are to be avoided. All punishments that bring raillery and ridicule upon the object of it, are not to be tolerated."[20]

In summary, penal reformers at the end of the nineteenth century used the reformatory plan to develop new ideas about the nature and purposes of imprisonment. The first to benefit from these innovations were adolescents and young adults who were more deserving of and more susceptible to reformation.[21] The reformatory plan embodied the following principles:[22] (1) Young offenders must be segregated from the corrupting influences of adult criminals. (2) "Delinquents" need to be removed from their environment and imprisoned for their own good and protection. Reformatories should be guarded sanctuaries, combining love and guidance with firmness and restraint. (3) "Delinquents" should be assigned to reformatories without trial and with minimal legal requirements. Due process is not required because reformatories are intended to reform and not to punish. (4) Sentences should be indeterminate, so that inmates are encouraged to cooperate in their own reform and recalcitrant "delinquents" are not allowed to resume their criminal careers. (5) Reformation should not be confused with sentimentality. Punishment is required only insofar as it is good for the punished person and only when other methods have been exhausted. (6) Inmates must be protected from idleness, indulgence, and luxuries through military drill, physical exercise, and constant supervision. (7) Reformatories should be built in the countryside and designed according to the "cottage

20. G. E. Howe, "The Family System," *PNCCC, 1880,* p. 223.

21. William Howard Neff, "Reformatories for Juvenile Delinquents," *PNCCC, 1890,* p. 231.

22. A good summary of the reformatory plan is to be found in A. E. Elmore, "Report of the Committee on Reformatories and Houses of Refuge," *PNCCC, 1884,* pp. 84–91.

plan." (8) Labor, education, and religion constitute the essential program of reform.[23] Inmates should not be given more than an elementary education. Industrial and agricultural training should predominate. (9) The value of sobriety, thrift, industry, prudence, "realistic" ambition, and adjustment must be taught.

THE NEW EDUCATION

Child saving and the new education were part of a larger social movement which went beyond mere instrumental reforms and set as its goal the revitalization and salvation of society. Common to both movements were a preoccupation with naturalism, an antithetical view of personality and culture, a belief in the value of self-help, and a romantic exaggeration of the importance of experience in learning.

Progressive education had at its core something new and important. Contrasted with traditional educational methods, it refused to accept the passivity of the child in the classroom, reduced some authoritarian features of the teaching role, and deemphasized the importance of rote learning. "It had the great merit," wrote Hofstadter, "of being experimental in a field in which too many people thought that all the truths had been established."[24]

John Dewey, whose ideas influenced the child savers, told a Chicago audience in 1899 that it was the task of teachers to dispose of the myth that education is reserved for an intellectual aristocracy. Education, he said, must be modernized to adjust to the tremendous social transformations accompanying industrialism. Dewey took note of the great scientific advances of his century, the growth of vast manufacturing centers, the development of cheap and rapid means of communication, the emergence of the metropolis, and the commercialization of manners and tastes. "Even our moral and religious ideas and interests, the most conservative because the deepest-lying

23. *Second Biennial Report of the Board of State Commissioners of Public Charities of the State of Illinois*, pp. 199–204.
24. Richard Hofstadter, *Anti-intellectualism in American Life*, p. 369.

things in our nature, are profoundly affected. That this revolution," said Dewey, "should not affect education in other than a formal and superficial fashion is inconceivable." He warned his audience that "it is useless to bemoan the departure of the good old days of children's modesty, reverence, and implicit obedience, if we expect merely by bemoaning and exhortation to bring them back."

Dewey was not opposed to modernization and scientific progress; he welcomed "the increase in toleration, in breadth of social judgment, the larger acquaintance with human nature, . . . and contact with greater commercial activities." These gains, however, were not generally beneficial to children and had to be measured against the accompanying decline in family unity and intimacy which had important disciplinary, educational and character-building consequences:

Those of us who are here today need go back only one, two, or at most three generations, to find a time when the household was practically the center in which were carried on, or about which were clustered, all the typical forms of industrial occupation. . . . There was always something which really needed to be done, and a real necessity that each member of the household should do his own part faithfully and in co-operation with others. Personalities which became effective in action were bred and tested in the medium of action. Again, we cannot overlook the importance for educational purposes of the close and intimate acquaintance got with nature at first hand, with real things and materials, with the actual processes of their manipulation, and the knowledge of their social necessities and uses.[25]

The conception of the child formed by spokesmen for the new education was, as Hofstadter has observed, "more romantic and primitivist than it was post-Darwinian. Theirs was a commitment to the natural qualities of childhood as against the artificiality of society.[26] The emphasis on naturalism encouraged a naïve sentimentalism in less sophisticated educators. One child saver felt that "in-

25. John Dewey, "The School and Social Progress," in Ray Ginger, ed., *American Social Thought,* pp. 19–21, 27.
26. Hofstadter, *Anti-intellectualism in American Thought,* p. 363.

creased mechanization" was the source of children's corruption. "Children," said Miriam Van Waters, "should deal with elemental things of the world—earth, stones, trees, animals, running water, fire, open spaces—instead of pavements, signboards, subdivided lots, apartment houses, and electric percolators. Civilization has been hardest on children."[27] Dewey was never very clear about the goals at which the new educational techniques were aimed and, in authoritarian institutions, they were used as a rationale for taming the "spirit of youth." The romanticism of the new education meant that the simplest trade could be given poetic stature.[28]

The idea that children should learn from life as well as from books was a progressive innovation, but it lent itself too easily to the anti-intellectualism of the "life-adjustment" educators. The most consequential deficiency of the new education was that it was primarily individualistic and used to reconcile the poor and deviant to their lot in life.[29] Ambition, self-help and independence were to be rewarded only so long as aspirations were consistent with status and capacity. Social Darwinists, new educators, and child savers agreed that education should be child-centered, not teacher-centered, so that students could make their own investigations and be encouraged to discover as much as possible through their own efforts. "The marked success of the self-made man," advised Herbert Spencer in an essay republished in the United States, was testimony to this approach:

27. "The Juvenile Court from the Child's Viewpoint," in Jane Addams, ed., *The Child, the Clinic and the Court*, p. 221.

28. See T. J. Charlton, "Report of the Committee on Juvenile Delinquents," *PNCCC, 1890*, pp. 227–29, for an account of the "worthy" qualities of basically menial jobs.

29. According to Hofstadter, "*Democracy and Education*, for all its generalized discussion of leisure and working classes, had almost nothing to say about the specific class structure of American society or the relation of educational opportunity to increase social mobility and break down class barriers. In short, his view of the problem of education and democracy was not economic or sociological, or even political, except in the broadest sense of that term. . . . In Dewey's theory, the ends of democratic education are to be served by the socialization of the child, who is to be made into a co-operative rather than a competitive being and 'saturated' with the spirit of service" (*Anti-intellectualism in American Life*, p. 379).

This need for perpetual telling is the result of our stupidity, not of the child's. We drag it away from the facts in which it is interested, and which it is actively assimilating of itself; we put before it facts far too complex for it to understand, and therefore distasteful to it; finding that it will not voluntarily acquire these facts, we thrust them into its mind by force of threats and punishment; by thus denying the knowledge it craves, and cramming it with knowledge which it cannot digest, we produce a morbid state of its faculties, and a consequent disgust for knowledge in general; and when, as a result partly of still continued unfitness in its studies, the child can understand nothing without explanation, and become a mere passive recipient of our instruction, we infer that education must necessarily be carried on thus. Having by our method induced helplessness, we straightaway make the helplessness a reason for our method.[30]

Spencer believed that the child who is encouraged to learn independently and to test out his own discoveries is guaranteed a "vividness and permanency of impression which the usual methods can never produce. Any piece of knowledge which the pupil has himself acquired, any problem which he has himself solved, becomes by virtue of the conquest much more thoroughly his than it could else be." By making learning a "process of self-education," children become aware that life is a struggle for existence in which success comes to those who are capable of independent inquiry, self-instruction and imaginative use of limited resources.[31]

The issue of educational discipline was of the utmost importance because it provided a realistic criterion of democratic education. Spencer did not favor cruel punishments because they were likely to accustom students to despotism and arbitrariness, thus impeding the "natural" progress of democracy. Nevertheless, teachers were required to impose discipline at their own discretion because students needed to be taught the inevitable consequences of their misbehavior.[32] The new education did not dispute the absolute authority of the teacher over his pupils. The relationship between child and parent, student and teacher, and delinquent and correctional worker

30. Herbert Spencer, *Education: Intellectual, Moral and Physical*, pp. 124–26.
31. *Ibid.*, pp. 155, 166.
32. *Ibid.*, pp. 174–75.

was viewed only as a cooperative process in the sense that children were to be impressed that adults had their best interests at heart. In reformatories certainly, and even in most schools, the authoritarian impulse was dominant. The idea that a "teacher" may be both a friend and a disciplinarian had far-reaching consequences for the child-saving movement.

Since progressive educators failed to confront the full implications of their assumptions about the educational process in a democracy, they must be held partly responsible for the misuse that others made of their ideas.[33] Penal reformers exploited the rhetoric of the new education to give respectability and legitimacy to programs of agricultural and industrial training in reformatories. Most reformatories in the United States, reported T. J. Charlton in 1890, taught at least twelve trades and manual skills.[34] Ideally, said Brockway, "when there are a thousand or more prisoners confined, thirty-six trades and branches of trades may be usefully taught."[35] The anti-intellectualism of proponents of the reformatory plan was obvious: Brockway encouraged Hamilton Wey at Elmira to make inmates muscular rather than educated; the International Penitentiary Congress favored manual labor over higher education; the majority of reformatory administrators felt that delinquents did not deserve more than an elementary education; and the ideal reformatory was built in the countryside and equipped like an agricultural training school. The Superintendent of the New Jersey Reform School considered it his job, for example, "to get the idea out of the heads of city boys that farm life is menial and low. . . . Though the work may be hard, and usually done by men or boys working alone or in small companies, this is one of its beneficial features."[36]

Industrial education, as it was euphemistically called, was derived

33. Hofstadter, *Anti-intellectualism in American Life*, p. 367.
34. Charlton, "Report of the Committee," pp. 214–30. These twelve "general industries" were washing and ironing, cooking, bread- and cake-baking, tailoring, painting, shoe-making and shoe-repairing, carpentry, floriculture, caring for stock, farming, music, steam- and gas-fitting.
35. Brockway, *Fifty Years of Prison Service*, p. 421.
36. Ira D. Otterson, "General Features of Reform School Work," *PNCCC, 1892*, pp. 169–71.

from new developments in educational theory. The training of "delinquents" in manual and low-skilled jobs was justified as an educational enterprise because it was consistent with the rhetoric and aims of the child savers. The principles of the "new education" were misinterpreted and restyled to support the thesis that knowledge is subordinate to action and inferior to practice.[37] The educational benefits of industrial training, commented the Superintendent of the New York Orphan Asylum, lay in its capacity to train children for commonplace work. "No amount of instruction by a teacher of domestic science in the instruction school can rank in value with a thorough training through practical experiences in preparing, cooking, and serving the regular meals of the cottage from the individual cottage kitchen."[38] Bookishness was an undesirable attribute and the lowest form of menial labor was rationalized as an educational experience.[39] "We have in our Indiana reformatories a large number of colored boys and girls," Charlton told the National Conference of Charities and Correction in 1890.

In our boys' school, we aim to teach "cooking" and "waiting on tables" and laundry work to the colored boys. . . . This is a world for industry. It is our duty to do our part, to help the unfortunate, and to teach them how they may earn an honest living. If, after we do this, they still refuse to work, then they can never blame the State for their downfall. If they subsequently choose a life of crime, they must abide the consequences. . . . In all this life there is no room for the lazy person.[40]

From the new education, penal reformers took the assumption that the essential purpose of education is to indoctrinate children with the values of the middle-class, adult world. Social progress was to be achieved by "improving the quality of men's private lives," by confronting social, economic, and political problems with personal

37. Hofstadter, *Anti-intellectualism in America*, p. 362.
38. R. R. Reeder, "To Cottage and Country," *Charities* 13 (January, 1905): 365.
39. Dewey felt that books were harmful if substituted for experience but indispensable in interpreting and expanding experience. Most of Dewey's followers failed to appreciate this distinction. See Ray Ginger, *Altgeld's America: The Lincoln Ideal Versus Changing Realities,* pp. 203–8.
40. Charlton, "Report of the Committee," pp. 228–29.

solutions, and by redirecting the spirit of youth into socially accept-able channels.[41] What the more sensitive educational theorists sug-gested about children's capacity for originality, pride in discovery and self-direction had only the slightest influence on educational techniques in schools and reformatories. Instead, what most ap-pealed to teachers and correctional workers was the paternalistic premise of the new education, its belief in social progress through individual self-help, and its nostalgic allusion to the stability and intimacy of a pre-industrial way of life. The movement to cottage and country represented yet another way in which the principles of progressive education were translated into action by penal reformers.

TO COTTAGE AND COUNTRY

The trend from congregate housing in the city to group living in the country represented a significant change in the organization of penal institutions for young offenders. Salvation for the "city waif" and "gamin of the alley" was only possible if they were returned to a "simpler and saner life," "the normalities of the country," and "the simplicities of the farm." In order to truly help delinquents, said the President of the Illinois Conference of Charities in 1898, "they must be given simplicity, protection, and seclusion."[42]

Most penologists agreed that children living under "normal parental conditions" should not be committed to reformatories. "The discipline of a somewhat inferior home," wrote William Douglas Morrison, "is always better than the discipline of an insti-tution, and the efforts of parental solicitude are much more likely to be effectual in the ultimate reclamation of a wayward child than

41. Christopher Lasch, *The New Radicalism in America, 1889–1963*, p. 163 (New York: Alfred A. Knopf, 1965).
42. Jenkin Lloyd Jones, "Who Are the Children of the State?" *Proceedings of the Illinois Conference of Charities* (1898), in *Fifteenth Biennial Report of the Board of State Commissioners of Public Charities*, pp. 283, 286–87 (Springfield: Phillips Brothers, 1899).

any kind of State machinery."[43] In an address before the National Conference of Charities and Correction in 1891, Homer Folks pointed out that reformatories were not in many cases a substitute for parental affection and that they might even encourage parents to evade moral and financial obligations to their children.

Folks, anticipating recent sociological theories on the labeling of deviants, pointed out that an "inherent evil" of the reformatory system was its tendency to fasten an "enduring stigma" on its inmates:

The reformatory is, first and foremost, a place to which criminal children are sent to be reformed; and the implication is, in the case of every child thus committed, that the community was obliged in self-defense to place it behind bars. Just as the criminal discharged from prison finds it difficult or impossible to reinstate himself in society, so the boy discharged from the reformatory finds himself branded with the trademark of crime. This perpetuates the evil of association, since the discharged boy seeks as his companions those who by similar discipline and education have the same interests and sympathies.

The reformatory, said Folks, does not prepare a youth for the outside world. At the moment of his release, he is "thrown into the midst of temptation, doubly powerful because of novelty. Just at this moment the strict discipline must be withdrawn. The routine of life by which he has been carried along is removed."[44]

Although Folks was the most articulate and consistent critic of the American reformatory system, he was more dissatisfied with its execution than its underlying principles. He had to admit that institutions were a necessary evil which could be made to approximate the spirit of family life. Most penologists, however, had few reservations about the usefulness and benefits of reformatories; to them a cottage-plan reformatory in the country was more "natural" and wholesome than a slum tenement. "In removing a boy from an inadequate or bad home into a better or good one," noted G. E. Howe,

43. Morrison, *Juvenile Offenders*, p. 289.
44. Homer Folks, "The Care of Delinquent Children," *PNCCC, 1891,* pp. 137–39.

we are not acting in violation, but in harmony with natural law. . . . So that if we remove a child from parents who have virtually orphaned him by their inadequacy, neglect, or cruel usage, and from a home unnatural and hateful, and bring him into the adoption of a wiser and better parentage, and into the more natural home of comfort and benevolence, then, again, we are not going contrary to, but in unison with, natural principles.[45]

The cottage plan differed in several important respects from the congregate style of traditional prisons and jails. According to William Letchworth, in an address delivered before the National Conference of Charities and Correction in 1886, reformatories should encourage individuality and an awareness of family responsibilities.[46] Howe outlined the requisites of an ideal cottage plan:

. . . the inmates are classified, and limited numbers are placed in modest but well built cottages, which are free from anything like the usual prison appliances, and furnished with all the necessaries and comforts of a well ordered home, presided over by a Christian gentleman and lady, who, as husband and wife, hold the relation of father and mother toward the youth of the household. Each family is distinct from the other families in all matters of its own particular management, but is united with all the others under one central head. Every family having its own school-room, dining-room, dormitory and play-ground. The government of each family is to be thoroughly parental, and physical coercion must never be used until other means have failed, and even then, to be administered under the humanizing spirit and genius of the family.[47]

R. R. Reeder, Superintendent of the New York Orphan Asylum, observed that the ideal reformatory should contain the "essential elements of a good home."[48] Several years earlier, Mary Carpenter had also suggested that "the loving spirit of the family [should be] infused by the resident officials and voluntary benevolent effort. The surroundings of the young persons thus brought into an artificial

45. Howe, "The Family System," pp. 209–10.
46. William P. Letchworth, "Children of the State," *PNCCC, 1886*, pp. 151–56.
47. Howe, "The Family System," p. 210.
48. Reeder, "To Cottage and Country," p. 366.

atmosphere should correspond with their natural mode of life, as far as possible as is compatible with sanitary conditions, order, and propriety."[49]

The traditional principles of prison discipline were considered abhorrent to youthful offenders and an "outrage [to] the nature of child life." The prison, with its "bolted door, barred window, walled yard, shadowy cell" and "brute force," said Howe, are antagonistic to the reform of young children. "The child loves and pants for freedom. His every contact with nature is but his communion with a second mother." The prison is an "unnatural home" and its officers are "never parental or fraternal, but suspicious constables and taskmasters."

In institutions based on the family plan, it was important that the staff be carefully selected for their character, intelligence, and "strong natural love for children." They should be "Christian gentlemen and ladies" with common sense, "natural refinement," and good education. "Love and enthusiasm for the work are ever the great requirements to be insisted upon in the choice of those to be in authority and parentage over these children and youth, and anything like the hireling spirit in the candidate for these places is to be abhorred, and the mere seekers of place and salary to be rejected as unworthy." In reply to the criticism that under the open or family system children are tempted to escape, Howe noted that a "wise liberty becomes its own defender." If the institution is as comfortable and kind as a natural home why should a child wish to escape? "But suppose that if even five or ten per cent of the worst boys should irretrievably run away, should the remaining percentage never be trusted to the beneficence of freedom? . . . The boy or man in need of reformatory treatment," he continued, "is well-nigh hopeless if he is to be continually suspected. Such policy of perpetual suspicion is irritative, hateful, and a bondage that blunts and blights whatever desire he may have to be *worthy* of confidence." In the traditional

49. Mary Carpenter, "Suggestions on Reformatory Schools and Prison Discipline, Founded on Observations Made During a Visit to the United States," *Proceedings of the National Prison Reform Congress, 1874,* p. 158.

prison, "suspicion and spying are reduced to a science, and the child is never in a position to have his honor fairly tried."[50] What the congregate plan offered in terms of economy and efficiency was sufficiently compensated by the preservation of the child's social instincts and familial obligations under the cottage plan.

The new penology emphasized the corruptness and artificiality of the city; from progressive education it inherited a concern for naturalism, purity, and innocence. It is not surprising, therefore, that the cottage plan also entailed a movement to a rural location. The aim of penal reformers was not merely to use the countryside for teaching agricultural skills. The confrontation between depraved delinquents and unspoilt nature was intended to have a spiritual and regenerative effect. "Under a new atmosphere of kindness, sympathy, comfort and self-respect," said Charles Loring Brace, "many of their vices drop from them like the old and verminous clothing they left behind. . . . The entire change of circumstances seems to cleanse them from many bad habits." Out in the country "they are not so liable to fall in with bad company and idleness does not leave them to its dangers."[51]

In his famous study of *The Dangerous Classes of New York,* Brace contributed to the myth that "the cultivators of the soil are in America our most solid and intelligent class. . . . It is, accordingly, of the utmost importance to them to train up children who shall aid in their work and be associates of their own children."[52] It was important that institutions for children be located in the country far from the "noisy, bustling, dirty city" with its "saloons, low dives, and gangs of bad boys." Rural purity as opposed to urban corruption was a recurring theme in the child saving movement. John P. Sloan, Superintendent of the John Worthy School in Chicago, complained to the Illinois Conference of Charities in 1901 that it was impossible

50. Howe, "The Family System," pp. 211–21.
51. Charles Loring Brace, "The 'Placing Out' Plan for Homeless and Vagrant Children," *PNCCC, 1876,* p. 137.
52. Charles Loring Brace, *The Dangerous Classes of New York and Twenty Years' Work Among Them,* p. 225.

to reform children in the city where there were temptations all around and children were not taught by their parents to respect the rights and property of others. He suggested that a change of environment was the only proper remedy. "From the crowded slum-life of a noisy, disorderly settlement, where seventy per cent of the population is of foreign parentage, these boys should be sent to the open country, with a regular methodical existence and a training and education that will develop and promote habits of industry."[53]

Ophelia Amigh, Superintendent of the Illinois State Home for Juvenile Female Offenders, substantially agreed with her professional colleagues that "the only plan, the only way for saving these boys and girls is to get them away from the large cities."[54] Nelson McLain, the newly appointed Superintendent of the Illinois State Home for Delinquent Boys, also suggested that delinquents be "taken away from evil associations and temptations, away from the moral and physical filth and contagion, out of the gaslight and sewer gas; away out into the woods and fields free from temptation and contagion; out into the sunlight and the starlight and the pure, sweet air of the meadows. . . ."[55]

The preoccupation with the "simple, natural life" reflected reformers' concern for the corrupting influences of technology and city life, and the unrestrained exuberance of adolescence.[56] But the child savers were quick to point out that naturalness was not to be equated with permissiveness. The problem with the city was that it offered too many temptations and insufficient supervision. A reformatory was not a "mere pleasure home" but a place where "wayward" children were taught the value of discipline and "sturdy habits of thrift."[57]

53. *Proceedings of the Illinois Conference of Charities* (1901), in *Seventeenth Biennial Report of the Board of State Commissioners of Public Charities*, p. 232 (Springfield: Phillips Brothers, 1902).
54. *Ibid.*, p. 230.
55. *Ibid.*, p. 300.
56. The transfer of the reformatory from city to country also meant that delinquents became "invisible" and removed from "civilized" society.
57. Howe, "The Family System," pp. 212–17.

TREATMENT AND RESTRAINT

The goal of the new penology was reformation or, in Brockway's words, "education of the whole man, his capacity, his habits and tastes, by a rational procedure."[58] The program of reform was not possible without discipline and supervision. Thus, the indeterminate sentence was introduced to encourage cooperation on the part of inmates.[59] Although the reformatory was intended in theory to function as an exemption to punitive force, it was characterized in practice by a regime of coercion and restraint. Since the child savers professed to be seeking the best interests of their "wards," there was no need to formulate legal regulation of the right and duty to treat in the same way that the right and duty to punish had formerly been regulated. In effect, the new penology reified the dependent status of children by disenfranchising them of legal rights.

The "Age of Treatment" made "people-changing" a profession and a moral injunction.[60] "Reformation," said Brockway, "is socialization of the anti-social by scientific training while under completest governmental control."[61] Hamilton Wey, Elmira's resident physician, implemented this philosophy through a regime of physical training, hot baths, and "all the modern appliances for scientific culture."[62] Brockway similarly required all inmates to observe regular army tactics, drill, and daily dress parade. "The reformatory," wrote Brockway with pride,

became like a garrison of a thousand prisoner soldiers. . . . By means, mainly of the military organization . . . the general tone had gradually

58. Brockway, *Fifty Years of Prison Service*, p. 423.
59. *Ibid.*, pp. 401–2.
60. Robert Martinson, "The Age of Treatment: Some Implications of the Custody-Treatment Dimension," *Issues in Criminology* 2 (Fall, 1966): 275–93.
61. Brockway, *Fifty Years of Prison Service*, pp. 308–9, 393.
62. Hamilton D. Wey, "A Plea for Physical Training of Youthful Offenders," *Proceedings of the Annual Congress of the National Prison Association, 1888*, p. 193.

changed from that of a convict prison to the tone of a conscript fortress.
. . . [I]t was a convict community under martial law garrisoned with its
own inhabitants. Vigorously and thoroughly the grand object of the
reformatory was pursued; every incipient disintegration was promptly
checked and disinclination of individual prisoners to conform was overcome. The regime was planned to both arouse and restrain.[63]

Although Elmira was considered the model American reformatory, it suffered such serious overcrowding that the job of reforming
became incidental to problems of management and control. Elmira
had been built with 500 cells, but by 1899 it housed as many as
1,500 inmates. "What had begun as a bold experiment," wrote
Grünhut, "lost the inspiring impulse of its first promoters, and
became routine work and mass treatment."[64] Nevertheless, the reformatory movement spread rapidly through the United States,
and European visitors crossed the Atlantic to inspect and admire
achievements of their pragmatic colleagues.[65] Mary Carpenter, who

63. Brockway, *Fifty Years of Prison Service*, pp. 310–11, 421. "The military system . . . when placed in command of Colonel Bryan, who had the
advantage of previous cadetship at the West Point National Military Academy, quickly produced precision of military organization and movements
with corresponding benefits to the entire disciplinary regime" (*ibid.*, p. 302).
    64. Grünhut, *Penal Reform*, p. 92. Grünhut's adulation of Brockway,
Dwight, Sanborn, and Wines is somewhat overstated. There is a tendency in
histories of American penology to regard progressive innovations as the result of charismatic individuals rather than of social systems. It is easy to
note that the new penology did not live up to the ideas of its sponsors and
that new ideas were spoilt by routine and conformity. But it is more difficult
to analyze the contributions that penal reformers made to the corruption
of their own ideas. What seems even more likely, from this brief examination
of Brockway and Wines, is that the new penology was not altogether "new"
and that it incorporated many authoritarian features of the "old" penology.
    65. See, for example, the *Proceedings of the Eleventh National Confer-
ence of Charities and Correction* (the Conference was held in St. Louis in
1884). Madame Concepción Arenal read a paper on the "abandonment of
children" in Spain; the presiding judge of the Warsaw high court, Alexandre
de Moldenhauer, discussed problems of guardianship in Poland; G. F. Alm-
quist, Inspector-General of Swedish prisons, gave a paper on the reformatory
system; Arthur G. Maddison, secretary of the reformatory and refuge union
in England, described the English treatment of juvenile offenders; and T. B.
Baker discussed the objections and alternatives to sending delinquents to
reformatories on their first conviction.

toured American institutions in 1873, gave an account of her impressions to the National Prison Congress in St. Louis. She was generally satisfied with the "generous and lavish expenditures freely incurred to promote the welfare of the inmates, and with the love of religion." Most correctional problems with regard to delinquents, she advised, could be remedied if reformatories were built like farm schools or "true homes." At the Massachusetts Reform School in Westborough, she found an "entire want of family spirit," and in New York, she complained, there was no "natural life" in the reformatory. "All the arrangements are artificial," she said; "instead of the cultivation of the land, which would prepare the youth to seek a sphere far from the dangers of large cities, the boys and young men were being taught trades which will confine them to the great centers of an overcrowded population." She found similar conditions in Philadelphia, where "hundreds of youths were there congregated under lock and key," but praised the Connecticut Reform School for its "admirable system of agricultural training."[66] If she had visited the Illinois State Reformatory at Pontiac, she would have found a seriously over-crowded "minor penitentiary" where the inmates were forced to work ten hours a day manufacturing shoes, brushes, and chairs. On the whole, foreign visitors tended to identify Brockway's ideas with *the* American policy. But some German penologists criticized the rigidity of reformatories based on a military regime. They suggested that the grading system was too mechanical and that "the breathless strain and competition which pervaded the whole life was exclusively directed towards the selection of the successful."[67]

The reformatory plan required the teaching of lower-class skills and middle-class values. "Delinquents" were characterized by "carelessness about the rights of others," "lack of moral distinctions," "lack of ambition to become something worthy," "lack of stamina" and "covetousness." These deficiencies could only be recti-

66. Carpenter, "Suggestions on Reformatory Schools," pp. 157–73.
67. Cited by Grünhut, *Penal Reform*, p. 93. For a detailed account of the grading system, see Zebulon R. Brockway, "Prison Discipline in General," *PACC, 1878*, p. 109.

fied by character building—"a great deal of training and drill in self-control"—and changes in personality.[68] "Point out to the children," exhorted a delegate to the annual conference of the National Prison Association in 1898, "all that is beautiful in nature and art. . . . Teach them to love mother and the home, and to hope for heaven. . . . Give the little fellows good companionship, decent, comfortable quarters, clean beds and wholesome food. Smile on them, speak to them, and let sunshine into their souls."[69] Delinquents, suggested another charity worker, should be trained in "the use of money, economy, thrift, and self-reliance."[70] A supporter of the kindergarten system of education suggested that children should be trained "to speak gently, to act politely, to show courtesy, to allow no rudeness or roughness in speech or action."[71]

The Horatio Alger myth prevailed: a poor, delinquent child could rise to a position of social and economic importance by determination, hard work, and individual effort.[72] When it was proposed at the Second International Prison Congress in 1878 that education in special institutions for children "ought to correspond to the conditions in which the working class live," an American Commissioner to the Congress, Caleb C. Randall, rejected this recommendation on the grounds that it was based on the "caste idea." Randall said that "no such idea for an instant is tolerated in America, where equal rights prevail, and where the child of the humblest origin may attain the highest position."[73] Talks at national conferences, annual cor-

68. F. H. Nibecker, "The Influence of Children in their Homes after Institution Life," *PNCCC, 1895*, pp. 220–23, 229.
69. R. C. Buckner, "Child Saving," *Proceedings of the Annual Congress of the National Prison Association, 1898*, p. 279.
70. Lynde, "Prevention in Some of its Aspects," p. 165.
71. R. Heber Newton, "The Bearing of the Kindergarten on the Prevention of Crime," *PNCCC, 1886*, p. 27.
72. R. Richard Wohl, " 'The Rags to Riches Story': An Episode of Secular Idealism," in Reinhard Bendix and Seymour Martin Lipset, eds., *Class, Status and Power: A Reader in Social Stratification*, pp. 388–95.
73. Teeters, *Deliberations*, pp. 47–48. Many penologists, however, maintained that delinquent children should be trained only for menial tasks. One leading penologist-educator observed that "the poverty, misery, and vice of the next generation will to a large extent come from slum children. Their

rectional reports, and pamphlets often included short vignettes and anecdotes about children who had graduated from a reformatory or orphanage to become financial and social successes. If children were taught "the customs of neat, frugal American homes" while in reformatories, their chances of success would be much greater when released.[74]

In practice, however, it was well recognized that correctional workers were concerned with "pacifying" delinquents and exposing them to the value of "self-denial and productive personal exertion."[75] The real test of reformation in a delinquent, as William Letchworth told the National Conference of Charities and Correction in 1886, was his uncomplaining adjustment to his former environment. "If he is truly reformed in the midst of adverse influences, he gains that moral strength which makes his reform permanent."[76]

Recalcitrant delinquents who refused to appreciate the value of reformation were taught through "vigorous treatment" to "learn the benefits that will accrue from following the path of rectitude."

---

need is education in habits of decency, cleanliness, self-respect, the rudiments of civilization and domestic life; their instruction should not be too abstract, nor technical in the sense of fitting them for competitive examinations, clerkships, or college; but rather for the workshop, factory, trades or the home" (Arthur MacDonald, *Abnormal Man*, p. 14). Another example is the suggestion of a reformatory superintendent in Illinois that "nine-tenths of the people should be trained to do commonplace work. . . ." *Seventeenth Biennial Report of the Board of State Commissioners of Public Charities,* p. 301 (Springfield: Phillips Brothers, 1902).

74. James Allison, "Juvenile Delinquents: Their Classification, Education, Moral and Industrial Training," *PNCCC, 1898,* p. 414. Success stories usually took the same form: "Of the large number that passed out of the institution to care for themselves, a mass of wonderful and most gratifying statistics could be gathered. Among the number may be found eminent lawyers, doctors, and members of other honorable professions; some passed through college with high honors; some have become editors and proprietors of influential journals; others, skilled mechanics and tradesmen, while scores have become industrious farmers and horticulturists, acquiring their taste and knowledge of these noble industries at the school" (Howe, "The Family System," p. 214).

75. Brockway, *Fifty Years of Prison Service,* pp. 404–5.

76. Letchworth, "Children of the State," p. 152.

Card-playing and the telling of "obscene" stories were severely punished.[77] "A reformatory," said J. C. Hite of the Ohio Boys' Industrial School,

> is a place of discipline, which means to educate, to instruct, to correct, and in some cases to chastise. . . . The principle that labor is honorable should be faithfully taught and upheld, but every wayward boy in a reformatory ought to be provided with such kinds of labor as will arouse his mind most and get him to thinking soonest. . . . Labor produces muscle, and muscle produces brain.[78]

The "treatment" ideology of the reformatory was further complicated by a romantic and sentimental repudiation of the urban-technological complex. Programs of "industrial education" were quite divorced from economic and agricultural realities. They suffered, like most public schools in the 1890's, from outmoded machinery and old-fashioned craftsmen who "too easily isolated themselves from the mainstream of industrial innovation."[79] Advocates of the reformatory plan ignored the economic attractiveness of city work and the redundancy of farming skills. As one economist cautioned reformers in 1902:

> Whatever may be said about the advantages of farm life for the youth of our land, and however much it may be regretted that young men and young women are leaving the farm and flocking to the cities, there can be no doubt that the movement cityward will continue, just so long as improvements in the methods of agriculture make it possible for a constantly decreasing percentage of the population to furnish the food and

77. P. H. Laverty, "The Management of Reformatories," *PNCCC, 1884,* pp. 88–89.

78. J. C. Hite, "Moral Elevation in Reformatories: What is Required to Produce it," *PNCCC, 1886,* pp. 60–61.

79. "In the cities problems of skyrocketing enrollments were compounded by a host of other issues. In school buildings badly lighted, poorly heated, frequently unsanitary, and bursting at the seams, young immigrants from a dozen different countries swelled the tide of newly arriving farm children. Superintendents spoke hopefully of reducing class size to sixty per teacher, but the hope was most often a pious one" (Lawrence A. Cremin, *The Transformation of the School: Progressivism in American Education, 1876–1957,* p. 57).

raw materials required by the rest of mankind. Under such circumstances it is doubtful if the boy who had been turned out from such a home . . . and was left to find employment in agriculture, would be able to do so, especially when it is remembered that it is every year becoming more difficult for agricultural laborers to find steady and remunerative employment throughout the year. There is great danger that many who had left the home, unable to find employment in agricultural callings, would drift back to the city and not finding there an opportunity to make use of the technical training secured in the institution, would become discouraged and resume their old criminal associations and occupations.[80]

Although the reformatory plan was "corrupted" in practice by overcrowding, mismanagement, "boodleism," inadequate financial resources and staff hiring problems, it is important to understand that its basic ideology was tough-minded and uncompromising. Restraint and discipline were an integral part of the "treatment" program and not merely expedient approximations.[81] Military drill, "training of the will," and long hours of tedious labor were the essence of the reformatory plan. Correctional workers combined the functions of a public health doctor and insurance company agent: their job was to treat clients, but their primary obligation was to report recalcitrant and troublesome clients to the "company."[82]

It seems clear that the child saving movement went beyond mere

80. *Proceedings of the Illinois Conference of Charities* (1901), pp. 232–33. This point was also made by Cremin: "Those who labored in the soil had been 'God's chosen people.' Now, somehow, the old slogans rang a bit hollow as farm prices hovered at pitiful lows and the number of abandoned homesteads multiplied. Despite all the talk about the nobility of agriculture, there was no ignoring the hard facts of life: the cheap land was gone; the jobs, the money, and the opportunity had moved to the city" (*The Transformation of the School,* p. 75).
81. A similar argument is made by Harvey Powelson and Reinhard Bendix, "Psychiatry in Prison," in Arnold M. Rose, ed., *Mental Health and Mental Disorder,* pp. 459–81.
82. James Carey and Anthony Platt: "The Nalline Clinic: Game or Chemical Superego?" *Issues in Criminology* 2 (Fall, 1966): 223–44. See also Lee Rainwater's comment that "the proliferation of policemen in schools, of special schools for 'incorrigible' children, and the like, testify to the prison-like functions that undergird the educational rhetoric and increasingly call into question the natural ideology that 'education' cures all ills" ("The Revolt of the Dirty-Workers," *Trans-action* 5 [November, 1967]: 2).

instrumental reforms in the social control of youth. It was also a symbolic movement which seemed to be defending the sanctity of fundamental institutions—the nuclear family, the agricultural community, Protestant nativism, women's domesticity, parental discipline, and the assimilation of immigrants. The next chapter examines how these expressive concerns were related to the needs of those enterprising reformers who participated in the child saving movement.

Chapter 4: *Maternal*

Justice

A WOMAN'S PLACE

The child-saving movement in Chicago was mobilized through the efforts of a group of feminist reformers who helped to pass special laws for juveniles and create new institutions for their reformation. Their activities were essentially a "moral enterprise," for they were hoping to strengthen and rebuild the moral fabric of society.[1] There was broad public support for the idea that it was a woman's business to be involved in regulating the welfare of children. Women were considered the "natural caretakers" of wayward children and the new penology incorporated maternalistic roles into its reformatory plan. Women's claim to the public care of children had some historical justification during the nineteenth century and their role in child rearing was considered paramount.[2] Women were generally

1. Howard S. Becker, *Outsiders: Studies in the Sociology of Deviance*, p. 145 (New York: Free Press paperback ed., 1966).
2. Geoffrey Gorer claims that the vestigial role of the father and dominant role of the mother in child rearing is responsible for the matriarchal dominance of American society. "The idiosyncratic feature of the American conscience is that it is predominantly feminine. Owing to the major role played by the mother in disciplining the child, in rewarding and punishing it, many more aspects of the mother than the father became incorporated. Duty and Right Conduct became feminine figures" (*The American People: A Study in National Character*, pp. 54–56).

75

regarded as better teachers than men and were also more influential in handling disciplinary problems at home. The fact that public education came more under the direction of women teachers in the schools increased the predominance of women in the raising of children.[3]

Child saving was regarded even by anti-feminists as female domain. The social circumstances behind this appreciation of maternalism were women's emancipation and accompanying changes in the character of traditional family life. Middle-class women were now better educated and had more leisure time, but their choice of careers was limited. Child saving, however, was a reputable task for any woman who wanted to extend her housekeeping functions into the community without denying anti-feminist stereotypes of woman's nature and place.[4] "It is an added irony," writes Christopher Lasch in his study of American radicalism,

that the ideas about woman's nature to which some feminists still clung, in spite of their opposition to the enslavement of woman in the home, were the very clichés which had so long been used to keep her there. The assumption that women were morally purer than men, better capable of altruism and self-sacrifice, was the core of the myth of domesticity against which the feminists were in revolt. . . . [F]eminist and anti-feminist assumptions seemed curiously to coincide.[5]

3. Robert Sunley, "Early Nineteenth-Century American Literature on Child Rearing," in Margaret Mead and Martha Wolfenstein, eds., *Childhood in Contemporary Cultures*, p. 152. See also, Orville G. Brim, *Education for Child Rearing*, pp. 321–49.

4. "But if their existence inclined some women to piety, it spurred others to rebellion. Veblen pointed out that this result was especially common among the well-to-do. Lower-class women were tied to a life of drudgery, which gave them 'something tangible and purposeful to do' and occupied their lives so fully that they had no time or energy for revolt. But upper-class women were forced into a life of vicarious leisure to honor their husbands; the canons of good repute excluded them from all useful work and condemned them to spend their days in 'ceremonial futility.' In these circumstances the 'ancient habit of purposeful activity,' the instinct of workmanship, began to assert itself, and some women sought to fashion for themselves a mode of life that had meaning" (Ray Ginger, *Altgeld's America: The Lincoln Ideal versus Changing Realities*, p. 236 [Chicago: Quadrangle Paperbacks, 1965]).

5. Christopher Lasch, *The New Radicalism in America, 1889–1963*, pp. 53–54.

Middle-class women at the turn of the century experienced a complex and far-reaching status revolution. Their traditional functions were dramatically threatened by the weakening of domestic roles and the specialized rearrangement of family life.[6] The child savers were aware that their championship of social outsiders such as immigrants, the poor, and children, was not wholly motivated by disinterested ideals of justice and equality. Philanthropic work filled a void in their own lives, a void which was created by the decline of traditional religion, increased leisure and boredom, the rise of public education, and the breakdown of communal life in impersonal, crowded cities.

The background, pattern of life, and interests of the child savers were remarkably similar and cut across political affiliations. Career women and society philanthropists, women's clubs and settlement houses, and political and apolitical groups worked together on the problems of child care. Militant organizations regarded child saving as a problem of women's rights, whereas their opponents seized upon it as an opportunity to keep women in their proper place. Child saving was essentially a middle-class movement, launched by the "leisure class" on behalf of those less fortunately placed in the social order.[7]

The child savers were generally well educated, widely traveled, and had access to political and financial resources. Louise Bowen and Ellen Henrotin were both married to bankers; Mrs. Potter Palmer's husband was an influential broker and hotel owner; Mrs. Perry Smith's husband was Vice-President of the Chicago and Northwestern Railroad; and the fathers of Jane Addams and Julia Lathrop were both Republican senators in the Illinois legislature. Legal expertise was available to the child savers through Julia Lathrop's father, Lucy Flower's husband, and Alta Hulett, the first woman lawyer in Illinois. Professional women—such as Dr. Sarah Hackett Smith, Dr. Julia Holmes Smith, and Mrs. Andrew MacLeish, Principal of the fashionable Rockford Seminary—added to the profes-

6. Talcott Parsons and Robert F. Bales, *Family, Socialization and Interaction Process,* pp. 3–33.
7. For a similar analysis of the temperance movement, see Joseph R. Gusfield, *Symbolic Crusade: Politics and the American Temperance Movement.*

sional reputation of the child-saving movement. The public efforts of women reformers was further recognized during the administration of Governor Altgeld who appointed Julia Lathrop to the state board of charities and Florence Kelly as the first woman factory inspector in Illinois.

The executives of the child-saving movement relied on philanthropists and civic clubs for legitimate endorsement. The Chicago Woman's Club, founded in 1876, supported the juvenile court legislation, campaigned for better jail conditions and special institutions for children, and raised money for child welfare causes. The members of the Club were predominantly middle-class housewives living with small families of two or less children in suburban residential areas.[8] Louise Bowen, one of the Club's more socially prominent members, worked closely with Jane Addams and Julia Lathrop at Hull House, thus providing an important link between grass-roots organizations and the world of wealth and political influence.

Although the child savers were bored at home and unhappy with their lack of participation in the "real world," they vigorously defended the virtue of traditional family life and emphasized the dependence of the social order on the proper socialization of children. They promoted the view that women were more ethical and genteel than men, better equipped to protect the innocence of children, and more capable of regulating their education and recreation. "Women with a sense of responsibility for public affairs," said Louise Bowen, "naturally resent having the door shut in their faces when the work they have initiated and long maintained is taken over into the halls of the state."[9]

Feminist reformers used anti-feminist stereotypes to advance their own fortunes. To Francis Lieber, for example,

The influence of women, as wives and mothers, upon their family . . . is, generally speaking, greater than that of men. . . . A prudent and moral mother may, in great degree, counteract in her family the unhappy consequences of her husband's intemperate or dissolute life, much more than

8. Dorothy Edwards Powers, *The Chicago Woman's Club*, pp. 55–58.
9. Mary E. Humphrey, ed., *Speeches, Addresses, and Letters of Louise de Koven Bowen*, 1: 164–67 (hereafter cited as *Bowen Speeches*).

it is possible for an honest and industrious husband to counteract the melancholy effects of the bad conduct of an immoral wife. . . . If she is unprincipled, the whole house is lost. . . .[10]

The participation of the child savers in public affairs was justified as an extension of their housekeeping functions, so that they did not view themselves—nor were they regarded by others—as competitors for jobs usually performed by men. At a meeting of the Friday Club in Chicago, Mrs. Bowen told her audience that, even if a woman's place was in the home, she was certainly entitled to give her opinion on garbage disposal, cleanliness of the streets, and the care and education of children. "If, on our charity boards, we had more women who were conversant with the daily lives of the poor, they would be a great asset in the work of relief and construction. If a woman is a good housekeeper in her own home, she will be able to do well that larger housekeeping. . . ."[11]

The child savers argued that women were especially suited to working with delinquents. A reformatory without a woman, suggested Lucy M. Sickels of the State Industrial School for Girls in Michigan, is "like a home without a mother—a place of desolation. In reformatory work woman is the good mother. The pulse of the school or home throbs in her breast. She is the one to whom all look for comfort and relief."[12] The cottage plan also required a woman's touch. According to G. E. Howe:

. . . here the way opens to the most ample opportunities for woman's transcendent influence. The universal heart of men will acknowledge the strange potency of the mother upon the growing character of a child, and especially in lasting influence upon a boy. Here, then, in this system we

10. Francis Lieber, "Introduction" to Gustave de Beaumont and Alexis de Tocqueville, *On the Penitentiary System in the United States,* pp. 8–9. For similar comments to this effect, see *Eighth Biennial Report of the Board of State Commissioners of Public Charities of the State of Illinois,* pp. 162–74 (Springfield, Illinois: H. W. Rokker, 1885).
11. Humphrey, *Bowen Speeches,* 2: 633.
12. Lucy M. Sickels, "Woman's Influence in Juvenile Reformatories," *Proceedings of the National Conference of Charities and Correction, (PNCCC), 1894,* p. 164.

give the boy to be *mothered* by giving him a *home,* such as the necessities of the penal plan know nothing about; and especially does this consideration rise into momentous importance as we know that many of the commitments are of children of tender age. Then if we can have a reformatory system that will give us woman's ear to listen to little ailments; woman's hand to soften the rigors of the young orphaned life, and the sceptre of woman's soft and winning love to rule in that strange kingdom, the heart of a child, then it is immeasurable gain![13]

George Hoover, Superintendent of the American Home-Finding Association, told the Illinois Conference of Charities in 1898 that "no institution is so well adapted to develop the better elements of human character as is God's institution, namely, the family home, where there is a mother to love and a father to guide and control."[14] James Allison, Superintendent of the Cincinnati House of Refuge, said at the National Conference of Charities and Correction that it was the task of those interested in the welfare of children to rebuild families and protect children from corrupt families. "We must surround [a child] with the warm sunshine of a true home life. It must of necessity be a humble home, . . . pervaded with the elements of paternal and directive force, with the warmth and earnestness of motherly affection."[15] Frederick Wines also felt that "the security of society depends upon the safeguarding of the home, which must first of all be a sanitary home."[16]

Female delegates to national philanthropic and penal conferences realized that the reformatory plan suggested possibilities for useful careers. Mrs. W. P. Lynde told the National Conference of Charities and Correction in 1879 that children's institutions offered the "truest and noblest scope for the public activities of women in the time which they can spare from their primary domestic duties." Women with husbands and children to look after were not expected to neg-

13. G. E. Howe, "The Family System," *PNCCC,* pp. 212–13.
14. *Fifteenth Biennial Report of the Board of State Commissioners of Public Charities,* p. 322 (Springfield, Illinois: Phillips Brothers, 1899).
15. James Allison, "Juvenile Delinquents: Their Classification, Education, Moral and Industrial Training," *PNCCC, 1898,* p. 413.
16. *Proceedings of the Annual Congress of the National Prison Association, Chicago, 1907,* p. 11.

lect their own homes, but most women had ample leisure time in which to pursue their philanthropic interests:

They neither have nor desire political influence or place, but are ready to give of their talent and time to work for such benevolent or charitable purposes as may lie within the circle of their lives. These are largely women with no higher duty of domestic life demanding their first thought; widows, unmarried women, or women without children, with ability, and often money, and a conscientious desire to do something that will fill their own lives, and make for the good of humanity. . . . The benefit of that experience, that can be learned so well nowhere else as in their own homes, beside the cradle of their own children, the state can never buy, but they are willing to give.[17]

Saving children also required "self-sacrifice and patient labor" on the part of married women involved in correctional work. It was a job for middle-class women who possessed intelligence, a sense of altruism, and were willing to work. "By simplifying dress and amusements, by cutting off a little here and there from our luxuries," accordng to Clara T. Leonard, "we may change the whole current of many human lives."[18] Women were exhorted to make their lives useful by participating in welfare programs, by volunteering their time and services, and by getting acquainted with less privileged groups. They were encouraged to seek jobs in institutions which were "like family-life with its many-sided development and varied interests and occupations, and where the woman-element shall pervade the house and soften its social atmosphere with motherly tenderness."[19]

C. D. Randall told a national conference in 1884 that women were responsible for many social reforms. A woman, he said, has a unique capacity for understanding human problems and for unselfish devotion to social engineering. "Whenever and wherever we find her, she is always the fearless and uncompromising apostle of truth and the inspired prophet of a higher and better humanity."

17. Mrs. W. P. Lynde, "Prevention in Some of Its Aspects," *Proceedings of the Annual Conference of Charities, 1879,* p. 167.
18. "Family Homes for Pauper and Delinquent Children," p. 175.
19. Lynde, "Prevention in Some of its Aspects," pp. 165–66.

In institutions, women are indispensable, said Mr. Randall, because "the strongest nation is one where the love of home is strongest. Every benevolent effort to purify and strengthen home-life is well directed."[20] Reformatories, noted a superintendent of a state reform school, should be divided up into families and led by a "God-fearing man and wife." Women should be appointed as educators and administrators, for

the influence of a pure Christian woman in the permanent reformation of [delinquents] cannot be overestimated. With other accomplishments, she should possess a knowledge of music, at least sufficient to play her accompaniments, and sing with the children and teach them to sing. . . . These female heads of families in our school act in the dual capacity of mother and housekeeper and teacher.[21]

"Women in Philanthropy" was the subject of discussion at the National Conference of Charities and Correction in 1892. Anne B. Richardson, a member of the Massachusetts Board of Lunacy and Charity, appeased the delegates by promising that professional women would not in any way neglect their duties as "keepers at home." Women, she said, do not claim to "usurp the rights and privileges of the sterner sex and their so-called better halves." Mrs. Richardson disassociated herself from the "dreadful doctrines" of the suffragette movement and distinguished between political rights and social services as a justification for the involvement of women in public positions. This argument was a dubious kind of rationalization, reflecting the professional woman's conflict and guilt over abandoning her domestic duties. Nevertheless, it was a good practical strategy to stress the fact that public institutions, such as reformatories, needed housewifely skills, maternal guidance, and female tenderness in order to supplement, not replace, paternal authority. "The only claim to rights here made," said Anne Richardson,

is the equal right with men to minister to and labor for the sick, the suffering, the helpless, the depraved. . . . Because of fitness for the posi-

20. C. D. Randall, "Child-Saving Work," *PNCCC, 1884,* p. 116.
21. Ira D. Otterson, "General Features of Reform School Work," *PNCCC, 1892,* p. 172.

tions referred to should both men and women, one just as much as the other, be appointed, and not at all as a question of sex. . . . It is not intended to advocate the appointment of women on boards with a view to their advancement as women, but as a means of bringing into useful activity all feminine qualities which shall supplement those of men and round out to harmonious proportions organizations formed for facilitating charity work.[22]

In summary, the child-saving movement was heavily influenced by middle-class women who extended their housewifely roles into public service and used their extensive political contacts and economic resources to advance the cause of child welfare. The child savers defended the importance of the home, of family life, and of parental supervision, since it was these institutions which had traditionally given purpose to a woman's life. The child-saving movement was organized according to class interests rather than political parties and transcended factionalism among feminist and civic groups.

PORTRAIT OF A CHILD SAVER:
LOUISE DE KOVEN BOWEN

Louise de Koven Bowen was typical of the wealthy, civic-minded philanthropists who transformed child saving from a respectable hobby into a passionate, full-time commitment.[23] Like many of her

22. Anne B. Richardson, "The Cooperation of Woman in Philanthropy," pp. 216–22.

23. The following books and manuscripts have been consulted for this portrait of Louise Bowen: Henriette Greenbaum Frank and Amalie Hofer Jerome, *Annals of the Chicago Woman's Club for the First Forty Years of its Organization;* Mary E. Humphrey, ed., *Speeches, Addresses, and Letters of Louise de Koven Bowen;* Bowen, *Safeguards for City Youth at Work and at Play;* Bowen, *Growing Up With a City;* Bowen, *The Road to Destruction Made Easy in Chicago;* Bowen, *The Straight Girl on the Crooked Path: A True Story;* Bowen, *The Colored People of Chicago;* Bowen, *Our Most Popular Recreation Controlled by the Liquor Interests: A Study of Public Dance Halls;* Bowen, *Open Windows.* These references will be cited only for lengthy quotations.

contemporaries in the Chicago Woman's Club and various civic associations, Louise Bowen came from a rural Protestant family, had been formally educated at a private school and college, was widely traveled, maintained traditional associations with the Republican party, and moved in the highest social and political circles.

A pale and anemic-looking child, Louise Bowen spent a quiet childhood in the comfort and seclusion of an affluent Chicago suburb. She later attended the fashionable Dearborn Seminary, where she was taught to appreciate the value of gentility and self-sacrifice —qualities which later served her well in her contacts with the poor. Her life at home was sophisticated and luxurious. At the age of twelve, she asked her father to hire a coachman and footman for the family carriage so that she would not be disgraced by her stylish cousin who visited them from New York. Her father allowed her to spend her own money on decking out the servants in exotic livery, even though the coachman said that it reminded him of slavery. The Bowens were country people at heart, prone to evangelical Protestantism and strong moral convictions. "After all, if we *were* countrified," reminisced Louise Bowen, "we had certain standards and ideals which we all tried to live up to and which certainly made for sterling character and sound citizenship. There was no liquor served at any of the parties given in Chicago in these early days and a young man ever seen under the influence of it was never invited anywhere again."[24]

Many of Louise Bowen's relatives were prominent socialites in the Midwest and East. Two of her aunts in New York were married to professional men and another to a businessman. Her grandfather Edward Hadduck, who came to Chicago from Ohio in 1830, made his fortune in land speculation and later owned several mills. Louise used to meet her imposing grandfather when he returned home from work.

He was an interesting figure, wearing black broadcloth clothes with a high collar, and old fashioned black stock, and, alas, a large diamond solitaire in his shirt front. His high hat was always shiny as well as his

24. Bowen, *Growing Up With a City,* p. 44.

right coat sleeve, which served instead of a hat brush. When he came at night he was all covered with white dust from his mill.... As I came running down the stairs he would take off his hat, which was full of papers of all descriptions, leases, deeds, mortgages, bank notes, even the morning paper, and usually something he had brought home for me.

He provided her with a considerable income, making her independently wealthy. One day he returned from work and told his grand-daughter: "I sold the corner of Washington Street and Wabash Avenue [to Marshall Field and Company] for a good sum and I am going to divide it between you and your mother." With that he pulled out numerous bank notes and checks and made a fair division.[25]

Louise Bowen was gradually converted to charity work after her marriage to a banker. Aside from caring for four children and organizing philanthropic ventures, she took time to learn to play the piano and laboriously studied needlework and tapestry. Together with her husband, she had traveled to Egypt, Greece, France, Italy, Turkey, and Mexico. She was accustomed to meeting and entertaining high officials and had met Presidents Lincoln and Arthur, and had known Roosevelt, Wilson, and Harding. Recalling her first meeting with a President, she wrote:

Abraham Lincoln was President when I was a little girl, and I used to see a good deal of him because his little boy, Tod Lincoln, was about my age, and a great friend of mine. The Lincolns, when they came to Chicago, always stopped at a little hotel known as Clifton House, on the corner of Madison Street and Wabash Avenue. It was only two doors away from my grandfather's house where I lived, and Tod and I often played together in the Lincolns' apartments, where Mr. Lincoln would sometimes go in and out, giving me a kind word as he passed.[26]

Louise Bowen's youth was generally devoted to idleness and ostentatious frivolity, entertaining her friends, attending lavish parties, and traveling. Until her marriage to a wealthy banker and her contact with fashionable women's clubs in Chicago, she was un-

25. *Ibid.*, pp. 8–9.
26. *Ibid.*, p. 142.

interested in charity work.[27] Her earliest writings concerned the fertilization of flowers, travel in Europe, and "society" affairs. What she later discovered about the conditions of slum life through her membership in the Chicago Woman's Club was a troubling experience that was to preoccupy her for the rest of her life.

Louise Bowen was a nineteenth-century benefactress in the true sense. She was generous with her money and supported a variety of causes and organizations. One day in 1924, she received some 69 letters including everything from a request to found a school of music to an invitation to give a political speech on behalf of candidates up for reelection. As a young Sunday School teacher, she discovered that many of her pupils had little opportunity for recreation; she found an old studio, refurnished it and equipped it with pool tables and other amusements. She even hired a manager to take care of the building every night. When she became President of the Board of Managers of the Maurice Porter Hospital, she was upset by the sight of suffering children and, to ease her own suffering, donated money for the building of an extra wing.

She describes a revealing incident which happened one Christmas during her affiliation with Hull House. It was the custom of the settlement to distribute turkeys to the poor for one of the Chicago newspapers, but on this particular day the gift baskets had not arrived by evening. The poor waited anxiously outside until Jane Addams phoned the newspaper—and was told that all the turkeys had been given away. Finally, she phoned Louise Bowen, who told her to give everybody two or three dollars instead. But there was no money at the settlement and all the banks were closed. "It was ten o'clock Christmas Eve," writes Mrs. Bowen.

I got hold of the druggist in my neighborhood and asked his advice. He said there was an all-night bank open in his neighborhood. I went, gave my check and drew out some money, but unfortunately, it was only in one-hundred dollar bills. They had no small ones. I then telephoned to the president of my own bank and told him my trouble. He said, "Those

27. In her autobiography, Louise Bowen suggests that even as a child she was philanthropically inclined. This retrospective explanation of her "calling" is inconsistent with known facts about her youth and upbringing.

poor people shall have their money tonight." He telephoned a clerk, got him out of bed, sent him down to the bank and several hundred dollars was given me in one-dollar bills. We got over to Hull-House about midnight, and the four hundred people who were waiting went home happy, because they could purchase a Christmas dinner at one of their neighborhood stores the following morning.[28]

Louise Bowen got the most gratification from performing this kind of public service. She joined the Hull House Woman's Club and, when its membership suddenly expanded, she built an auditorium, "Bowen Hall," which comfortably seated 800 people.

Although Louise Bowen was conventionally religious, attended church every Sunday, supported church charities, and taught Sunday School, she preferred the secular atmosphere of a slum settlement to the tranquillity and meditation of a church. "I often felt at this Hull-House club that not even in church did I ever get the inspiration or the desire for service, so much as when I was presiding at a meeting of the club and sat on the platform and looked down on the faces of 800 or 900 women gathered together, all intensely in earnest and all most anxious perhaps to put over some project in which they were interested."[29] Hull House seemed to Louise Bowen the essence of philanthropy and comraderie; "it opened for me a new door into life." She showed her gratitude by buying seventy-two acres of land in the country where she built a Hull House country club for poor city children.

Louise Bowen acted on her conscience and, once convinced that a wrong needed righting, attacked the problem with all her resources and energy. She greatly admired Jane Addams for her dedication, altruism, hard work, and sadness; she too wished to be a "receptacle into which all the troubles of the district were poured." Social work was doing "something worth while" for the poor, a means of establishing a sympathetic relationship between "the well-to-do and those less well off." What was needed was a complete understanding of both sides rather than the championing of one class against another. "Miss Addams in these early days was really an interpreter between

28. Bowen, *Growing Up With a City*, pp. 77–78.
29. *Ibid.*, p. 85.

working men and the people who lived in luxury on the other side of the city and she also gave the people of her own neighborhood quite a different idea about the men and women who were ordinarily called 'capitalists.' "[30]

For some time Louise Bowen was ashamed of being recognized in her charity work as a person of great wealth, and on her visits to Hull House she always wore her simplest, least ostentatious clothes and drove an unpretentious buggy. Later, she realized this was a mistake because the poor, like children, wanted to be patronized and indulged by their superiors:

The women wanted good clothes, they liked to see me dressed smartly, they liked to see me drive up in a motor and to see it standing in front of the club house on Polk Street. I always told my friends that I had to keep up a certain number of social activities in order to get my name in the papers to please the Hull-House Woman's Club. Many a time they would say, "We saw your name in the paper as being at the opera." "We were glad to know our club president was at a ball." "It is a pleasure to know we have for a president a lady who goes so much into society."[31]

Mrs. Bowen had numerous philanthropic and civic affiliations, including over thirty official positions, among which were President of Hull-House Woman's Club, Chairman of Lower North-Side District United Charities, President of the Juvenile Protective Association, Auditor of the National Woman's Suffrage Association, President of Chicago Woman's City Club, President of Woman's Roosevelt Republican Club, only woman member of Illinois State Council of Defense, President of Woman's World Fair, and Illinois delegate to the White House Conference on Dependent Children and Child Health.

Most of the child savers believed that women were obligated to spend their time "usefully," to stay removed from partisan politics but to purify corrupt political practices, and to participate in public life by virtue of their peculiarly female skills. Louise Bowen had little sympathy for the woman who "wishes to remain in the

30. *Ibid.*, pp. 81–93.
31. *Ibid.*, p. 101.

'sanctity of the home' walled away from the real interests and concerns of the age in which she lives.''[32] She was more active in conventional politics than most of her friends in the child-saving movement, and occasionally worked for the Republican party as a speaker for local candidates. She was once approached to run for Mayor of Chicago but felt uneasy in the role of political decoy:

There were headlines saying that I had been asked to become the Republican nominee, and the reporters were extremely nice to me. They spoke of my ability, my knowledge of public affairs, and everything of that kind.

Meanwhile, the Republican Party was scurrying around to find a man in case I did decline. Finally when I learned that they had selected a good man, Arthur Leuder, who later became our Postmaster, I gave my reply, which was that I thought they should find a good man for the office. The whole affair was interesting and enlightening. They asked no promises of me, and were most polite, but in politics there is too much compromise to suit me. I would never be a good politician.[33]

Although she was on good terms with local public officials, and could call upon 6,000 members of the Chicago Woman's Republican Club, her independent political strength was only effective when her views coincided with those of the conventional party machines. She made a political fool of herself when she tried to get a reputable legal firm to indict the Governor of Illinois, Len Small, for appointing corrupt politicians as heads of state institutions. She was even willing to pay a retainer's fee of $10,000 out of the Club's treasury. The lawyer told her that most of his clients would leave his firm if he accepted the case. "They are the large utilities," he said, "who cannot get on without concessions from the State officials. We could not possibly go against them all. It would ruin our business."[34]

While devoting herself to the "social problems" of the poor, the unemployed, and deprived children, Louise Bowen remained neutral in party political battles. She did not see herself acting politically when she brought hope to the helpless and made free meals for the

32. Humphrey, *Bowen Speeches*, 1: 164.
33. Bowen, *Open Windows*, p. 174.
34. *Ibid.*, p. 177.

unemployed. "I was much pleased to have a man once tell me," she wrote, "that he had been going to commit suicide but what I had said to him the previous Sunday had kept him from it." As chairman of a committee at Hull House, she was able to raise $12,000 to pay for milk which was distributed free to the children of garment workers who had gone on strike. "I made many speeches," she writes, "at this time to raise this money, not taking either side in the controversy but feeling that the children were non-combatants and were entitled to have food enough on which to sustain life."[35]

Most of the child savers agreed that women had a right to vote, though there was considerable difference of opinion over the means of achieving equal rights. Some influential members of the Chicago Woman's Club still believed that delegates sent to seek reforms from city, county, and state officials would be received with greater respect if their intentions were seen·as nonpolitical and impartial. Others felt that voting power would give respectability and legitimacy to their demands. Louise Bowen conceded that "politics is a dirty game," but she argued that it was a woman's duty to help exercise control over graft and corruption in government. At a suffrage rally in New York, she criticized the sentimental notions of anti-suffragists who "failed to take notice of the march of events and of changing conditions. They think of woman in the home as she was years ago when she lived in a detached house on a village street. . . ."[36] According to the child savers, women were urgently required to participate in public life because of their unique capacity to act as custodians of public morality.[37]

35. Bowen, *Growing Up With a City,* pp. 96–97.
36. Humphrey, *Bowen's Speeches,* 1: 282.
37. "Another hoary argument similar to the military one is the contention that women cannot perform police duty, yet every student of social conditions in a large city realizes that the absence of women on the police force is perhaps responsible for some of our social dangers. Even conservative students of municipal administration are now advocating morales police, of whom a certain number should be women, if a city would properly protect young girls from the many traps and pitfalls which are purposely set for their unwary feet; if it would deal in any sense adequately with prostitution, that grave menace to public health and morals; if it would treat even decently the women who are constantly brought into the police courts for slight mis-

Louise Bowen's primary philanthropic interest was the protection and welfare of children. Her husband regarded her interest in child welfare as just another new hobby. What could be more admirable and nonpolitical than women using their civic organizations to find resources for poor city children? The child savers attributed the rise of youthful crime to the corrupting influences of city life, where dirt, crowding, artificiality, and impersonality robbed children of their innocence.[38] Children were quickly "beguiled" into "all sorts of wickedness" and immorality.[39] They were exploited and faced with unexpected temptations wherever they turned:

Here we are, Chicago, a great city sprawling over a vast territory, peopled with many nationalities, calling ourselves the commerce center of the world. Our great buildings are lifting their towers toward heaven. Our parks and playgrounds lead the world. We are fast becoming the center of literature, art, music and medicine. It is said that we are going to be the largest and most beautiful city in the world, but what is it going to profit us if our children lose their souls![40]

The child savers were horrified that the "road to destruction" was made so easy in Chicago. Brothels, comic books, alcohol, amusement parks, and other "commercialized vices" were seen as a ubiquitous threat to the fragility of youth. "Unless this condition is soon remedied," said Louise Bowen, "the children, in order to quench their

---

demeanors but who are too often subjected to the contempt and contumely accorded to 'women of the streets.' Certainly a beginning has now been made here in Chicago, with police matrons in every station, and it would be a mere extension of their functions to require them to seek out young girls who may have been decoyed into disreputable lodging houses or hotels; to be present in court when girls are tried; and to conduct those who have been convicted and sentenced to the institutions to which they have been committed" (*ibid.,* 1: 161–62).

38. *Ibid.,* 1: 110–11.

39. "We found photograph galleries which were being used for immoral purposes, catering to all that was bad for children. We had our people in the waiting rooms of the department stores, where we found men plying the white slave trade. In all of these cases the people were arrested, the violators of the law prosecuted. It seemed to me that there were years when I was just wading in the mud!" Bowen, *Open Windows,* p. 144.

40. Humphrey, *Bowen's Speeches,* 2: 799.

thirst for joy, will take deep draughts of the poisonous stuff which is everywhere offered to them, and which ultimately will end in their complete demoralization."[41]

Louise Bowen and her friends defined this crisis as a problem of personal and social hygiene rather than of political power.[42] Their solution to the "crime problem" was playgrounds, supervised recreation, "morales police," kindergartens, visits to the country, stricter laws, and more efficient law enforcement. The problem of juvenile crime, said Louise Bowen, would be diminished by stringent enforcement of laws and the development of resolute "character" in youth.[43]

PORTRAIT OF A CHILD SAVER:
JANE ADDAMS

If Louise Bowen was a typical example of conventional philanthropy, Jane Addams was the personification of professional philanthropy. Women like Jane Addams, Julia Lathrop, the Abbott sisters, and Florence Kelly made a full-time career out of their reform interests. They approached social problems with a tough-

41. *Ibid.*, 1: 144.
42. "What we need in this country," Louise Bowen told the Pan-American Congress of Women in 1922, "what we need in every country, is good government, and good government means clean alleys and clean streets; it means safety on the streets and in the home; it means health and happiness for the women workers; it means fine schools and wholesome recreation; it means a well-ordered community life that leads to national well-being" (*ibid.*, 2: 655).
43. "It isn't money nor houses nor lands that make a man, it is character; and it isn't what we do nor what we say, nor what we think, nor what we believe that will count for or against us when life is over, but it is what we are—it is character. The parents are the character-builders for the child, and upon them rests the responsibility of building well. They should also see to it that the child as he reaches manhood does not find himself, because of their injustice to him in his youth, shattered in strength and dulled in intellect, but strong and vigorous, both in mind and body, able and anxious to fight well the battles of life and to do his share in the world's work" (*ibid.*, 1: 97).

minded independence and an ethical code that they had learned as children after the Civil War.[44]

Jane Addams and Julia Lathrop both came from a family background of politics and Quaker idealism. William Lathrop was a Republican member of the Illinois senate as well as a successful lawyer and businessman. Julia Lathrop's mother was an ardent suffragist and "there was always a free atmosphere in the home where all the children freely expressed their opinions and were encouraged to work their own interests without parental interference."[45] Her father had a reputation for political honesty and "living up to his beliefs." The first woman lawyer in Illinois, Alta Hulett, read law in his office and drew up the bill permitting women to be admitted to the bar. Julia Lathrop was born in 1857, one of five children. Two years later and thirty-five miles away, Jane Addams was born.

Like most of the child savers, Jane Addams was country born and raised and she spent her childhood and adolescence in the pastoral community of Cedarville in northern Illinois.[46] Her earliest recollections were of a "scene of rural beauty" where she and her stepbrother "carried on games and crusades which lasted week after week, and even summer after summer, as only free-ranging country children can do." Whenever she discussed how the big cities were sapping the "spirit of youth" she would nostalgically return to her favorite theme, reminded of frontier villages where children played "naturally" in the surrounding woods.

Jane Addams' identification with the poor and downtrodden was partly due to her own estrangement from the genteel conventions of middle-class society. She was an ugly, pigeon-toed child with a deformed spine that prevented her from bearing children. Her mother died when she was a child; her father soon remarried a socially

44. Ginger, *Altgeld's America*, p. 113.
45. Jane Addams, *My Friend, Julia Lathrop*, p. 23.
46. Much of this discussion about Jane Addams is based on the following books and pamphlets: Addams, *Twenty Years at Hull-House;* Addams, *The Spirit of Youth and City Streets;* Addams, *My Friend, Julia Lathrop;* Addams, ed., *Hull-House Maps and Papers.* Studies by Christopher Lasch and Ray Ginger were used as secondary sources.

prominent widow. Her education at Rockford Seminary, which had a strong missionary tradition, left her with an ambivalent attitude to conventional Protestantism which she ultimately resolved by deciding to establish Hull House. Following the death of her father and a nervous breakdown, she allowed herself to be belatedly baptized as a Presbyterian at the age of twenty-five. But she found little consolation in this ritualistic conversion and left for a long trip to Europe with her stepmother and some family friends.

Traditional nineteenth-century theology did not have much appeal for Jane Addams and her contemporaries at college. As progressivism represented a different form of New England moralism, so philanthropy provided the secular equivalent of what were essentially religious impulses. Many of Jane Addams' friends devoted themselves to "the duties of good citizenship and to the arousing of the social energies which too largely lie dormant in every neighborhood given over to industrialism." One of her colleagues founded a school in Japan, another became a missionary in Korea, and another taught in a school for blind children. The new professional women brought a "moralized energy" to bear upon the complicated problems of industrial cities, and thus compensated for the "fatal want of harmony between their theory and their lives, a lack of coordination between thought and action."[47]

For Jane Addams, theological rhetoric could only become meaningful in the activity of a settlement house. It is not surprising, then, that Jane Addams was described by her friends as a "deeply religious woman" who did not show it by church going but "by following the footsteps of the Founder of the Christian Religion. Even during the war when, following her Quaker teachings, she declared herself a pacifist, she endured a perfect martyrdom because of the storm of disapproval directed against her. She never resented the manner in which she was sometimes treated and often misrepresented. . . ."[48]

Many of Jane Addams' writings reflect a preoccupation with making amends for her own good fortune at being born into wealth and luxury. She inherited her father's forthright moral integrity and

47. Addams, *Twenty Years at Hull-House,* pp. 91–100.
48. Bowen, *Growing Up With a City,* p. 92.

self-righteousness. A story was told of her father's political career that he had "never been offered a bribe because bad men were instinctively afraid of him." She remembered this many years later when she was approached by an informal association of manufacturers and asked to stop agitating for a sweatshop bill in return for a philanthropic donation of fifty thousand dollars. "As the fact broke upon me that I was being offered a bribe," wrote Jane Addams in her autobiography, "the shame was enormously increased by the memory of this statement. What had befallen the daughter of my father that such a thing could happen to her?"[49]

Jane Addams recognized that her generation, especially the women, lacked a "heritage of noble obligation" and were driven by a "desire for action" and "the wish to right wrong and alleviate suffering." The new religion of social service—"this renaissance of the early Christian humanitarianism"—was designed to provide an outlet for the "active faculties" of a "fast-growing number of cultivated young people" whose lives lacked vitality and purpose. Jane Addams commented sadly on the tendency of so many young girls to surrender their "altruistic" talents and withdraw into their homes:

There are a few girls who, by the time they are "educated," forget their old childish desires to help the world and play with poor little girls "who haven't play things." Parents are often inconsistent; they deliberately expose their daughters to knowledge of the distress in the world; they send them to hear missionary addresses on famines in India and China; they accompany them to lectures on the suffering in Siberia; they agitate together over the forgotten region of East London. In addition to this, from babyhood the altruistic tendencies of these daughters are persistently cultivated. They are taught to be self-forgetting and self-sacrificing, to consider the good of the whole before the good of the ego. But when all this information and culture show results, when the daughter comes back from college and begins to recognize her social claim to the "submerged tenth" and to evince a disposition to fulfill it, the family claim is strenuously asserted; she is told that she is unjustified, ill-advised in her efforts.[50]

49. Addams, *Twenty Years at Hull-House*, p. 39.
50. *Ibid.*, pp. 93–94.

Jane Addams' interest in children was similar to that of Louise Bowen. She felt that children were forced into premature independence because their labor power was prized more than their "innocence" and "tender beauty." She found Chicago to be "gaudy and sensual" with its "trashy love stories, the feathered hats, the cheap heroics of the revolvers displayed in the pawn-shop windows." The city deceived and exploited children. "Never before have such numbers of young boys earned money . . . and felt themselves free to spend it as they choose in the midst of vice deliberately disguised as pleasure." Jane Addams warned her working colleagues not to be deceived by the city's false glamour: "Let us know the modern city in its weakness and wickedness, and then seek to rectify and purify it until it shall be free at least from the grosser temptations which now beset the young people who are living in its tenement houses and working in its factories."[51]

Paradoxically, Jane Addams realized that city children were being overwhelmed by the "ideals of Puritanism" and yet she encouraged the "standardizing of pleasure" at Hull House by insisting on strict chaperoning of single girls, prohibiting the use of liquor and "certain types of dancing," and regulating most dances and parties. The trustees of Hull House also restricted membership in the social clubs to certain kinds of children, and two fourteen-year-old girls who had been rescued from a brothel in Virginia were refused entry, "not so much because there was danger of contamination, as because the parents of the club members would have resented their presence most hotly."[52]

According to Jane Addams, recreation would alleviate the problems of delinquency, and education would solve labor disputes. It was the aim of educational and social reformers "to feed the mind of the worker, to lift it above the monotony of his task, and to connect it with the larger world outside of his surroundings."[53] Public recreation, she further suggested, would "bring together all

51. Addams, *The Spirit of Youth and City Streets*, p. 14.
52. Addams, *Twenty Years at Hull-House*, p. 112.
53. *Ibid.*, p. 299.

classes of a community in the modern city unhappily so full of devices for keeping men apart."⁵⁴ Jane Addams appealed to men's good will and sought to establish a society based on Christian brotherhood. Personal relationships were more important to her than economic arrangements and she implicitly argued that the latter could only be achieved if the quality of men's private lives was enriched. "It would seem obvious," she wrote, "that in order to secure relief in a community dominated by industrial ideals, an appeal must be made to the old spiritual sanctions for human conduct. . . ."⁵⁵ Even her support of the labor movement was cautious, subject to sporadic self-recriminations, and often ambivalent. Although she was upset that "the capitalist should have been so slow to accord [the] right [of representation] to workingmen," she felt that the democratic relation of employer to employee was jeopardized by the tendency of unions to lack "ethical power" and a "sense of proportion." Her sympathies with the labor movement were guilt-ridden because she could not accept "dirty" political tactics from either the poor or the rich:

A glance at the labor movement shows that the preponderating force has been given to what may be called negative action. Unions use their power to frustrate the designs of the capitalist, to make trouble for corporations and the public, such as is involved, for instance in a railroad strike. It has often seemed to be the only method of arresting attention to their demands; but in America, at least, they have come to trust it too far.⁵⁶

Although Jane Addams wrote perceptively of the numerous ways in which children were being objectified by modern industrialism, she always avoided unconventional political solutions and resisted the logical consequences of her arguments which pointed to an indictment of capitalism. She remained within the bounds of orthodox political action—one historian suggests that she was politically naïve and "accepted unthinkingly the genteel Republicanism of her

54. Addams, *The Spirit of Youth and City Streets*, p. 96.
55. *Ibid.*, p. 148.
56. Addams, *Hull-House Maps and Papers*, pp. 183–204.

family"—and her reform activities were aimed at consoling the unfortunate and adapting them to a way of life which, she admitted, was oppressive and unjust.[57]

THE DEPENDENCY OF YOUTH

The child-saving movement provided middle-class women with a vehicle for promoting acceptable "public" roles and for restoring some of the authority and spiritual influence that women had seemingly lost through the urbanization of family life.[58] Child saving may be understood as a crusade which served symbolic and ceremonial functions for native, middle-class Americans. The movement was not so much a break with the past as an affirmation of faith in traditional institutions.[59] Parental authority, home education, rural life, and the independence of the family as a social unit were emphasized because they seemed threatened at this time by urbanism and industrialism. The child savers elevated the nuclear family, especially women as stalwarts of the family, and defended the family's right to supervise the socialization of youth.

Although child saving had important symbolic functions for preserving the prestige of middle-class women in a rapidly changing society, it also had considerable instrumental significance for legitimizing new career openings for women. The new role of social worker combined elements of an old and partly fictitious role— defender of family life—and elements of a new role—social servant. Social work and philanthropy were thus an affirmation of cherished values and an instrumentality for women's emancipation.

57. Lasch, *The New Radicalism*, p. 35.
58. Richard Hofstadter makes the same point about the clergy at the end of the nineteenth century (*The Age of Reform*, pp. 151–52).
59. One historian, Alan P. Grimes, suggests that the woman suffrage movement was coopted by conservative and nativist organizations, and that it was predominantly an instrumentality of white, Protestant Americans to counteract the growing immigrant vote (*The Puritan Ethic and Woman Suffrage*).

One of the significant consequences of the child-saving movement was the successful reification of youth. Many of the child
savers' reforms were aimed at imposing sanctions on conduct unbecoming youth and disqualifying youth from the benefit of adult
privileges. The child savers were more concerned with restriction
than liberation, with the protection of youth from moral weaknesses
as well as from physical dangers. The austerity of the criminal law
and criminal institutions were not their major target of concern, nor
were they especially interested in problems relating to "classical"
crimes against person and property. Their central interest was in the
normative behavior of youth—their recreation, leisure, education,
outlook on life, attitudes to authority, family relationships, and
personal morality.

Although the child savers were responsible for minor reforms in
jails and reformatories, they were most active and successful in ex-
tending governmental control over a whole range of youthful activities that had been previously ignored or dealt with informally. Their
reforms were aimed at defining and regulating the dependent status
of youth.[60] The child savers were prohibitionists in a general sense
who believed that social progress depended on efficient law enforcement, strict supervision of children's leisure and recreation, and the
regulation of illicit pleasures. Their efforts were directed at rescuing
children from institutions and situations (theaters, dance halls,
saloons, etc.) which threatened their "dependency." The child saving movement also raised the issue of child protection in order to

60. The consequence of this dependency is well described by the novelist
Frank Conroy: "Children are in the curious position of having to do what
people tell them, whether they want to or not. A child knows that he must
do what he's told. It matters little whether a command is just or unjust since
the child has no confidence in his ability to distinguish the difference. Justice
for children is not the same as justice for adults. In effect all commands are
morally neutral to a child. Yet because almost every child is consistently
bullied by older people he quickly learns that if in some higher frame of
reference all commands are equally just, they are not equally easy to carry out.
Some fill him with joy, others, so obviously unfair that he must paralyze himself to keep from recognizing their quality, strike him instantly deaf, blind,
and dumb. Faced with an order they sense is unfair children simply stall"
(*Stop-Time,* p. 50).

challenge a variety of "deviant" institutions: thus, children could only be protected from sex and alcohol by destroying the brothels and saloons.[61]

The child savers defined delinquency as a problem of social rather than political policy, calling for "therapeutic" remedies rather than a redistribution of power. Child saving was viewed as an ethical and humanitarian calling, removed from the world of political compromise and party disputes. Yet, as Horowitz and Liebowitz have indicated, "the decision to treat deviance as a social problem is itself a political decision. It represents the political ability of one group of decision-makers to impose its value sentiments upon decisions concerning deviance."[62] Furthermore, the child savers used extensive political and professional contacts to implement their reforms and thus remove youth from the political arena. The consolidation of the dependent status of "problematic" youth was complete. Young people were denied the option of withdrawing from or changing the institutions which governed their lives. Their opposition to or disenchantment with the school or reformatory or recreation center was treated as a problem of personal maladjustment which evoked "therapeutic" programs from the child savers. The next chapter examines in detail the fate of one such program.

61. "Children of all ages need guidance and protection. While many children develop into useful citizens in spite of evil surroundings, a few eventually become a menace to society in spite of every effort in their behalf. Next to religious influence, the rule still holds that a good home, a good education and environment, healthful employment and recreation under moral conditions, are very much to be desired, and it is a great misfortune when these have not been given. Immoral influences are frequently thrust upon children through the pernicious activities of immoral people, and because of lack of protection, proper instructions of guidance from those who should have the child's welfare at heart" (The Vice Commission of Chicago, *The Social Evil in Chicago,* p. 235).

62. Irving Louis Horowitz and Martin Liebowitz, "Social Deviance and Political Marginality: Toward a Redefinition of the Relation Between Sociology and Politics," *Social Problems* 15 (1968): 281.

Chapter 5: *The Child-Saving*

Movement in Illinois

DELINQUENT CHILDREN

Special provisions for the protection and custody of "delinquent" children apart from adult offenders existed in the United States long before the enactment of the juvenile court in 1899. Nineteenth-century legal doctrines and sentencing policies made allowances for the immaturity and disabilities of children.[1] When Illinois was admitted to the Union in 1817, a child under seven years was not considered responsible for a criminal act, though he could be whipped like a slave for refusing to obey his parents.[2] A revision of the state code in 1827 raised the age of criminal responsibility to ten,[3] and, four years later, children under eighteen were excluded by statute

1. See Appendix, pp. 183–202.
2. This subject is cursorily treated by Andrew A. Bruce, "One Hundred Years of Criminological Development in Illinois," *Journal of Criminal Law and Criminology* 24 (1933): 11–49. For a more general analysis, see Wiley B. Sanders, "Some Early Beginnings of the Children's Court Movement in England," *National Probation Association Yearbook* 39 (1945): 58–70. See also, Leslie A. Cranston, *Early Criminal Codes of Illinois and their Relation to the Common Law of England.*
3. "An infant under the age of 10 years shall not be found guilty of any crime or misdemeanor" (Revised Laws of Illinois, 1827, sect. 4).

from the state penitentiary. Typical sanctions against children included corporal punishment, fines, and short jail sentences.[4]

In 1833, the criminal code included for the first time a provision that "persons under 18 shall not be punished by confinement in the penitentiary for any offense except robbery, burglary, or arson; in all other cases where a penitentiary punishment is or shall be provided, such a person under the age of 18 shall be punished by imprisonment in the county jail for any term not exceeding 18 months at the discretion of the court."[5] There was no further legislation pertaining to the treatment of juvenile offenders until 1867 when an act was passed providing for the establishment of the State Reform School at Pontiac for boys between the ages of eight and eighteen who lived outside Cook County.[6] A reform school (established in 1855) already existed in Chicago and was used for Cook County boys until 1871 when it was destroyed in the great fire. An act of 1872 authorized the transfer of all boys who were serving any definite sentence in the Chicago Reform School to the State Reformatory.[7] The Pontiac reformatory was created for "the discipline, education, employment, and reformation of juvenile offenders and vagrants." The 1867 act further provided that "all courts of competent jurisdiction are authorized to exercise their discretion in sending juvenile offenders to the county jails, in accordance with the laws made and provided, or in sending them to Reform School."[8] The establishment of the State Reform School made unnecessary the use of the penitentiary for persons under eighteen who were convicted of robbery, burglary, or arson. Commitment to the county jail for these and other offenses was left to the discretion of the courts. The obvious implication of this provision was that the county jails were to be used for minor offenders, the reform school being reserved for more dangerous delinquents.[9]

4. Revised Laws of Illinois, 1827, sects. 29, 46, 47, 48, 50. See also, Helen Rankin Jeter, *The Chicago Juvenile Court*, pp. 1–2.
5. Revised Laws of Illinois, 1833, sect. 158.
6. *Ibid.*, 1867, sect. 16.
7. *Ibid.*, 1872, sects. 1, 2, 3.
8. *Ibid.*, 1867, sect. 16.
9. This point is suggested by Elizabeth Francis Hirsh, *A Study of the Chi-*

The Reform School at Pontiac was in every sense a minor penitentiary. "The real purpose of the General Assembly," commented the Illinois Board of Public Charities, "was to provide for the erection of a prison . . . with a view to relieving the penitentiary and jails of the state from the various evils incident to overcrowding."[10] This view was indirectly supported by the Illinois Supreme Court in a case involving the Chicago Reform School, which was administered by a board of guardians appointed by the city judiciary. The reformatory, at an approximate annual cost to the city of $35,000, was designed for boys between the ages of six and sixteen who had committed minor criminal offenses. Sentences were indeterminate and boys could be held in the institution, depending on their conduct and attitude, until they were twenty-one. Parents and guardians had the power to commit their children to the Reform School with the permission of the board of guardians and superintendent.[11] The courts could also commit children who were found to be "destitute of proper parental care, or growing up in mendicancy, ignorance, idleness or vice."

On September 9, 1870, a mittimus was issued by the clerk of the Supreme Court of Cook County committing Daniel O'Connell to the Chicago Reform School. The boy's father applied to the Supreme Court for a writ of habeas corpus and, in his decision, Mr. Justice Thornton held that the act in question was unconstitutional because the boy had been committed without benefit of trial to what was really an "infant penitentiary" and "a necessary evil, the neighborhood of which decent people desire to avoid." The judge also asked:

Can the State, as parens patriae, exceed the power of the natural parent, except in punishing crime? These laws provide for the "safe keeping" of the child; they direct his "commitment" and only a "ticket of leave" or the uncontrolled discretion of a board of guardians, will permit the im-

cago and Cook County School for Boys, pp. 3–13, and by Evelyn Harriet Randall, *The St. Charles School for Delinquent Boys,* pp. 2–13.

10. *First Biennial Report of the Board of State Commissioners of Public Charities of the State of Illinois* (hereafter *BRPCI*————), p. 72 (Springfield: Illinois Journal Printing Office, 1871).

11. *Ibid.,* p. 167.

prisoned boy to breathe the pure air of heaven outside his prison walls, and to feel the instincts of manhood by contact with the busy world. . . . The confinement may be from one to fifteen years, according to the age of the child. Executive clemency cannot open the prison doors for no offense has been committed. The writ of habeas corpus, a writ for the security of liberty, can afford no relief, for the sovereign power of the State as parens patriae has determined the imprisonment beyond recall. Such a restraint upon natural liberty is tyranny and oppression. If, without crime, without the conviction of an offense, the children of the State are thus to be confined for the "good of Society," then Society had better be reduced to its original elements and free government acknowledged a failure. . . . The welfare and rights of the child are also to be considered. . . . Even criminals cannot be convicted and imprisoned without due process of law.[12]

Child-saving organizations regarded the O'Connell case as an irresponsible decision designed to discredit and retard their efforts. The State Teachers' Association wanted an institution to which parents and other "responsible" adults could commit children for indeterminate sentences.[13] The Board of Public Charities argued that the Reform School was in fact a "house of refuge" where juveniles were treated with "tender pity." The Supreme Court decision, said Frederick Wines, "greatly injured the morale and utility of the institution" and "cast an irremediable blight upon the inmates." Despite the protests of the child savers, the State Reform School act was revised in 1873 to incorporate the O'Connell decision and make it consistent with constitutional guarantees. The right to sentence during minority was taken from the courts as was the right to commit a child for want of proper parental care, mendicancy, ignorance, idleness, or vice. The right of guardianship was also revoked from the trustees. Instead, it was provided that any boy between the ages of ten and sixteen who was convicted of any crime which, if committed by an adult, would be punishable by imprisonment in the county jail or penitentiary, could be committed to the Reform School for not less than one year or more than five years. The courts were

12. *People v. Turner*, 55 Ill. 280 (1870).
13. *BRPC4*, p. 149 (Springfield, Illinois: D. W. Lusk, 1877).

also given discretionary power to authorize jail sentences for minor offenses.

After land and money had been appropriated, the State Reform School was finally opened in 1871 at Pontiac, about a hundred miles from Chicago. Dr. J. D. Scouller, who was formerly a physician and Assistant Superintendent at the St. Louis Reform School, was appointed Superintendent and immediately contracted with private industry for the cheap labor of inmates. Although the trustees of the reformatory were prevented by law from "leasing the labor" of inmates for more than six hours a day, a contract was made with a Chicago shoe firm for the labor of fifty boys who were to be employed seven hours a day. A similar contract was made with Clark and Hill and Company for the manufacture of brushes. After these contracts were dissolved due to legal difficulties, many of the inmates were employed in cane-seating chairs for the Bloomington Manufacturing Company under the direction of the officers of the School. Such was the main "educational" program in the new reformatory. In the first four years after the opening of the institution, the legislature appropriated about $23,000, most of which was spent on developing land and farmstock rather than on improving living conditions.[14]

On September 30, 1876, the State Reform School housed 180 boys.[15] Six years later, the School was seriously overcrowded with a population of about 250. "The insufficiency of room in the institution is such that the boys sleep in bunks touching each other. . . . The dining room, the school rooms, and chapel are all overcrowded."[16] By 1888, the population had nearly doubled and, five

14. *Ibid.*, pp. 152–56.
15. *BRPC10*, p. 10 (Springfield: Springfield Printing Company, 1888).
16. *BRPC7*, p. 92 (Springfield: H. W. Rokker, 1883). Two years later, it was reported that "the boys sleep in double-deck bunks, one over the other, placed close to each other, side by side and end to end, with passages at the ends to enable them to crawl into bed. The dining room barely contains room enough for them to eat standing—not enough for them to sit down at their meals. From every point of view, sanitary as well as disciplinary, this arrangement is in the highest degree injurious and discreditable to a great and wealthy State" (*BRPC8*, p. 64 [Springfield: H. W. Rokker, 1885]).

years later, it was further increased when a law was passed permitting any criminal court in the state to sentence to the Reform School —now officially known as the Illinois State Reformatory—any male criminal between the ages of sixteen and twenty-one who had been found guilty of a first offense. The board of managers of the Reformatory were correspondingly empowered to transfer to the penitentiary any "apparently incorrigible prisoner, whose presence in the reformatory appeared to be seriously detrimental to the well-being of the institution."[17]

Frederick Wines, Secretary of the Illinois Board of Public Charities, was appointed a United States Special Commissioner to attend the International Penitentiary Congress held in Stockholm in 1878. He was greatly impressed with the Congress' recommendations for the treatment of juvenile offenders and visited several reformatories in England, including Hardwicke Court Reformatory—"a fine illustration of the possible results of intelligence and devotion in reducing the volume of crime. . . ." At other institutions, such as the Philanthropic Society's Farm School in Surrey, he was pleased to find the inmates "occupied in cultivating the fields with the spade—the use of the plough being prohibited in order that the boys may experience the healthy influence of personal contact with the soil." Wines came back from Europe convinced that it was the task of child-saving organizations to remove reformatories from the jurisdiction of the criminal law:

The object of reformatory institutions is well stated; it is not punishment for past offenses, but training for future usefulness. . . . [T]he operation of the Illinois law is positively injurious. It proceeds from a morbid sensibility on the subject of personal liberty, and from a false idea of the relation of the juvenile offender to society, as well as of the object sought in sending him to a reformatory. It destroys the potency of the agencies employed for his reformation, by encouraging in his mind the hope that obstinate resistance to their influence, for a comparatively short period, will enable him to triumph over authority and to enter upon a life of vicious indulgence. Another wise suggestion in conflict with the practice

17. Hirsh, *Study of School for Boys,* p. 5.

adopted in our state, is that to the utmost extent possible the placing of vicious children in families or in public institutions should take place without the intervention of a formal trial. The statutes of Illinois fail to recognize the fact that confinement and control have a humane as well as a severe aspect nor do they distinguish between confinement for the protection of society and for the protection of the individual himself. This distinction was clearly perceived by the Congress and the application of the principle in Illinois is much to be desired.[18]

By 1885, Illinois did not have a reformatory for delinquent girls and the boys' reformatory was essentially a miniature prison, based on the "stern principle of retribution for offenses committed against the criminal law."[19] Wines was commissioned by the Board of Public Charities to investigate private and public facilities for delinquent children. In 1886, the Board reported that the institutional facilities were inadequate in size and resources. They proposed that "delinquents" should be managed according to the law of guardianship and that institutional care should be extended to "those children and others who swarm in the streets, gather about docks and wharves, and are almost sure to take up crime as a trade."[20] Ideally, the child savers wanted to intervene in the lives of "pre-delinquent" children and maintain control over them until they were immunized against "delinquency":

If the prevention of crime is more important than its punishment, and if such prevention can only be secured by rescuing children from criminal surroundings before the criminal character and habits become firmly established, then it is evident that the state reform school can not accomplish all that we desire, since it does not receive children at a sufficiently early age, nor does it receive children who still occupy the debatable ground between criminality and innocence, who have not yet committed any criminal act, but who are in imminent danger at every moment of becoming criminals.[21]

18. *BRPC5*, pp. 273–99 (Springfield: Weber, Magie and Co., 1879).
19. *BRPC9*, p. 52 (Springfield: T. W. Rokker, 1887).
20. *Ibid.*, pp. 52–84.
21. *BRPC6*, p. 104 (Springfield: H. W. Rokker, 1880).

DEPENDENT CHILDREN

Prior to the latter part of the nineteenth century, the public care of
dependent children in Illinois was, for the most part, delegated to
county almshouses. By 1875, Illinois was far behind Ohio, Michigan, and Massachusetts, where county homes and state institutions
for dependent children had been established. Illinois was also extremely slow in passing legislation authorizing the removal of
children from almshouses.[22] The Cook County almshouse, which
was used as an asylum for all age groups, was described by a grand
jury investigation in 1853 as "entirely inadequate," especially since
"the section devoted to women and children is so crowded as to be
very offensive."[23] According to the 1880 Report of the Board of
Charities, about 13 per cent of the inmates of the county almshouses
in Illinois were children.[24]

Between 1850 and 1870, the almshouse system was supplemented
by private organizations and "rescuing" societies.[25] These self-
appointed guardians of children's physical and moral integrity provided the administrative machinery for policing and enforcing
welfare laws which would have been otherwise unenforceable. Rescue societies, beginning in New York with the creation of the Society
for the Prevention of Cruelty to Children in 1875, afforded "organized protection for dependent children" and "provision of an
official character for the prosecution of parents or others who ill-
used and brutally treated the young and defenseless."[26] Private

22. *Ibid.*, pp. 102–4. See also James Brown, *The History of Public Assistance in Chicago, 1833–1893,* pp. 32 f., and Arlien Johnson, *Public Policy
and Private Charities: A Study of Legislation in the United States and of
Administration in Illinois,* p. 91 f.
23. Brown, *History of Public Assistance in Chicago,* p. 33.
24. *BRPC6,* p. 290.
25. For an excellent overview of these organizations in Chicago, see Bessie
Louise Pierce, *A History of Chicago,* 3: 423–66 (New York: Alfred A.
Knopf, 1957).
26. Margaret Kenney Rosenheim, "Perennial Problems in the Juvenile
Court," in Rosenheim, ed., *Justice for the Child,* p. 5.

organizations and individuals had provided care since the 1850's in some of the eastern states, notably Charles Loring Brace in New York.

The authority and usefulness of the private child-saving societies was recognized by the Illinois legislature, which passed various laws to prevent and punish wrongs to children, to prohibit the sale of tobacco to minors, to prevent the abandonment of children (1877), to prevent the sale of liquor to and gambling in the presence of minors (1879), to prevent the sale of "deadly weapons" to minors (1881), and to provide for the payment of fines received from prosecutions for cruelty to animals or children to the support of private protective and humane societies (1885). Despite the passage of this legislation, the institutional care of dependent children continued to be left to private agencies, most of which were under sectarian auspices. James Brown, in a study of the history of public assistance in Chicago, commented on some implications of state subsidies to religious organizations:

The citizens who refused to permit the overcrowding of children in the common mixed almshouse, through their generosity in providing other, private asylums for part of them, probably did future generations of dependent children a disservice. They cannot be criticized for taking up the slack in the public provision for they were merely following in the footsteps of similar private groups in the older Eastern states. The possibility of developing a public program which would meet the needs of *all* dependent children was not considered. The setting was an ideal one for the growth of vested interests and the development of a subsidy system, and later years were to illustrate the enormous difficulties in the way of abandoning this course once launched upon it.[27]

The Illinois Board of Public Charities was aware of the demoralizing conditions under which children were kept in the almshouses and suggested alternatives such as adoption, indenture, and "placing out." The population of children in the Cook County almshouse gradually declined due to the large number of private child-caring agencies in Chicago. By 1880, there were twelve such organizations

27. Brown, *History of Public Assistance in Chicago,* pp. 36–37.

in Chicago, of which only five pursued a non-sectarian policy. But as Homer Folks observed, even these organizations were regarded by members of other than Protestant churches as sectarian and Protestant.[28]

In 1876, the first industrial school in Illinois was planned by the Women's Centennial Association, who "strangely finding themselves in possession of $500 at the end of their tasks," decided that "nothing could be more appropriate than to establish some sort of an institution for our girls."[29] Mrs. Louise R. Wardner, a member of the Centennial Association, had originally shown interest in the problem of dependent girls when she and her colleagues in southern Illinois experienced difficulty in "placing out" girls released from a local orphanage. She inspected several institutions for delinquent and dependent children in Wisconsin but "nowhere did she find any provision for girls over twelve who were liable to become delinquent if left unsupervised."

The idea of an industrial school for girls was enthusiastically supported by child-saving groups. After land was donated to the Centennial Association, a school was incorporated in 1876 and a statewide association formed to provide financial support.[30] By the end of the school's first year, forty-one girls had been enrolled and were being supervised under "purifying, refining influences" and in "the atmosphere of a Christian home." The aim of the school, Mrs. Wardner told the National Conference of Charities in Chicago in 1879, was to prevent "depraved," "unprincipled," and "unpure" girls from growing up to reproduce "their kind three to five fold."[31]

The financing of the school was a problem because the only source of income was a one-dollar annual membership, which was so inadequate that it was "only by the most untiring exertions of the founders of the institution that its life was maintained." Another

28. Johnson, *Public Policy and Private Charities*, p. 4.
29. Helen L. Beveridge, "Reformatory and Preventive Work in Illinois," *Proceedings of the National Conference of Charities and Correction, 1881*, p. 276.
30. Johnson, *Public Policy and Private Charities*, pp. 95–96.
31. Mrs. Louise Rockwood Wardner, "Girls in Reformatories," *Proceedings of the Annual Conference of Charities, 1879*, pp. 185–89.

difficulty which the association had to face was that it had no legal authority to retain dependent girls. In order to find solutions to these financial and legal limitations, the board of trustees appointed Judge and Mrs. Bradwell and ex-Governor Beveridge to an investigative committee. The outcome of their investigations was the drafting of the "Industrial School for Girls Bill," which, after some opposition, was enacted by the legislature in 1879.[32]

The act permitted any seven or more persons, the majority of whom were women, to establish an industrial school for girls and to accept dependent girls upon commitment from the county court. A dependent girl was defined as:

Every female infant who begs or receives alms while actually selling, or pretending to sell any article in public; or who frequents any street, alley or other place, for the purpose of begging or receiving alms; or, who having no permanent place of abode, proper parental care, or guardianship, or sufficient means of subsistence, or who for other cause is a wanderer through streets and alleys and in other public places; or, who lives with, or frequents the company of, or consorts with reputed thieves, or other vicious persons; or who is found in a house of ill-fame, or in a poor house.

The act authorized any "responsible" resident to petition the county court to inquire into the alleged dependency of a girl and specified that the question of her dependency be determined by a jury of six persons. If adjudged dependent because, for example, "the parent or guardian is not a fit person to have the custody of such infant," the girl could be committed to an industrial school until she reached the age of eighteen, unless sooner discharged. The county was required to pay $10.00 per month for her tuition and supervision.[33]

An effort was made in 1886 to transform the girls' industrial school into a state institution because the board of trustees was having difficulty in raising money without the help of large endowments. The bill, however, failed to pass the legislature because the Board of Public Charities raised several objections. "We have no question

32. *Annual Report of the Illinois Industrial School for Girls* (1885) cited by Johnson, *Public Policy and Private Charities,* p. 97.
33. Revised Laws of Illinois, 1879, pp. 309–13.

of the propriety and utility of such an institution," stated the Board. "To commit juvenile offenders of the female sex to a county jail, house of correction or penitentiary, is a gross and palpable wrong. . . . But we should greatly prefer that all such offenders should be committed not for a definite term, but during their minority, as in the case of girls who are simply dependent." The Board reiterated its position that "the necessity for guardianship on the part of the state is greater in the case of criminal than of non-criminal children. . . . The proposed home for juvenile offenders seems to us to be far too positively penal in its character, and in this respect the bill needs radical revision."[34]

The School continued to operate as a private organization with a program of industrial and school work. In 1884 the school housed 104 girls and was described by state inspectors as "well and neatly kept," though the buildings were in need of extensive repairs. Corporal punishment was allowed "such as a kind mother would inflict upon a refractory child" and "disobedient" girls were locked in their rooms.[35] The permanence of the School was assured after the passage of an 1879 act provided a minimum income from the county. In 1883, the board of trustees purchased forty acres of land fifteen miles outside of Chicago but did not acquire sufficient funds to build an institution there until 1909. The building of the institution was partly delayed by complaints that the School was a "breeding place for vice and laziness." The Cook County Board of Commissioners appointed an investigative committee which reported that the School was "sadly in need of repair" and poorly organized. They "found nothing to justify the title 'Industrial School' for the institution, as the only industry the inmates seem to be acquainted with appears to be such plain housework as is connected with the institution's management."[36]

Meanwhile, the Catholic Archbishop of Chicago, Patrick A. Feehan, had organized the St. Mary's Training School for Boys at Des Plaines, near Chicago, and representatives of this institution

34. BRPC9, pp. 83–84.
35. BRPC10, pp. 131–32.
36. Johnson, *Public Policy and Private Charities,* p. 140.

soon introduced the "Feehanville Training School Bill" to the legislature. As originally drafted, the bill included a section providing that the courts "in making the order committing a dependent boy to the proposed school, shall have regard to the boy's religion, and whenever practicable assign him to a school, where he will be in the charge of persons of the same religious belief as that to which the boy does or should belong. . . ." This clause was omitted in the bill as passed because, according to one member of the legislature, it "was calculated to foster sectarian schools, and . . . the legislature should steer entirely clear of that rock." The omission of this clause, however, did not prevent industrial schools from developing along sectarian lines, and by 1929 only six of the twenty-seven industrial and training schools in Illinois were under non-sectarian control.[37]

"An act to provide for and aid training schools for boys," which was passed in 1883, permitted the commitment of dependent boys until the age of twenty-one. A Protestant institution, the Illinois Industrial Training School for Boys, was organized in 1887 and celebrated its "first Fourth of July with twelve wild, untamed boys." Mrs. Ursula Harrison, the Superintendent, introduced a program of military drill as well as industrial shops for broom-manufacturing, shoemaking, and woodcarving. After six months, one hundred boys were in the overcrowded home, but problems of space and financing were suddenly alleviated by the patronage of Milton George who had made a fortune in the newspaper business. George donated to the school 300 acres of farm land which, according to the president of the board of trustees, had "fertile soil" and "beautiful groves." The land was estimated to be worth $90,000 and the board was able to raise another $40,000 for the erection of buildings. The President of the Board of Trustees, Oscar L. Dudley, told delegates to the National Conference of Charities and Correction in 1891 that

the training school is in no sense a prison, having no bolts or bars; but, instead, the boys are governed by love and kindness, it being our aim to cultivate in them good manners, cleanliness of person, decency of language, habits of industry, and an appreciation of good morals and in-

37. *Ibid.,* pp. 97–99, 135.

dustry, thus fitting them for entrance into homes where they can grow to manhood and develop the essential qualities of good citizenship.[38]

To these three institutions—St. Mary's Training School for Boys, Illinois Industrial School for Girls, and Illinois Industrial Training School for Boys—was added another Catholic organization, the Chicago Industrial School for Girls, which was established in 1855 for the purpose of entrusting the care of dependent girls to the House of the Good Shepherd, St. Joseph's Orphan Asylum, and St. Vincent's Foundlings' Home. The "School" was merely a nominal institution, representing Catholic interests at the county court. These four schools were the only ones organized under the industrial school legislation prior to 1910.[39]

Between 1882 and 1917, the Supreme Court of Illinois was called upon at least nine times to interpret the constitutionality of the industrial school acts. The validity of the acts was attacked on the following grounds: (1) that the institutions created under the act were really penal institutions, and, therefore, the commitment was a punishment resulting in the deprivation of liberty without the constitutional right to due process; (2) that the institutions violated Section 3 of Article VIII of the state constitution which prohibited the granting of public money to sectarian institutions by either state or local governments; (3) and that the liability for the support of dependent children could not be charged to the county.[40]

In two actions brought in 1882—one by an individual and the other by a county—the Supreme Court upheld the constitutionality of the Illinois Industrial Training School for Girls.[41] In the first case, Mr. Justice Sheldon decided that the School was not a prison:

We perceive hardly any more restraint of liberty than is found in any well regulated school. Such a degree of restraint is essential in the proper education of a child, and it is in no just sense an infringement of the

38. "The Illinois Industrial Training School for Boys," *Proceedings of the National Conference of Charities and Correction, 1891,* pp. 146–50.
39. Johnson, *Public Policy and Private Charities,* pp. 101 f.
40. Jeter, *The Chicago Juvenile Court,* p. 3.
41. *In the Matter of the Petition of Alexander Ferrier,* 103 Ill. 367 (1882); *County of McLean v. Humphrey,* 104 Ill. 379 (1882).

inherent and inalienable right to personal liberty. . . . The power conferred under the act in question upon the county court is but of the same character of the jurisdiction exercised by the court of chancery over the persons and property of infants, having foundation in the prerogative of the Crown, flowing from its general power and duty, as "parens patriae," to protect those who have no other lawful protector.

In another case in 1882, the act was attacked because it permitted the organization of schools for sectarian purposes. Mr. Justice Mulkey, in upholding the constitutionality of the Illinois Industrial School for Girls, held that "it is the unquestioned right and imperative duty of every enlightened government, in its character of parens patriae, to protect and provide for the comfort and well-being of such of its citizens as, by reason of infancy, defective understanding or other misfortune or infirmity, are unable to take care of themselves."[42] An interpretation of Section 3 of Article VIII of the state constitution was again necessary in 1888 when the Board of Commissioners of Cook County refused to pay a bill of nearly $20,000 for the tuition, maintenance, and clothing of seventy-three girls committed by the county court to the Chicago Industrial School for Girls. The School was proved to be a paper organization, "a mere tender to two institutions . . . under the control of the Roman Catholic Church." Mr. Justice Magruder, in giving judgment in favor of the county, held that the decision in no way reflected upon the officers and founders of the School:

The women, whose names are written in this record are animated by the purest motives. They are engaged in the best and holiest of works, that of reforming the wicked and caring for the unfortunate. . . . [But] any scheme, even though hallowed by the blessing of the church, that surges against the will of the people as crystallized into their organic law, must break in pieces as breaks the foam of the sea against the rocks on the shore.[43]

Frederick Wines and members of the Board of Public Charities, who were quite explicit in their disapproval of the industrial and

42. Quoted by Johnson, *Public Policy and Private Charities,* p. 106.
43. *County of Cook v. The Chicago Industrial School for Girls,* 125 Ill. 540 (1888).

training school acts, welcomed the decision of the Supreme Court.
By 1886, the Board was convinced that the Chicago Industrial
School for Girls was an unconstitutional organization.[44] When the
Supreme Court confirmed this impression in 1888, the Board rec-
ommended state control and supervision of dependent children:

> The state owes a duty to them, which it has neither performed nor even
> acknowledged. It cannot delegate the discharge of that duty to any other
> hands. . . . Governments which shirk their obligations are sure to forfeit
> the respect and confidence of the people. . . . If the government finds it
> necessary or expedient to establish and maintain a charitable or penal
> institution, let it do so wholly at its own charge and expense, and receive
> no form of aid from private parties. . . . Works to which the state grants
> pecuniary aid should be wholly under the control of the state, and it
> should be done by officers and employees of the state, in buildings owned
> by the state. . . . If it is proposed to take care of children by the instru-
> mentality either of religious orders of the Church or by associated efforts
> outside of the Church, well and good. That means that the religious orders
> and secular associations will find their own means of carrying it on, just
> as the father of the family does, without expecting state aid.[45]

However, despite the decision of the Supreme Court and the criticism of the Board of Public Charities, Cook County continued to
contract with sectarian institutions for the care of dependent children. In 1917, the Illinois Supreme Court circumvented its earlier
decisions, which had not been followed in any practical sense, and
refused to find the Catholic-controlled Chicago Industrial School for
Girls in violation of the constitution. Finally, the legislature and
the courts agreed that counties could give financial aid to private
organizations under sectarian auspices.

In summary, the development of state institutions for "dependent" children was delayed by the vested interests of sectarian
organizations[46] and the reluctance of the state legislature to provide

44. *BRPC9*, pp. 79–81.
45. *BRPC10*, p. 86.
46. "If the executives of the private societies, who were confident that
they understood the proper method of dealing with poverty, had interested
themselves and their influential boards in the administration of the public

funds which would in effect benefit only Chicago and Cook County. The Supreme Court reversed its position in the O'Connell case and endorsed the practice of committing potential delinquents to institutions without trial or due process. The child-saving organizations were in general agreement that no distinctions should be made between "dependent" and "delinquent" children if the prevention of crime was to be realistically achieved.[47]

CHILDREN IN JAIL

In 1869, the General Assembly of Illinois enacted legislation providing for the appointment of a Board of State Commissioners of Public Charities. The Illinois Board, the fourth such organization in the United States, was established "to consider new questions arising out of experience as to the best modes of treatment and improvement of the various classes of patients and inmates in our several benevolent institutions." Governor Oglesby, in recommending the legislation, urged the public to never "lose sight of the . . . ever-present claims of the vast multitudes in our midst" who are "afflicted with the terrible diseases which deprive them of sight, hearing and of reason."

The Board was composed of five persons appointed by the Governor to serve without salary for five years. These Commissioners hired Frederick Wines as Secretary to guide policy as well as to handle administrative matters. Although the Board was an integral

---

charities instead of ignoring them, progress might not have been so long delayed. It is true that during certain periods in the history of the county board, the interest and cooperation of these voluntary groups would probably have been strenuously resisted, but it is not easy to justify their refusal to extend their help when it was requested, as was true on more than one occasion" (Brown, *History of Public Assistance in Chicago*, p. 177).

47. Jane Addams reported that the courts minimized criminal offenses in order to commit children to industrial schools and thus "save [them] from the sure demoralization of imprisonment" (*My Friend, Julia Lathrop*, p. 133).

part of the charitable machinery of the state, it had almost no administrative powers and was limited in making inspections, suggestions, and recommendations. The main scope of the Board's work
was directed to the regulation of private organizations and they
were authorized and required to visit, at least twice a year, "all the
charitable and correctional institutions of the State, excepting prisons
receiving state aid, and ascertain whether the moneys appropriated
for their aid are or have been economically and judiciously ex-
pended. . . ."[48] In addition to these investigative powers, the commissioners were required to supervise the girls' industrial schools
(1879), boys' training schools (1883), private associations receiving children committed to them by the courts (1899), and agencies
and institutions placing children in foster homes (1905). By the
juvenile court law of 1899, the Board was also made responsible for
approving the charters of associations desiring to supervise the care
of dependent, neglected or delinquent children.

In the first ten years of the Board's work, the Commissioners
launched a critical and carefully documented attack on the county
and city jail system in Illinois.[49] In 1869, agents of the Board in-
spected 78 jails where they found 511 persons, of whom 408 were
awaiting trial. Ninety-eight children under the age of 16 were
discovered in 40 of the jails. The Cook County jail, which had
originally cost $120,000 to be built, consisted of 32 poorly venti-

48. *BRPC1*, pp. 2–3, 7. For a lengthy discussion of the Board's powers,
see Johnson, *Public Policy and Private Charities*, pp. 52 f.
49. "Mere suspicion of crime places the accused under ban, and deprives
him of all rights, except to those of an enemy. The conversion of a criminal
into an honest man seems to be looked upon as so hopeless an undertaking
as to be unworthy of even an effort. He is treated as an outlaw, a foe to
mankind, an Ishmaelite, whose hand is against every man, and every man's
hand against him. . . . A man who becomes a criminal . . . does not cease to
be a man. As a man, he has rights, which, as men, we are bound to respect.
We have no more right to infringe upon his rights, than he has to infringe
upon ours. We may demand restitution. We may use all wise and lawful
means to cure him of his weakness and criminal tendencies. But to outlaw
him, to cut him off as an unworthy member, is like amputating a sore finger,
without first endeavoring to heal the sore. Injustice to the criminal is an
injury to society" (*BRPC1*, pp. 126–27).

lated cells in the basement of the courthouse. On the day of inspection, there were 114 persons in the jail—107 were awaiting trial—and as many as seven inmates were confined in one cell, deprived of fresh air, light, and basic comforts. "The jail is so dark," reported the Board, "that it is necessary to keep the gas burning in the corridors both day and night. The cells are filthy and full of vermin." The Board was especially concerned over the fact that 14 children were found in the jail. "Here the insane are confined, awaiting trial and transportation to the almshouse or asylum. Here witnesses are detained who, perhaps have never seen a crime committed, but are too poor to give bail for their appearance in court."

The county jail was found to be based on a system of terror: "It is unjust and unloving, it assumes that a certain amount of suffering will expiate a certain amount of guilt, it confirms criminal tendencies instead of eliminating them, it is questionable whether it diminishes crime, and it is terribly expensive." The Board criticized the system for its lack of scientific classification and inadequate educational and labor programs. "The effect of this promiscuous herding together of old and young, innocent and guilty, convicts, suspected persons and witnesses, male and female, is to make the county prison a school of vice. In such an atmosphere purity itself could not escape contamination."[50]

The county jails in Illinois were found to be "moral plague spots" and "dark, damp, and fetid" places where the inmates' self-respect was brutalized and crushed.[51] "Such a policy makes great criminals out of little ones." The commissioners radically proposed that "nothing but the overthrow of the system will ever put an end to the present abuses, for they cannot be corrected by individual effort, but are inherent in the system itself."[52] The county jails were incapable of reforming "the children of thieves or prostitutes, of gamblers and drunkards" who are "exposed to a thousand corrupting influences" on the city streets. "The atmosphere which many of them breathe," commented the Board in 1872,

50. *Ibid.*, pp. 175–84.
51. *BRPC6*, p. 117.
52. *BRPC1*, p. 187.

is such that a future career of crime may be unerringly predicted for them. Shall we leave them to perish? And in perishing to prey upon society, to lead lives of violence, destructive alike to property and life? A thousand times, no. The state has a duty to perform towards its criminal population, no less sacred and obligatory than that which it owes to the simply unfortunate, and this duty rests upon the same double foundation of humanity and self-interest.[53]

Despite the Board's efforts, there were few noticeable improvements in the county jail system.[54] An attempt to regulate the conditions under which minors were detained was made in 1874 by adding to the law regulating jail conditions a clause providing for the separation of minors from older offenders and those convicted of felonies. But this provision was a tokenistic and ineffectual remedy which could not be implemented in overcrowded and poorly constructed institutions.[55] At a New York meeting of the National Prison Congress, in 1876, Frederick Wines indicted the Illinois county jail system as a "failure and a disgrace to the intelligence and humanity of the state. We know of no evil which so loudly calls for a remedy."[56] Illinois was not the only state to have a jail system "antagonistic to the theory of reformation." In Michigan, the statistics for 1873 revealed that 377 boys and 100 girls under 18 years were given jail sentences. Ohio, in 1871, committed 182 boys and 29 girls to county jails and Massachusetts had 2,029 minors in their jails during 1870; 231 of these children were under 15 years old. "One of the most painful features of this dreary picture," commented Wines, "is the large number of young people of both sexes,

53. BRPC2, pp. 197–98 (Springfield: State Journal Steam Print, 1873).
54. BRPC3, p. 51 (Springfield: State Journal Steam Print, 1875).
55. Randall, The St. Charles School, p. 5.
56. BRPC4, p. 81. "Thus society, by its own want of foresight, its indifference, its indolent self-indulgence and toleration of evils which it would cost more effort to obviate than society is willing to make, actually trains offenders, stimulates and qualifies them to become great criminals. In effect, crime is not punished at all, nor is any intelligent attempt made to reform the offender, so long as the crime assumes the form of a mere misdemeanor. Not until it reaches the stage of actual felony does society make any earnest attempt to grapple with the evil" (ibid., p. 188).

who are subjected to the contaminating influences of such a life."[57]

The Commissioners' fifth report included a comprehensive survey of all the county jails in Illinois, and it found little improvement in jail conditions.[58]

In a moral sense, the atmosphere of the jail is stifling to every better impulse and aspiration; it is profane, obscene, ribald; . . . it is defiant, reckless, bitter. . . . It is the state—the General Assembly—which is to blame for relinquishing its own duty into the hands of boards of county supervisors, who can no more grapple successfully with the criminal class than they can bail out Lake Michigan with a sieve.[59]

During the 1880's, penal reformers in Illinois shifted their interest from the general physical condition of jails to the effect that these conditions had on particular groups, especially children. Frederick Wines' visit to England caused him to think about the reformatory system as a means of rescuing children from jails, where they were contaminated by contact with older offenders. The Board of Public Charities slowly gave up the idea of "overthrowing the system," and instead concentrated on improving jail conditions for children who needed special care and attention.

Children were regularly detained in the Cook County jail and the Chicago House of Correction, both before and after their trial. Their presence in such places was to be "deplored" but it was the "fault of our laws" rather than the institutions themselves.[60] Sunday school and other elementary teaching was occasionally provided by philan-

57. *Ibid.,* pp. 186–87.
58. Although twenty-five new jails were built in six years from 1870 to 1876, the Board complained that many of them merely perpetuated the old evils. "If we had been consulted with reference to some of these jails, we could have saved some of the counties from serious mistakes and unnecessary expense. The building of so many new jails is, in one aspect of the question, to be regretted, for the reason that the amount of money spent in their erection, during ten years past, aggregating, as it does, three-quarters of a million dollars, might have been applied to better effect in the construction of district prisons, built by the state itself" (*BRPC5,* p. 180).
59. *Ibid.,* p. 176.
60. *BRPC7,* p. 307.

thropic individuals and organizations but this proved to be a superficial diversion.[61] Adelaide Groves, a Chicago socialite, informed the editor of a local newspaper that she visited "the boy's ward of the county jail, on Sunday afternoon usually, carrying with me books and writing material, stamps and pencils." She objected to the fact that "groups of idle boys and girls, teaching each other wickedness and sin, were permitted to roam at will through their town. . . . Shall we not, as a Christian city and people, stretch out a helping hand to the boys in the jail and bridewell?"[62]

Adelaide Groves suggested that Chicago needed special institutions—detention homes for before trial and reformatories for after trial—to replace the boys wards in the county jail and bridewell.[63] The existing reformatory at Pontiac was considered inappropriate because it was not a place of detention and it only housed children who had been convicted of a criminal offense. "Let a 'Detention Manual School,' with locks, and bolts, and bars, and keys, be provided by Cook County," wrote Mrs. Groves, "so that these boys who have broken the laws in a greater or less degree may not be driven to still greater crime and degradation. . . ."[64]

In 1890, the Board of Public Charities found on the day of inspection nine children under sixteen in Cook County jail and forty-five children in the Chicago House of Correction. "What a shame," they commented, "to place these little boys in such a school of vice."[65] Adelaide Groves, in conjunction with the Chicago Woman's Club,

61. "The so-called school room is furnished with three long benches, one table, a chair and a stool. These benches are so crowded that the boys who are attempting to write upon slates strike their elbows into their next neighbor, who vigorously resists, therefore the writing lesson is not a success. The books are from the attics of our friends and embrace much ancient literature. . . . Fortunately the singing books are alike, and that lesson is received and rendered with the vigor of boys; they beat the time with their feet and heads. . . . Miss Wright makes this her strong lesson, explaining the meaning of the gospel words, and letting them select the hymns to be sung" (letter from Adelaide Groves to *Chicago Inter Ocean*, November 12, 1884).
62. *Chicago Inter Ocean*, June 6, 1884.
63. *Ibid.*
64. *Chicago Tribune*, November 6, 1888.
65. *BRPCII*, p. 194 (Springfield: H. W. Rokker, 1890).

was successful in establishing a regular day school in the county jail and a movement was begun to separate children from adults in the House of Correction. Two years later, jail conditions had not improved and the Board of Public Charities observed that "one-half of the boys committed for first offenses, under seventeen years, may be saved if they were sent to a reform school, taught to work and educated while there, and when their term is served the stigma of 'jail-bird' will not forever stick to them as it does now."[66]

In summary, the Board of Public Charities found little public or political support for its efforts to reform conditions in county and city jails. The Board's policies were largely determined by its Secretary, Frederick Wines, who continued his father's work and introduced Illinois to the concepts of preventive penology. When the Board turned its interest to the problems raised by the detention of children in jails, it found allies in other child-saving organizations and a potential base from which successful reforms might be achieved.

CHILDREN OF THE STATE

Despite the failure to correct abuses in the industrial schools and to reform the county jail system, there was a general consensus of opinion among state welfare experts and private child-saving organizations that children should not be processed through the criminal courts or incarcerated with older offenders. In 1891, Timothy Hurley, president of the Catholic-controlled Visitation and Aid Society, was instrumental in introducing into the legislature a bill to authorize corporations "to manage, care and provide for children who may be abandoned, neglected, destitute or subjected to perverted training." The bill proposed that the county courts be empowered to commit to private child-saving organizations any dependent or neglected child or any child "being trained or allowed

66. *BRPC12*, p. 196 (Springfield: H. W. Rokker, 1893).

to be trained in vice and crime."[67] This bill failed to become law because its constitutionality was questionable and it failed to win the support of non-Catholic organizations.

The child-saving movement gained momentum in 1893, a year for great activity and agitation by state and private organizations. The Chicago Woman's Club worked to establish an efficient school in the city jail and to secure a central police station that could be used exclusively for women and children.[68] The sociologist Charles Henderson, who later supported the juvenile court movement, was teaching courses in criminology and child welfare at the University of Chicago.[69] The annual congresses of both the National Conference of Charities and Correction and the National Prison Association were held in Chicago in June; many Illinois representatives were present, notably Lucy Flower and Frederick Wines, who held executive positions.

In the same year that John P. Altgeld was elected Governor of Illinois, Julia Lathrop was appointed to the Board of Public Charities and Florence Kelly was appointed Chief Factory Inspector of Illinois. Both women were considered experts on the problem of dependent children and their appointment to positions of prestige gave the child-saving movement political power and helped to overcome factional disputes among sectarian organizations.[70] The pres-

67. Timothy D. Hurley, *Origin of the Illinois Juvenile Court Law*, pp. 139–40.

68. Henriette Greenbaum Frank and Amalie Hofer Jerome, *Annals of the Chicago Woman's Club for the First Forty Years of its Organization, 1876–1916*, pp. 125 f.

69. For an interesting survey of the teaching of sociology and criminology in American universities, see Daniel Fulcomer, "Instruction in Sociology in Institutions of Learning," *Proceedings of the National Conference of Charities and Correction, 1894*, pp. 67–85.

70. "Up to that time, visitation of State and County institutions had been largely perfunctory . . . and limited in the main to the State Institutions. Miss Lathrop determined to visit and see for herself and in the course of the work she went to every jail and poor house in the State, even in the most out-of-the-way localities. She was shocked at the conditions she found, young children shut up with the most depraved adults and being trained in crime instead of being kept away from it. She determined not to rest until some remedy for these conditions was found" (Hurley, *Origin of the Illinois Juvenile Court Law*, pp. 17–18).

ence of national reformers in Chicago and the efforts of Julia Lathrop were no doubt also responsible for the establishment of a state reformatory for delinquent girls in 1893.[71]

Governor Altgeld had a considerable influence on the child-saving movement. His political career, which was cut short by his pardoning the Haymarket "anarchists," was notable for its special interest in the welfare of minority groups, especially women, children, and criminals. He appointed women to political positions on the grounds that they were not as susceptible to bribery and corruption as men. He regarded children as innocent preys for industrial exploitation, and criminals as persons in need of guidance rather than repression. The penitentiaries, reformatories and jails, said Altgeld, were filled with "erring fellow-beings," whereas the "real" criminals were the industrialists and corrupt officials who were politically immune to criminal prosecution:[72]

No government was ever overthrown by the poor, and we have nothing to fear from that source. It is the greedy and powerful that pull down the pillars of the state. Greed, corruption and pharisaism are today sapping the foundations of government. It is the criminal rich and their hangers-on who are the real anarchists of our time. They rely on fraud and brute force. They use government as a convenience and make justice the hand-maid of wrong. We are developing a kind of carbonated patriotism which seems to derive its most sparkling qualities from respectable boodleism. Our country has great vitality, but these conditions must be arrested or else we are lost. Only those nations grow great which correct abuses, make reform, and listen to the voice of the struggling masses.[73]

Altgeld did not take a mere amateur interest in penology, for he was the author of a thoughtful pamphlet concerning *Our Penal Machinery and Its Victims* (published in 1884). It is a pamphlet in the true sense—a humanistic indictment of a "formal, iron-bound, and superficial" system, rather than a scholarly treatise. Alt-

71. Revised Laws of Illinois, 1893, pp. 119–23.

72. *Proceedings of the Annual Congress of the National Prison Association,* pp. 13–19 (Chicago: 1893). For an analysis of Altgeld's political career, see Ray Ginger, *Altgeld's America: The Lincoln Ideal Versus Changing Realities.*

73. Biennial message to the legislature by Governor Altgeld in the *Journal of the House of Representatives of Illinois* (1897).

geld was horrified by conditions in penitentiaries and "lock-ups," by the overcrowded jails filled with unconvicted petty criminals, and by the economic injustices of sentencing practices. "Only recently have we begun to recognize the fact," wrote Altgeld, "that every man is to a great extent what his heredity and early environment have made him, and that the law of cause and effect applies here as well as in nature." He agreed with Enoch Wines that "human justice is a clumsy machine, and often deserves the punishment which it inflicts." Adults and children alike are degraded, not improved, by harsh punishments.

Does clubbing a man reform him? Does brutal treatment elevate his thoughts? Does handcuffing him fill him with good resolves? Stop right here, and for a moment imagine yourself forced to submit to being handcuffed, and see what kind of feelings will be aroused in you. Submission to that one act of degradation prepares many a young man for a career of crime. It destroys the self-respect of others, and makes them the easy victim of crime.

Unlike most of the child savers, Altgeld was not afraid to acknowledge the economic inequalities behind the criminal law and its administration. He was not a sentimentalist when it came to the economic facts of life. The system, he wrote, "applies the *crushing process* to those who are already down; while the crafty criminal— especially if he be rich—is gently dealt with. . . ." What Altgeld was intimating was that the whole machinery of the criminal law was *politically* designed to intimidate and control the poor. Even the wealthy whores—"the petted children of sin [who] live in gilded palaces and dress in silks and satins"—were immune to prosecution. Altgeld was one of the first Illinois reformers to recommend the use of "probationary parole" and the indeterminate sentence, and he enthusiastically welcomed Enoch Wines' plan for establishing reformatories for young offenders.[74]

By 1893, the presence of hundreds of children in the jails was the central grievance of child-saving organizations. The Chicago

74. John P. Altgeld, *Our Penal Machinery and Its Victims,* pp. 20, 24, 34–37, 41–42.

Woman's Club became involved in jail reforms through the work of Adelaide Groves, who was made an honorary member of the Club for her philanthropic services. Mrs. Groves found the boys' wards of the jails to be "training schools" in crime, inhabited by "unkempt" and "vicious" children who would "soon be men, ripe for the penitentiary."[75] Discipline, hard work, silence, and segregation from adults were the answer to the problem. "We need a building and a yard," she wrote in one of her many letters to the press, "strongly constructed with a high wall, for these boys are great 'skippers.' "[76]

Chicago's eleven "police" courts typically handled children's cases and punished them with fines that were "laid out" in the House of Correction at the rate of fifty cents a day. In the first six months of 1899, 332 boys under the age of 16 were sent to the city jail, usually on charges of disorderly conduct which included everything from burglary to "flipping trains" and playing ball on the streets.[77]

In 1893, the Chicago Board of Education was persuaded to take over the supervision of boys under seventeen years who were committed to the city prison. The city council later authorized the Board of Education to use money from the "school fund" to equip and operate a manual training school within the city prison. In 1897, the school was renamed after John Worthy, a commissioner of the prison, who encouraged and provided funds for the building of separate dormitories for delinquent boys.[78] The interest of educational authorities in the city prison was prompted by the fact that a high percentage of the inmate population was committed for truancy. By laws of 1883 and 1889, children between the ages of seven and fourteen were compelled to attend a public school for at least sixteen weeks in the year. Truant officers were authorized to "arrest children of school-going age, who habitually haunt public

75. *Chicago Inter Ocean,* June 6, 1884.
76. *Ibid.,* December, 1884. Actual date is not known but a copy of the letter is available at the Chicago Historical Society.
77. Sophonisba P. Breckenridge and Edith Abbott, *The Delinquent Child and the Home,* pp. 1–2 (New York: Survey Associates Inc., 1916).
78. Robert M. Smith, "Boys in City Prison," *Proceedings of the Illinois Conference of Charities* (1898), in *BRPC15,* pp. 331–35 (Springfield: Phillips Brothers, 1899).

places, and have no lawful occupation, and also truant children who absent themselves from school without leave. . . ."[79] Although children under fourteen were prohibited by law from being employed, the truant officers or "attendance agents" were usually unable or unwilling to enforce this provision. In the second report of the Illinois factory inspectors in 1894, Florence Kelly reported that the job of rescuing children "from nicotine poisoning, from the miasma of the stock yards, and from the horrible conditions of the sweat shops" was frustrated by the lack of cooperation from the Board of Education. She complained that "unruly children are expelled from school to suit the convenience of teachers."[80]

The John Worthy School consequently became a glorified warehouse for school troublemakers who could not escape—as most boys did—the truant officers and factory inspectors. The School's Superintendent, Robert Smith, was quite candid about the fact that he had to deal with "mischievous and incorrigible boys who will not go to school when they ought, and whose behavior is so bad when there that the teachers are only too glad to be rid of their presence in the classroom and wish they had stayed away."[81] At the Illinois Conference of Charities in 1898, Smith complained that his institution could not possibly reform a diverse group of offenders who were herded together in miserable surroundings for only brief period of time:[82]

Under present conditions I do not wish to shoulder the responsibility of giving out to the citizens of Chicago that we have a place where mischievous and incorrigible boys are controlled and educated on the line of useful citizenship, when it is false. . . . The John Worthy School in its

79. Revised Laws of Illinois, 1883, pp. 131–32: "An Act to Secure to all Children the Benefit of an Elementary Education." Revised Laws of Illinois, 1889, p. 237: "An Act Concerning the Education of Children."
80. *Second Annual Report of the Factory Inspectors of Illinois* (1894).
81. Smith, "Boys in City Prison," p. 331.
82. "For the lack of proper sleeping quarters, where they could be properly confined and isolated from the old and hardened criminals, these boys pass their time harming themselves and injuring the community by careers of vice, diversified by occasional short terms in the county jail or house of correction" (Smith, "Boys in City Prison," pp. 328–37).

present condition is nothing more nor less than a school for crime, and until the city council of Chicago takes steps to isolate the boys from adult criminals, the evil will not be remedied.

Smith told the conference that the John Worthy School processed an annual average of 1,300 boys, of which over a quarter were truants. The average sentence in the institution was 29 days. "I would infinitely rather see my boy a truant," said Smith, "than run such a risk as having him imprisoned in the John Worthy School under present conditions."[83]

The concern for separate facilities for children was evident also in the juvenile court movement. According to the records of the Chicago Woman's Club, Mrs. Perry Smith recommended in 1891 the creation of a "juvenile court" so that children "might be saved from contamination of association with older criminals." Other influential members of the Club prevailed upon Judge Richard Tuthill to hold a separate court for children on Saturday mornings. The Club assigned a representative to this special court who acted in the capacity of probation officer and adviser to the judge.[84] By 1892,

83. *Ibid.*
84. "The work of this noble oganization was initial, persistent and effective. Well do I remember how many years ago, when it became my turn to hold the Criminal Court, I first visited the jail and found the cells of the old jail filled with boys, some of them under what was then called the age of responsibility, ten years. I requested the State's Attorney to have a calendar of all the boys' cases made out for me, telling him that I wished to dispose of their cases before I began on the adults. . . . Mrs. Lucy Flower, Mrs. Perry Smith and others . . . at once set to work to do what could be done to improve the situation. . . . The Club thereupon employed and paid for some two or three years a young lady who gave her service in behalf of the little children in the jail every day. No more loving and inspiring work was ever done by woman. . . . Then began the work of changing the law of Illinois with respect to the care and treatment of all boys and girls under 17 years of age, who were found in a condition of delinquency. In all the consultations and work done in the preparation of this law, which became the Juvenile Court Law of Illinois, the most humane and wisest law ever enacted in any state of the Union, the Woman's Club took a most important and effective part. . . . The first probation officer appointed by the Judge of the Juvenile Court was one of the remarkable women of Chicago, Mrs. Alzina P. Stevens, then residing at Hull-House. Mrs. Flower brought her to me and said that 'this lady, you will find, can be very helpful as a probation officer, and we will see that she

the New York courts were also hearing children's cases separately.[85]

The child savers recruited new members to their cause and spon-sored fact-finding expeditions to other states. Lucy Flower,[86] a for-mer president of the Chicago Woman's Club, visited Massachusetts to learn about their probation system; Jane Addams and Julia Lathrop attended the National Conference of Charities and Correc-tion held in Toronto in 1897; and Hastings Hart, Secretary of the Children's Home and Aid Society, was a delegate to the congress of the National Prison Association, where he recommended that de-pendent and delinquent children "be taken out of the slums and placed in clean homes, physically and morally, and put alone where they will not come into contact with their former associates."[87]

The child-saving movement was further legitimized by the Board of Public Charities, which, under the influence of Julia Lathrop, Ephraim Banning, and Frederick Wines, renewed its recommenda-tion that the "general assembly should make some provision for the care of the destitute, neglected and dependent children of the State." The Board warned that "every child allowed to grow up in ignorance and vice, and so to become a pauper or a criminal, is liable to become in turn the progenitor of generations of criminals." What was needed, said the commissioners in their biennial report, was a mas-sive effort to "rescue every child in the State exposed to destruction through neglect or abuse."[88]

Julia Lathrop, whose father was a lawyer, and Lucy Flower, who was married to one, realized that child-welfare reforms could only be accomplished with the support of political and professional or-

---

is paid for her service,' as there was no provision in the law for the payment of probation officers—not even one . . ." (Richard Tuthill, the first juvenile court judge in Illinois, quoted by Frank and Jerome, *Annals of the Chicago Woman's Club*, pp. 179–80).

85. Hurley, *Origin of the Illinois Juvenile Court Law*, p. 14.

86. For a portrait of this reformer, see Harriet S. Farwell, *Lucy Louise Flower, 1837–1920: Her Contribution to Education and Child Welfare in Chicago.*

87. *Proceedings of the Annual Congress of the National Prison Associa-tion, Indianapolis, 1899*, p. 382.

88. *BRPC15*, pp. 62–72.

ganizations. "This is a legal matter," Julia Lathrop is supposed to have said. "It must not go to the legislature as a woman's measure; we must get the Bar Association to handle it."[89] Ephraim Banning, who served with Julia Lathrop on the Board of Public Charities, introduced the following resolution at the annual meeting of the Chicago Bar Association in October, 1898:

WHEREAS, The State of Illinois and the City of Chicago, are lamentably deficient in proper care for delinquent children, accused or convicted of violation of law, lacking many of those reformatory institutions which exist in other progressive states of the union; and WHEREAS, Children accused of crime are kept in the common jails and police stations, and children convicted of misdemeanors are sentenced to the bridewell, where they are kept in immediate association with drunkards, vagabonds and thieves; and WHEREAS, The judges having charge of the trial of children are in our courts so overburdened with other work as to make it difficult to give due attention to the cases of children, particularly those of the dependent and neglected classes; and WHEREAS, The State of Illinois makes no provision for the care of most of the children dependent upon the public for support, other than the public almshouses—unlike many neighboring states which have long ago passed laws prohibiting the keeping of children in public almshouses: *Resolved,* That the president of this association appoint a committee of five of its members to investigate existing conditions relative to delinquent and dependent children, and to cooperate with committees of other organizations in formulating and securing such legislation as may be necessary to cure existing evils and bring the State of Illinois and the City of Chicago up to the standard of the leading states and cities of the Union.[90]

The President of the Bar Association, George Follansbee, appointed a committee consisting of Ephraim Banning, Harvey Hurd, Edwin Burritt Smith, John W. Ela, and Merritt Starr who cooperated with child-saving organizations to engineer a juvenile court bill through the legislature.

One month after the resolution of the Chicago Bar Association,

89. Hurley, *Origin of the Illinois Juvenile Court Law*, p. 18.
90. I would like to thank the Chicago Bar Association for providing me with a copy of the original document.

the Illinois Conference of Charities devoted most of its program to child-saving issues.[91] The juvenile court plan was endorsed by a number of speakers, including B. M. Chipperfield, President of the State's Attorneys Association, who called for state supervision of delinquents. Major R. W. McClaughry, Warden of Joliet State Penitentiary, stressed the importance of removing children from the jails. "You can not take a boy of tender years," he said, "and lock him up with thieves, drunkards and half-crazy men of all classes and nationalities without teaching him lessons in crime." This criticism was echoed by the Superintendent of the John Worthy School who recommended that delinquents be remanded to educational authorities after their trial in "juvenile court, presided over by a careful and most painstaking judge, empowered to commit them for longer terms than the present law permits. . . ." Frederick Wines best expressed the mood of the conference in his closing speech:

We make criminals out of children who are not criminals by treating them as if they were criminals. That ought to be stopped. What we should have, in our system of criminal jurisprudence, is an entirely separate systems of courts for children, in large cities, who commit offenses which would be criminal in adults. We ought to have a "children's court" in Chicago, and we ought to have a "children's judge," who should attend to no other business. We want some place of detention for those children other than a prison. . . . No child ought to be tried unless he has a friend in court to look after his real interests. There should be someone there who has the confidence of the judge, and who can say to the court, "Will you allow me to make an investigation of this case? Will you allow me to make a suggestion to the court?"

The conference ended on a note of optimism and unity. "If we could only act together during one session of the Legislature," said Julia Lathrop, "we could much improve the legislation of Illinois." Reverend Jenkin Lloyd Jones, Chipperfield, Wines, and George Hobson (a member of the Board of Supervisors of Vermilion County) were appointed to a committee for the purpose of cooperating with other child-saving organizations in drafting a juvenile court bill. Similarly, the Chicago Bar Association examined the legal rami-

91. *Proceedings of the Illinois Conference of Charities*, pp. 310–37.

fications of child-welfare legislation and asked Judge Harvey Hurd of Cook County Circuit Court to prepare a bill for the legislature. Hurd in turn consulted Timothy Hurley, of the Catholic Visitation and Aid Society, and Hastings Hart, of the Children's Home and Aid Society. On December 10, 1898, Judge Hurd called a meeting in his office; attending were Lucy Flower, Julia Lathrop, Timothy Hurley, Hastings Hart, State Representative John C. Newcomer, Superintendent A. G. Lane of the Public Schools system, County Jailor John L. Whitman, Carl Kelsey of the Children's Home and Aid Society, and Frank Soule, a businessman with philanthropic interests. Hurd was elected chairman and Hart secretary of this informal committee.[92]

The juvenile court bill, drafted by Judge Hurd in consultation with the Bar Association, Hurley, and Hart, was finally introduced by John Newcomer in the House of Representatives on February 7, 1889, and by Selon Case in the Senate on February 15. In March, a hearing was held before the judiciary committee of both houses sitting together in a joint session. To this hearing the Chicago Bar Association sent Hurd, Ephraim Banning, and Edwin Smith; "other interests" were represented by Judge Orrin Carter, Hurley, and Thomas MacMillan. The constitutionality of the bill was defended by the legal spokesmen, while the representatives of child-saving organizations stressed its humanitarian implications. The juvenile court bill was passed without much delay or difficulty in the Senate but, "owing to repeated delays, it was not put on its passage in the House until the last day of the session and not finally voted on until late in the afternoon of that day." At this point, the Bar Association committee approached Governor Tanner and Speaker Sherman, "explaining the objects of the bill and securing their support and cooperation." Without their help, the bill would probably have failed to be passed.[93] On April 14, both Houses of the legislature passed

92. Hurley, *Origin of the Illinois Juvenile Court Law*, pp. 21–22.
93. *Report of the Chicago Bar Association Juvenile Court Committee* (October 28, 1899). A copy of the original document was provided by the Chicago Historical Society. Louise Bowen gives another, more dramatic version of how the act was passed: "I happened to know at that time a noted

"an act to regulate the treatment and control of dependent, neglected and delinquent children."[94]

SUMMARY

The juvenile court act of 1899 culminated nearly thirty years of reform efforts by child-saving organizations in Illinois. Its success was due in large measure to the fact that it was widely sponsored and in turn satisfied diverse interest groups:

1. Sectarian organizations supported the act because juvenile court judges were required to sentence children to institutions in accordance with their religious preference.

2. The industrial school legislation was not repealed by the act and industrial schools retained the power to release their wards or place them in foster homes without the court's consent.

3. The Board of Public Charities regarded the juvenile court act as a confirmation of basic principles of preventive penology—comprehensive governmental control over "delinquent" youth, segregation of delinquents from adult offenders, access to "pre-delinquent" youth, indeterminate sentencing, and minimal judicial formality.

4. Administrators of reformatories welcomed the act as a means of facilitating the commitment and release of "delinquents" in a manner consistent with the requirements of the "new penology."

The juvenile court was not, as some writers have suggested, a

---

Illinois politician; I asked him to my house and told him I wanted to get this law passed at once. The legislature was in session; he went to the telephone in my library, called up one of the bosses in the Senate and one in the House and said to each one, 'There is a bill, number so and so, which I want passed; see that it is done at once. One of the men whom he evidently called said, 'What is there in it?' and the reply was, 'There is nothing in it, but a woman I know wants it passed.' And it was passed. I thought with horror at the time, supposing it had been a bad bill, it would have been passed in exactly the same way" (*Growing Up With a City*, p. 107).

94. Revised Laws of Illinois, 1899, pp. 131–37.

"radical reform,"[95] but rather a politically compromised reform which consolidated existing practices. Conservative in origins, the act was passed with the help of influential members of the judiciary, the Chicago Bar Association, elite civic and feminist groups, state and private child-saving organizations, and politicians interested in "non-political" causes. Three themes in the juvenile court movement further reflect its conservatism and middle-class bias:

1. "Delinquents" were depicted as needing firm control and restraint if their reform was to be successful. The child savers were not indulgent sentimentalists, they recommended increased imprisonment as a means of removing delinquents from corrupting influences. Thus, it did not seem inconsistent to the President of the Illinois Humane Society that he should support the juvenile court for young offenders and corporal punishment and the whipping post for older offenders.[96] It is inaccurate to regard the child savers as liberal reformers and their opponents as staunch conservatives, for the authoritarian impulse was implicit in the child-saving movement.

2. Although the child savers affirmed the value of the home and family as the basic institutions of American society, they facilitated the removal of children from "a home which fails to fulfill its proper function." The child savers set such high standards of family propriety that almost any parent could be accused of not fulfilling his "proper function." In effect, only lower-class families were evaluated as to their competence, whereas the propriety of middle-class families was exempt from investigation and recrimination.

3. The blurring of distinctions between "dependent" and "delinquent" children and the corresponding elimination of due process for juveniles, served to make a social fact out of the norm of adolescent dependence. "Every child is dependent," held the Board of Public Charities. "Dependence is a child's natural condition." It

95. Rosenheim, *Justice for the Child,* p. 7. A similar inference is made by Herbert H. Lou, *Juvenile Courts in the United States,* pp. 1–31, and Board of Commissioners of Cook County, Illinois, *Juvenile Court of Cook County: Fiftieth Anniversary Report* (1949).
96. *New York Evening Journal,* May 17, 1899.

was one task of the child savers to punish premature independence in children and restrict youthful autonomy. Proponents of constitutional protections for children were rebuked for impeding the "systematic and adequate effort for the salvation of all the children who are in need of savior."[97]

97. *BRPC15*, pp. 62–72.

Chapter 6: *The Fate of the Juvenile Court*

A FRIEND IN COURT

The essential preoccupation of the child-saving movement was the recognition and control of youthful deviance. It brought attention to and thus "invented" new categories of youthful misbehavior which had been hitherto unappreciated. The efforts of the child savers were institutionally expressed in the juvenile court, which is generally regarded as their most significant contribution to the new penology.

The juvenile court was a special tribunal created by statute to determine the legal status of "troublesome" children. Underlying the juvenile court act was the concept of *parens patriae* by which the courts were authorized to use wide discretion in resolving the problems of "its least fortunate junior citizens."[1] The administration of juvenile justice differed in many important respects from the criminal court process. A child was not accused of a crime but offered assistance and guidance; intervention in his life was not supposed to carry the stigma of a criminal record; judicial records were not generally available to the press or public, and hearings were conducted in relative privacy; proceedings were informal and due process safe-

1. Gustav L. Schramm, "The Juvenile Court Idea," *Federal Probation* 13 (September, 1949): 21.

137

guards were not applicable due to the court's civil jurisdiction.[2]

The original juvenile court statutes enabled the courts to investigate a wide variety of youthful needs and misbehavior. As Joel Handler has observed, "the critical philosophical position of the reform movement was that no formal, legal distinctions should be made between the delinquent and the dependent or neglected."[3] Statutory definitions of "delinquency" included (1) acts that would be criminal if committed by adults, (2) acts that violated county, town or municipal ordinances, and (3) violations of vaguely defined catchalls—such as "vicious or immoral behavior," "incorrigibility," "truancy," "profane or indecent language," "growing up in idleness," "living with any vicious or disreputable person," etc.— which indicated, if unchecked, the possibility of more serious misconduct in the future.

The Illinois juvenile court act of 1899, which specifically authorized penalties for "pre-delinquent" behavior,[4] was favorably received by the judiciary and legal profession. "The whole trend and spirit of the act," noted the Chicago Bar Association, "is that the State, acting through the Juvenile Court, exercises that tender solicitude and care over its neglected, dependent wards, that a wise and loving parent would exercise with reference to his own children under similar circumstances." Albert Barnes, an Assistant State's Attorney of Cook County, explained to a meeting of the State's Attorneys Association in Ottawa that, under the 1899 Act,

the State must step in and exercise guardianship over a child found under such adverse social or individual conditions as develop crime. To that end it must not wait as now to deal with him in jails, bridewells and reformatories after he has become criminal in habits and tastes, but must seize

2. Monrad G. Paulsen, "Fairness to the Juvenile Offender," *Minnesota Law Review* 41 (1957): 547–67. See also "Rights and Rehabilitation in the Juvenile Courts," *Columbia Law Review* 67 (1967): 281–341.

3. "The Juvenile Court and the Adversary System: Problems of Function and Form," 1965 *Wisconsin Law Review,* p. 9.

4. Revised Laws of Illinois, 1899, pp. 131–37. See also, Revised Laws of Illinois, 1901, pp. 141–42.

upon the first indications of the propensity as they may be evinced in his conditions of neglect or delinquency. . . .[5]

The act's constitutionality was somewhat in doubt because it was designed to be "liberally construed" so that "the care, custody and discipline of a child shall approximate as nearly as may be that which should be given by its parents." The informality of juvenile court proceedings, however, was upheld by the Pennsylvania and Illinois Supreme Courts.[6] The other, more technical objection—that the juvenile court would exercise jurisdiction already assigned to particular courts by the state constitution—was circumvented by conferring jurisdiction on existing courts. The Illinois act was considered a prototype for legislation in other states and juvenile courts were quickly established in Wisconsin (1901), New York (1901), Ohio (1902), Maryland (1902), and Colorado (1903). By 1928, all but two states had adopted a juvenile court system.

The juvenile court movement went far beyond a humanitarian concern for the special treatment of adolescents. It brought within the ambit of governmental control a set of youthful activities that had been previously ignored or handled informally. It was not by accident that the behavior selected for penalizing by the child savers—drinking, begging, roaming the streets, frequenting dance-halls and movies, fighting, sexuality, staying out late at night, and incorrigibility—was primarily attributable to the children of lower-class migrant and immigrant families.

This focus was apparent in the composition of court personnel and charges by which children were brought before the court. The personnel of Cook County juvenile court consisted of (1) six probation officers paid from private sources, particularly the Chicago Woman's Club, (2) "one colored woman who devotes her entire time to the work, free of charge, and whose services are invaluable to the court as she takes charge of all the colored children," (3)

5. *Report of the Chicago Bar Association Juvenile Court Committee,* October 28, 1899.
6. *Commonwealth v. Fisher,* 213 Penn. 48 (1905); *Lindsay v. Lindsay,* 257 Ill. 328 (1913).

twenty-one truant officers paid by and responsible to the Board of Education, (4) sixteen police officers, paid by the Chicago police department, assigned to "assist the general probation officers in their visitation work," and (5) thirty-six private citizens who were occasionally responsible for supervising children on probation.[7] In effect, the court staff was primarily composed of police and truant officers, thus facilitating the arrest and disposition of "delinquent" youth. The juvenile court provided its own policing machinery and removed many distinctions between the enforcement and adjudication of laws.

An analysis of charges further demonstrates that the juvenile courts were originally intended to handle "crimes without victims" as well as classical crimes against property and person. During the earliest years of the Cook County juvenile court, over 50 per cent of the delinquency cases arose from charges of "disorderly behavior," "immorality," "vagrancy," "truancy" and "incorrigibility."[8] In his first annual report as Chief Probation Officer, Timothy Hurley reported that the more prominent causes of delinquency were truancy, "junking"[9] and begging. "Truancy seems to be at the foundation of most children's delinquency; they stay out of school, idle away their time, find bad company in their neighborhood, and then commit some petty offense."[10]

Cook County juvenile court's early records also show that institutional commitment was a basic tenet of the child-saving philosophy. One-third of all juveniles charged with delinquency were sent to the John Worthy School, the state reformatory, or transferred to the criminal courts. Almost two-thirds of the "delin-

7. Timothy D. Hurley, *First Annual Report of the Cook County Juvenile Court*, p. 1 (1900). I am grateful to Henry D. McKay for making the early juvenile court reports available to me.

8. *Ibid.*, p. 3. See also, Hurley, *Second Annual Report of the Cook County Juvenile Court*, p. 2 (1901).

9. "The junk man often encourages delinquency by purchasing from the boy lead pipe, brass from cars, and railway equipment and other fixtures, which he knows he ought not to buy. The Juvenile Court has assisted in the prosecution of several junk men who deserve punishment" (Hurley, *First Annual Report*, p. 5).

10. *Ibid.*

quent" girls were committed to state and local institutions.[11] Commenting on the achievements of the juvenile court in its first year, Hurley said that "it has saved hundreds from lives of shame and crime; taken hundreds from homeless life or from so-called homes that were utterly unfit, and placed them in good institutions or the care of societies to find them suitable homes."[12]

The juvenile court system attracted judges with philanthropic interests and appetites for crusading, notably Ben Lindsey in Colorado, Harvey Baker in Boston, and Richard Tuthill in Chicago. Tuthill, for example, was a fifty-eight-year-old judge of high repute when he was appointed to Cook County's juvenile court. He had previously been a State's Attorney in Nashville and City Attorney for Chicago before he was elected a judge in 1884. He was described in an official biography as "active in every movement which has for its object the general welfare of the city in which he lives, and is closely identified with charitable organizations seeking to promote the moral and mental training of poor and destitute children."[13] Tuthill cooperated with child saving organizations before and after the juvenile court act, even inviting members of the Chicago Woman's Club to sit with him on the bench and help in the disposition of cases.[14]

The juvenile court movement was "anti-legal" in the sense that it encouraged minimum procedural formality and maximum dependency on extra-legal resources. The judges were authorized to investigate the character and social background of both "predelinquent" and "delinquent" children. They examined personal motivation as well as criminal intent, seeking to identify the moral reputation of problematic children.[15] The requirements of preven-

---

11. *Ibid.,* pp. 1–2. See also, *Second Annual Report,* p. 2, and John N. McManaman, *Fourth Annual Report,* p. 1 (1903).

12. *First Annual Report,* p. 3.

13. Weston A. Goodspeed and Daniel D. Healy, *History of Cook County, Illinois,* 2: 989–91.

14. See letters from Judge Richard Tuthill to Adelaide Groves, December 21, 1899, and November 9, 1901, in Chicago Historical Society.

15. "We should make it our business to study and know each particular case, because it will generally demand treatment in some little respect differ-

tive penology and child saving further justified the court's intervention in cases where no offense had actually been committed but
where, for example, a child was posing problems for some person
in authority, such as a parent or teacher or social worker.[16] According
to Harvey Baker, of the Boston juvenile court:

The court does not confine its attention to just the particular offense
which brought the child to its notice. For example, a boy who comes to
court for some such trifle as failing to wear his badge when selling papers
may be held on probation for months because of difficulties at school;
and a boy who comes in for playing ball on the street may . . . be committed to a reform school because he is found to have habits of loafing,
stealing or gambling which can not be corrected outside.[17]

The role model for juvenile court judges was doctor-counselor[18]
rather than lawyer. "Judicial therapists" were expected to establish a
one-to-one relationship with "delinquents" in the same way that a
country doctor might give his time and attention to a favorite
patient. The courtroom was arranged like a clinic and the vocabulary
of the participants was largely composed of medical metaphors. "We
can not know the child without a thorough examination," wrote

ent from any other case. . . . (a) Is the child simply mischievous or criminal
in its tendencies? (b) Is the case simply an exceptional or isolated instance
in which a really good boy or girl has gone wrong for the first time because
too weak to resist a strong temptation? (c) Is the child a victim of incom-
petent parents? Does the home or parent need correction or assistance? (d)
What of environment and association, which, of course, may embrace sub-
stantively all of the points of study? How can the environment be improved?
Certainly by keeping the child out of the saloon and away from evil ex-
amples. (e) Is the child afflicted with what we call 'the moving about fever'
—that is, is he given to playing 'hookey' from school, or 'bumming' and
running away, showing an entire lack of ambition or desire to work and settle
down to regular habits?" (Ben B. Lindsey,"The Boy and the Court," *Charities*
13 [January, 1905]: 352).
   16. The idea that attitudes to norms rather than their violation underlies
the labeling of "delinquent" behavior is supported by Carl Werthman,
Delinquency and Authority.
   17. "Procedure of the Boston Juvenile Court," *Survey* 23 (February,
1910): 649.
   18. For an analysis of the beliefs that underlie the "helping professions,"
see Paul Halmos, *The Faith of the Counsellors.*

Judge Julian Mack. "We must reach into the soul-life of the child."[19]
Another juvenile court judge from Los Angeles suggested that the
juvenile court should be a "laboratory of human behavior" and its
judges trained as "specialists in the art of human relations." It was
the judge's task, said Miriam Van Waters, to "get the whole truth
about a child" in the same way that a "physician searches for every
detail that bears on the condition of a patient."[20]

The idea that justice can be "personalized"[21] was a significant
feature of the child-saving movement and offers some interesting
clues as to what the child savers hoped to achieve. An examination
of the early literature of the juvenile court, during the period from
1899 to 1910, shows that the child savers were preoccupied with the
physical setting of the courtroom and tried to devise ways of making
it more personal and private. The new juvenile court building in
Chicago, opened in 1907, was designed so that "the hearings will
be held in a room fitted up as a parlor rather than a court, around a
table instead of a bench. . . . The hearing will be in the nature of a
family conference, in which the endeavor will be to impress the
child with the fact that his own good is sought alone."[22]

Since juvenile offenders were considered helpless children in need
of care and attention, it was important that the courtroom, the officers of the court, the routine methods of operation, and the ultimate
goals of the juvenile court should in no way resemble police courts
or the traditional criminal courts. An ideal juvenile court should be

19. Julian W. Mack, "The Chancery Procedure in the Juvenile Court," in
Jane Addams, ed., *The Child, the Clinic and the Court*, p. 315.
20. "The Socialization of Juvenile Court Procedure," *Journal of Criminal
Law and Criminology* 21 (1922): 61, 69.
21. According to Judge Stubbs of the Indianapolis juvenile court, "it is
the personal touch that does it. I have often observed that if I sat on a high
platform behind a high desk, such as we had in our city court, with the boy
on the prisoner's bench some distance away, that my words had little effect
on him; but if I could get close enough to him to put my hand on his head
and shoulder, or my arm around him, in nearly every case I could get his
confidence" (Samuel J. Barrows, ed., *Children's Court in the United States:
Their Origin, Development and Results*, p. xiii).
22. *Programme of Ceremonies on Dedication of the Juvenile Court and
Detention Home Building*, August 7, 1907. (The original document is available in the Chicago Historical Society).

more like a parlor or study than an official courtroom. Judge Tuthill, speaking before the National Prison Association in 1902, observed that the Illinois act was based on the assumption that children should not be "branded with the indelible stain of criminality. . . . I have always felt, and endeavored to act in each case, as I would were it my own son who was before me in the library at home, charged with some misconduct."[23]

In 1905, Charles Henderson published in *Charities* the results of an informal survey of juvenile court practices which suggested that the hearing "must carry out consistently the purely educational principles of the court, and any suggestion of an old-fashioned criminal trial should be avoided." Henderson approvingly cited Ben Lindsey's comment that "a child's case is not a legal case" and therefore it was not necessary for the child to be legally represented.[24]

The child savers proposed that the paternal, equitable and noncriminal aspects of the hearing should be symbolically reproduced in the physical construction of the court. "The court room," commented the editors of *Survey,* "should be not a court room at all; just a room, with a table and two chairs, where the judge and the child, the probation officer and the parents, as occasion arises, come into close contact, and where in a more or less formal way the whole story may be talked over."[25] The judge should sit at a desk rather than a bench so as to "evoke a sympathetic spirit" from the child. If the judge can occasionally "put his arm around his shoulder and draw the lad to him" he will "gain immensely in effectiveness, while losing none of his judicial dignity." Although Judge Mack advised juvenile court judges to dispense with the "ordinary trappings of the court room," he also stressed that a child should be made aware of his confrontation with the "power of the state."[26]

Harvey Baker, who was judge of the Boston juvenile court for many years, also suggested that the atmosphere of the courtroom

23. Richard S. Tuthill, "The Chicago Juvenile Court," *Proceedings of the Annual Congress of the National Prison Association, 1902,* p. 121.

24. Charles R. Henderson, "Juvenile Courts: Problems of Administration," *Charities* 13 (January, 1905): 340–41.

25. *Survey* 23 (February, 1910): 594.

26. Julian W. Mack, "The Law and the Child," *Survey* 23 (February, 1910): 642.

should be relaxed and informal so as to encourage trust and cooperation on the part of the offender. "The officials of the court," wrote
Baker, "believed it is helpful to think of themselves as physicians in
a dispensary." The Boston court had no uniformed officials, clerks, or
stenographers, and the judge heard most of the cases in his chambers.
This room was small, private, and "without decorations or objects
which might distract the attention of a child." Aside from the fact
that the judges sat on a slightly raised platform, "much like a school
teacher's platform," there was no more formality than there was in a
"physician's examination room." Yet, children and their parents
were required to keep standing while appearing before the judge so
that "the fact of the court being a department of public authority
and having power to compel compliance should be indicated
distinctly."[27]

In summary, the juvenile court system brought attention to and
thus "invented" new categories of youthful deviance, particularly
behavior in which the actor was seen as his own "victim." Organizational distinctions between the police and judiciary were diminished
so that the child savers could carry on their "life-saving" work without bureaucratic hindrance. "Delinquents" were increasingly committed to institutions on the grounds that their reformation was more
likely if they were removed from "immoral" parents and a "vicious"
environment. Juvenile court judges shared the missionary passion of
the child savers and approached their work in medical-therapeutic
terms. In their effort to impress juvenile offenders that the court was
seeking only their best interests, they were both friendly and firm,
offering hope of a better life without abandoning their position of
authority and power.

RHETORIC AND REALITY

The passage of the Illinois juvenile court act in 1899 prompted a
flood of optimistic rhetoric from child-saving organizations. Ephraim
Banning, attending the National Conference of Charities and Cor-

27. Baker, "Procedure of the Boston Juvenile Court," pp. 646, 650.

rection in Cincinnati, described the act as "the chief event of the year."[28] A delegate to a meeting of the State's Attorneys' Association claimed that the juvenile court would "minimize crime by striking at its roots" and "prove the dawn of a new era in our criminal history. . . ."[29]

The act, however, did little to change the quality of institutional life for delinquents, though it facilitated the means by which juvenile offenders could be "reached" and committed. Contrary to a specific provision in the act, children continued to be imprisoned with adult criminals in county and city jails.[30] Some Chicago reformers soon realized that there was a wide difference between idealized goals and operating realities. Judge Tuthill told a national audience that the John Worthy School was a "well-equipped public school," while acknowledging to his professional colleagues at home that it was overcrowded, poorly equipped, badly situated, and more like a prison than a school.[31]

The 1899 act declared that children under twelve years should not be committed to a jail or police station and provided that "if such child is unable to give bail it may be committed to the care of the sheriff, police officer or probation officer, who shall keep such child in some suitable place provided by the city or county outside of the inclosure of any jail or police station." However, the legislature did not provide funds for the establishment of "some suitable place" and private organizations were required to find and equip a temporary detention home. The John Worthy School was also used for pre-trial detention and its superintendent complained that he had to

28. *Proceedings of the National Conference of Charities and Correction, 1899*, p. 53.
29. *Report of the Chicago Bar Association Juvenile Court Committee,* October 28, 1899.
30. *Seventeenth Biennial Report of the Board of State Commissioners of Public Charities of the State of Illinois,* p. 193 (Springfield, Illinois: Phillips Brothers, 1902).
31. Richard S. Tuthill, "The Chicago Juvenile Court," *Proceedings of the Annual Congress of National Prison Association,* pp. 115–24; "State Home for Delinquent Boys," *Proceedings of the Illinois Conference of Charities* (1901), in *Seventeenth Biennial Report of the Board of State Commissioners of Public Charities,* pp. 220–27.

parole boys in order to make room for new arrivals.³² In 1903, the Juvenile Court Committee—consisting of representatives of various private child-saving organizations—established a Detention Home two miles from the county courthouse. In its first year it housed over 2,600 children. "It is clear," commented Julia Lathrop, "that no one can be expected to exercise much more than the somewhat humorously designated 'official parenthood' over most members of such a brood." She was well aware that "the Chicago method is hardly a 'system' so far as its mechanism is concerned. It is rather a series of contrivances which have grown up to meet the situation as necessity demanded."³³

Although the city and county partly subsidized the Detention Home, it was very difficult to get funds, and the Juvenile Court Committee raised most of the money privately. The city gave eleven cents a day per child and the county provided transportation and the services of a county physician. The "transportation"—an old omnibus drawn by horses—eventually fell to bits. Despite the efforts of Julia Lathrop and Louise Bowen, the county did not replace the omnibus and "the whole thing ended in the committee buying its own omnibus, its own horses, renting its own stable and furnishing its own horsefeed." Although the Committee was justifiably indignant over the lack of facilities for children before and after trial, this at least allowed them to make a meaningful contribution to the public effort. The women's clubs regularly sent representatives to the Detention Home, where "they pulled down the covers of the beds to see if they were clean; they tasted the food to see if it was good. . . . [I]t certainly tended to keep us alert and active on the job," said Louise Bowen.³⁴

32. *Proceedings of the Illinois Conference of Charities* (1901), p. 231.
33. Julia C. Lathrop, "The Development of the Probation System in a Large City," *Charities* 13 (January, 1905): 346.
34. Mrs. Joseph T. Bowen, "The Early Days of the Juvenile Court," in Jane Addams, ed., *The Child, the Clinic and the Court,* pp. 302, 305. According to one chief probation officer of the Cook County juvenile court, children under detention were kept in a transformed barn where "there was plenty of opportunity for telling vile stories, experiences with the police and, violations of the law, so that boys came to court in a spirit of bravado or in-

In 1905, the legislature appropriated money to pay probation officers and, two years later, the county erected a new juvenile court building containing detention facilities.[35] Due to these successes, the Juvenile Court Committee disbanded and re-formed as the Juvenile Protection League, which worked "to create a permanent public sentiment for the establishment of wholesome uplifting agencies, such as parks, playgrounds, gymnasiums, free baths, vacation schools, communal social centers and the like."[36] This nominal change marks the beginning of the decline of child saving by volunteers and civic organizations. There was no place for amateurism or unsupervised philanthropy in "professional" probation work.[37] "There can be no possible doubt," wrote Bernard Flexner, "that the indiscriminate use of volunteers is to be condemned. . . . The fewer children given to a volunteer the better."[38]

In 1901, the state legislature provided an appropriation for the establishment of a State Home for Delinquent Boys to be built at St. Charles. For lack of sufficient funds and an overall construction

---

timidation. No provision was made for the detention of delinquent girls, except that afforded by the so-called annex to the Harrison Street Police Station, where women of all degrees of degradation were also confined" (Henry W. Thurston, "Ten Years of the Juvenile Court of Chicago," *Survey* 23 [February, 1910]: 662–63).

35. Revised Laws of Illinois, 1905, pp. 151–52. For a description of the Detention Home, see *Annual Report of the Board of Commissioners of Cook County*, p. 29 (Chicago: Henry O. Shepard, 1907), and *Programme of Ceremonies on Dedication of the Juvenile Court and Detention Home Building*, August 7, 1908. (The original document is available in the Chicago Historical Society.)

36. *Annual Report of the Board of Commissioners of Cook County* (1907), pp. 29, 112–13. As Howard Becker has observed, it is often the fate of successful crusades to leave a crusader without a vocation, thus requiring him to become a "professional discoverer of wrongs to be righted, of situations requiring new rules" (*Outsiders* [New York: Free Press, 1963], p. 153).

37. Homer Folks, "Juvenile Probation in New York," *Survey* 23 (February, 1910): 667–73.

38. "The Juvenile Court as a Social Institution," *Survey* 23 (February, 1910): 619–20.

plan, the Home was not officially opened until July, 1905.[39] The mission of the Home, according to its Superintendent, was to train delinquent children "to do commonplace work well." Nelson Mc-Lain estimated that there were nearly 10,000 children in Chicago in need of supervised industrial training, but said that the Home would only receive those children capable of completing the "course."[40] Many child savers were upset by this professional realism and expressed doubts about the future of the new institution. By 1927, the St. Charles School for Boys, as it was now called, housed about 300 delinquent boys between the ages of ten and seventeen.[41] In 1915, the General Assembly had passed a law excluding from Pontiac all boys under sixteen years of age and raising the upper age to twenty-five years.[42] This provision served to expand the population of the St. Charles School as well as to transform the Pontiac reformatory into a small, tough prison with limited educational facilities.[43]

The new reformatory again demonstrated that child saving was a job for tough-minded professionals who realized that sentimental humanitarianism had no place in their work. In 1927, the Superintendent of the St. Charles School was transferred to another job on the grounds, among other things, that he was an ineffective disciplinarian. The new Superintendent, Major Butler, enlarged the military staff, marched everybody to and from school, and required all

39. Evelyn Harriet Randall, *The St. Charles School for Delinquent Boys*, pp. 22–26

40. Nelson W. McLain, "The Care of Delinquent Boys," *Proceedings of the Illinois Conference of Charities* (1902), in *Seventeenth Biennial Report of the Board of State Commissioners of Public Charities*, pp. 301–4.

41. John H. Wigmore, ed., *The Illinois Crime Survey*, p. 713.

42. Randall, *The St. Charles School*, pp. 8–10.

43. Wigmore, *Illinois Crime Survey*, pp. 478–90. According to Andrew Bruce, E. W. Burgess, and Albert J. Harno (the authors of the section on parole and probation in Illinois), the Pontiac reformatory was mismanaged, overcrowded and overroutinized. Concerning educational training, they reported that a considerable number of teachers "are really hired as guards and do guard duty after school and on Sundays and holidays. To assume that their qualifications are those for guards rather than for teachers would be, generally speaking, fair; and it must be borne in mind that guards are politically appointed."

boys to observe rules of military courtesy. "If any of you just can't learn these things," Second Lieutenant Butler—Major Butler's son —lectured the inmates, "we'll build a bull-pen out there on the grounds and put you in it until you do learn." For infractions of the numerous rules, boys were punished with a leather strap. "During the early months of Major Butler's regime," according to the Illinois Crime Commission, "all whippings were administered by a disciplinary officer who, in company with the military officer of the day, went to each cottage each evening after supper and whipped any boys who had been reported earlier by the house father, or for whom the house father requested punishment at the time." Some boys were punished by being locked up in the "hole" for up to thirty-two days with no shoes and no mattress. They slept on wooden boards nailed to the concrete floor. Some were handcuffed to iron pipes and kept manacled day and night.[44]

Other children's institutions in Illinois were similarly overcrowded, regimented, and poorly equipped.[45] In 1915, the John Worthy School was closed and replaced outside the city by the Chicago and Cook County School for Boys. This reformatory, used for "minor" offenders, essentially provided a short, sharp punishment for the least troublesome delinquents.[46] The new Detention Home, welcomed with exuberant optimism by the child savers, was later found by the Illinois Crime Commission to contain "a great mixture of tremendously varying children, held for a variety of rather unnecessary and unidentified purposes, most of whom stay too long and

44. *Ibid.*, pp. 713–25.
45. Private and public institutions for the care of dependent and delinquent children suffered similar problems and continued to provide inadequate and sometimes highly punitive supervision. The inadequacies of the private organizations, from about 1900 to 1926, are catalogued by Arlien Johnson, *Public Policy and Private Charities*, pp. 133–78 (Chicago: University of Chicago Press, 1931). For a revealing, but uncritical, account of problems of racial segregation and homosexuality in a large public institution, The State Training School for Girls at Geneva, see *The Illinois Crime Survey*, pp. 718–22.
46. Elizabeth Francis Hirsh, *A Study of the Chicago and Cook County School for Boys*, pp. 59–61.

each of whom adds to the complexity of the problem of handling, constructively and sanely, this already socially complex situation."[47] In 1925, Louise Bowen sadly noted that the Detention Home had "every appearance of being a jail, with its barred windows and locked doors. . . . The children have fewer comforts than do criminals confined in the county jail. They are not kept sufficiently occupied and have very little fresh air."[48]

The bleakness and impersonality of the institutions were matched by the uncompromising professionalism of juvenile court officials. "Troublemakers" were characterized as ungrateful and malicious, requiring swift measures of retaliation. Henry Thurston, Chief Probation Officer of the Cook County juvenile court from 1906 to 1908, warned that the "persistent repeater will bring inevitable disorganization into the district work of a probation officer and arouse resentment in the hearts of many of the best friends of the probation idea. All right-minded people are willing to have boys and girls have chances to do the right thing, but after they persistently throw chances away, the same people have a right to insist that these young people be really controlled, even if it takes a criminal court process to do it."[49] Thurston and his chief assistant, John Witter, suggested that some "unresponsive boys" could be made to "respond" to treatment if threatened with a criminal prosecution. "In any event," they wrote, "it is a duty of probation officers, for the sake of boys and girls who improve under probation, to ask the judge to make some other

47. *The Illinois Crime Survey,* p. 681.
48. Mrs. Joseph T. Bowen, "The Early Days of the Juvenile Court," p. 309. The findings of Breckenridge and Abbot in *The Delinquent Child and the Home* also troubled Julia Lathrop and made her aware that the juvenile court was not a cure-all. "The results of this investigation," she writes in the introduction to that volume, "lack that precise definition which is comforting to the reforming spirit. The study shows that there are many elements combined in uncertain numbers and quantity. . . . It makes the question of youthful delinquency very searching and subtle, not to be solved by any court or system of institutions, or probation, or other wise contrivances attempted as substitutes for wholesome, orderly, decent family life."
49. *Annual Report of the Board of Commissioners of Cook County* (1907), p. 123.

order in those cases where an honest and persistent effort at kindly
aid has been spurned by the probationer."[50]

If the child savers were alive today, they would find that little has
changed in the institutions for delinquents. The St. Charles School
for Boys, which is now planned for 550 maximum occupancy, has a
population that averages about 800. The Superintendent of the
School complains that his staff is so overworked and underpaid that
"they finally accept jobs from industry with higher wages and
shorter hours."[51] Chicago's youth welfare agency has been disrupted
by striking Negro staff members who claim that they are not properly represented in formulating agency policies.[52] Similar criticism
has been voiced by black employees of the juvenile court detention
home,[53] and a local newspaper has charged that the detention home,
the Arthur Audy Juvenile Home, "has the chilling, barren, alien
look of a day room in a mental hospital."[54]

MORALISM AND CONSTITUTIONALISM

Criticism of the juvenile court system over the last fifty years has
come from persons expressing two diametrically opposed ideological
perspectives. To the "legal moralists," the juvenile court is a politically ineffective and morally improper means of controlling juvenile
crime. To the "constitutionalists," the juvenile court is arbitrary, un-

50. *Annual Report of the Board of Commissioners of Cook County*, p.
171 (Chicago: Henry O. Shepard, 1908). Witter was later involved in a
public scandal in which, among other things, he was accused of incompe-
tence and brutality. See *Report of a Committee Appointed Under Resolution
of the Board of Commissioners of Cook County* (August 8, 1911).
51. *Chicago's American*, December 11, 1965.
52. *Chicago Sun-Times*, June 15, 1968; *Chicago Daily Defender*, June
17, 1968.
53. *Chicago Daily Defender*, July 16, 1968. See also, the comments of
the detention home's superintendent with regard to overpopulation and
understaffing (*Chicago Sun-Times*, December 7, 1967).
54. *Chicago Daily News*, December 18, 1967.

constitutional, and violates the principles of fair trial.[55] The former view concerns the protection of society, the latter addresses the safeguarding of individual rights.

The retributive justification of punishment has traditionally been associated by its opponents with irrationality and revenge.[56] Retributive justice, however, is not necessarily an impulsive reaction to crime. Its conditions are not satisfied by giving vent to personal desires for revenge.[57] On the contrary, it envisions an objective principle of justice that must be enforced regardless of sentiment or expediency. Thus, according to Kant, "judicial punishment can never be imposed merely for the purpose of securing some extrinsic good, either for the criminal himself or for civil society; it must in all cases be imposed (and can only be imposed) because the individual upon whom it is inflicted has committed an offense. . . . The right of retaliation . . . is the only principle which . . . can definitely guide a public tribunal as to both the quality and quantity of a just punishment."[58]

According to the retributive position, society has a moral right and duty to inflict punishment on offenders who consciously commit crimes. In a sense, the offender is entitled to be punished and it is a restriction of his moral freedom and a slur upon his rationality to deny it to him.[59] While the idealistic philosophers and moralists of the early nineteenth century argued frankly on metaphysical grounds, latter-day proponents of retributive justice speak about its

55. The term "legal moralism" is used by H. L. A. Hart, *Law, Liberty and Morality.*

56. Part of the following discussion is taken from my paper with Egon Bittner, "The Meaning of Punishment," *Issues in Criminology* 2 (1966): 79–99.

57. For the traditional, acrimonious view of retributive punishment, see Henry Weihofen, "Retribution Is Obsolete," *National Probation and Parole Association News* 39 (1960): 1 f. A more reasonable statement of this position is formulated by Alex Comfort, *Authority and Delinquency in the Modern State,* p. 102.

58. As quoted in James Heath, *Eighteenth Century Penal Theory,* p. 272.

59. Hegel, for example, argued somewhere in his *Philosophy of Right* that by being punished the criminal is "honored as a rational being."

"functional" equivalence. In their view, punishment is a constitutive element in the symbolism of morality. That is, the ultimate purpose of punishment is to reveal the heinous and evil character of crime, and to establish the balance of right and wrong in the cosmos.

The retributive position has been most fully articulated in recent years by the proponents of legal moralism, a primarily defensive philosophical movement which at the beginning of this century self-consciously embraced common sense criteria of morality and exploited a growing skepticism of the efficacy of "scientific" solutions to social problems. James Stephen, the English legal historian, complained of the weakening of religious sanctions and moral imperatives in an increasingly secular and industrial society.[60] For Stephen, the criminal law proceeds upon the principle that "it is morally right to hate criminals" and that punishment "gives definite expression and a solemn ratification and justification to the hatred which is excited by the commission of the offense."[61] Oliver Wendell Holmes agreed with Stephen that the first requirement of the criminal law is that it should "correspond with the actual feelings and demands of the community."[62] It is felt by many legal moralists that punishment should be proportional to the revulsion or indignation felt for particular crimes by "reasonable citizens." "The ultimate justification of any punishment," said Lord Denning, "is not that it is a deterrent but that it is the emphatic denunciation by the community of a crime."[63] Critics of this view have often emphasized its non-

60. "A man may disbelieve in God, heaven and hell, he may care little for mankind or society or for the nation to which he belongs—let him at least be plainly told what are the acts that will stamp him with infamy, hold him up to public execration and bring him to the gallows, the gaol or the lash" (James Fitzjames Stephen, *History of the Criminal Law in England*, 3: 366–67).
61. *Ibid.*, 2: 81.
62. Oliver Wendell Holmes, *The Common Law*, p. 41.
63. Quoted by the Royal Commission on Capital Punishment, *Final Report* (1949–1953), p. 53. One modern lawyer, in support of this argument, has noted that "it is perhaps unfashionable these days to link justice with retribution. Much more accent is placed upon treatment and training for offenders, so that the consequence of conviction becomes less and less a 'punishment' in a layman's sense. Yet it is submitted that there is nothing inherently wrong with the idea of retribution as the basis for punishment, that

rational and nonutilitarian aspects. This criticism is correct insofar as it points to the fact that the punitive function is endorsed without consideration for its instrumental value. But the proponents do not maintain that punishment works to protect society or to reform offenders; rather, they maintain that it expresses the moral judgments of society.

In a real sense, the theorists of retributive justice do not think of crime as an act that can be independently defined and which calls for a considered measure of retribution; instead, they hold that the act of punishment defines the behavior, to which it is fittingly related, as criminal. Accordingly, to abandon punishing means to abandon the very idea of crime. In particular situations we may wish to be guided by considerations based on mercy or practicality, but in general, the concept of crime implies the concept of punishment. Therefore, as long as we choose to call some forms of conduct criminal, we already provide for the fitness of punitive sanctions and the search for added justification merely confuses the issue. To say that we could have crimes which we shall not punish, or which we shall punish exclusively for some extrinsic purpose, is a contradiction in terms. In the last analysis, retributive justice is based on the Kantian categorical principle or some equivalent of it. It presupposes that good and evil are moral absolutes which are imprinted on the mind of man, defining his duties, without the need for added justifications.

With regard to juvenile delinquency, the legal moralists argue that it is socially undesirable to allow predatory and harmful behavior to go unpunished. They further point out that most ordinary citizens view delinquency with "intolerance, indignation and disgust" and that it is the proper function of the law to give ceremonial expression to this moral revulsion.[64] Some writers claim that failure to punish delinquency and immoral behavior is likely to weaken the moral fabric of society; according to A. L. Goodhart, for example,

---

the punishment should fit the crime rather than the individual" (David C. M. Yardley, "Current Attitudes to Capital Punishment," *The Lawyer* 4 [1961]: 34).

64. Sir Patrick Devlin, *The Enforcement of Morals.*

"a community which is too ready to forgive the wrongdoer may end by condoning the crime."[65]

The legal moralists stress the important psycho-social functions of "theatrical justice," which are predicated upon the expressive capacity of the criminal law to ritually uphold institutionalized values.[66] The resentment shown by many lawyers toward the juvenile court system embodies many of the traditional features of legal moralism: there is vigorous criticism of the ineffectiveness of the juvenile court in the "war against crime,"[67] an implicit hostility directed toward professional rivals,[68] and a stern disapproval of permissive ideologies. Although the legal moralists do not necessarily advocate harsh punishments, their theoretical perspective is often used by law-enforcement officials, political campaigners and com-

65. *English Law and the Moral Law*, pp. 92–93.

66. In an analysis of the ritualistic aspects of the criminal law, Michael Balint suggests that "the offender is expected to show signs of guilt and repentance, to admit so to speak that he sinned against the community. His treatment may be lenient or cruel, but it is always a 'theatrical public affair.' . . . Every community feels that certain offenses must be considered as major ones, necessitating the staging of a 'public drama.' . . . In all such instances there are, at least in theory, three acts of the public drama: a) isolation, b) punishment and penance, c) readmission" ("On Punishing Offenders," in *Psychoanalysis and Culture*, p. 225).

67. Judge Oliphant has vigorously stated this argument as follows: "I cannot comprehend the reasoning that suggests that marauding gangs of little hoodlums armed with guns, knives, switch knives or other illegal weapons are to be considered as a matter of law incapable of committing the crime of murder. Infants under the age of 21 years, according to statistics, perpetrate a high percentage of the heinous crimes committed throughout the country, and the situation has reached such serious proportions that it is a threat to the public welfare and safety of law-abiding citizens. . . . Murder by an individual criminal is bad enough but when it appears that a confirmed criminal has organized a group of teenagers for the sole purpose to murder and rob, then the time has come to examine the underlying philosophy of the treatment of juvenile offenders" (*State v. Monahan*, 15 N.J. 34, 104A 2d 21 [1954]).

68. For example, the English Chief Justice Goddard once advised "justices to remember that the sending of children for examination by psychiatrists may do more harm than good, as it is so apt to make children think they are interesting cases when they are only naughty boys or girls" (F. T. Giles, *Children and the Law*, Foreword).

munity organizations who seek severer penalties or corporal punishment as an answer to the "crime problem."[69] The following manifesto by John Wigmore captures the essence and spirit of the legal moralists' argument with regard to juvenile justice:

... the social workers and the psychologists and the psychiatrists know nothing of crime or wrong. They refer to "reactions" and "maladjustments" and "complexes." ... The people need to have the moral law dinned into their consciences every day in the year. The juvenile court does not do that. And to segregate a large share of daily crime into the juvenile court is to take a long step toward undermining the whole criminal law. ... [T]here is no deterrence of the multitude; merely a "treatment" of the "maladjustment." Its actions have no more effect on the multitude than the surgical operations of the hospitals—not so much, to be sure, because many a citizen has been deterred from submitting to the surgeon's knife because of rumors of what happened to his friend. And so we say to the devoted social workers and the cold scientists: "Do not think that you have the right to demand that all crimes be handed over to your charge until you have looked a little more deeply into the criminal law and have a better comprehension of the whole of its functions."[70]

The legal moralists view the criminal law as the symbolic expression of the institutionalized values which the criminal violates, so that punishment has an educative function which unites all non-criminals and conformists in the "emotional solidarity of aggression."[71] Punishment—for the legal moralists—is not intended to have instrumental value other than to promote a sense of moral

69. Take, for example, the following statement attributed to General Eisenhower: "Let us not be guilty of maudlin sympathy for the criminal who, roaming the streets with the switchblade knife and illegal firearm, seeking a helpless prey, suddenly becomes upon apprehension, a poor underprivileged person who counts upon the compassion of our society and the laxness or weaknesses of too many courts" (*San Francisco Chronicle,* July 15, 1964).
70. "Juvenile Court vs. Criminal Court," *Illinois Law Review* 21 (1926): 375–77.
71. George H. Mead, "The Psychology of Punitive Justice," *American Journal of Sociology* 23 (1918): 577–602. See also, Talcott Parsons, *The Social System,* pp. 309–14.

solidarity in the citizenry. The juvenile court, according to this perspective, fails to make juvenile delinquency unattractive as a role
model and has deprived the criminal law of its efficacy as an instru-
ment of moral education because it does not formally express
condemnation of anti-social behavior.[72]

Advocates of the constitutionalist perspective, on the other hand,
are skeptical of the juvenile court's humanitarian goals and are particularly concerned about the invasion of personal rights under the
pretext of "welfare" and "rehabilitation."[73] Edward Lindsey, one
of the earliest spokesmen for this point of view, observed in 1914
that, despite the sonorous rhetoric of "socialized justice," there had
been no effort to provide proper care and protection for children.
"There is often a very real deprivation of liberty," said Lindsey, "nor
is that fact changed by refusing to call it punishment or because the
good of the child is stated to be the object."[74] This constitutional

72. F. L. Ludwig, "Considerations Basic to Reform of Juvenile Offenders,"
St. John's Law Review 29 (1955): 226.

73. The constitutionalist literature is too vast to be completely cited, but
the most significant contributions include: Sol Rubin, "Protecting the Child
in the Juvenile Court," *Journal of Criminal Law, Criminology and Police
Science* 43 (1952): 425–40; Matthew J. Beemsterboer, "The Juvenile
Court—Benevolence in the Star Chamber," *Journal of Criminal Law, Crim-
inology and Police Science* 50 (1960): 464–75; Stephen M. Hermann,
"Scope and Purposes of Juvenile Court Jurisdiction," *Journal of Criminal
Law, Criminology and Police Science* 48 (1958): 590–607; Robert G.
Caldwell, "The Juvenile Court: Its Development and Some Major Problems,"
Journal of Criminal Law, Criminology and Police Science 51 (1961): 493–
511; Henry Nunberg, "Problems in the Structure of the Juvenile Court,"
Journal of Criminal Law, Criminology and Police Science 48 (1958): 500–
16; Lewis Diana, "The Rights of Juvenile Delinquents: An Appraisal of
Court Procedures," *Journal of Criminal Law, Criminology and Police Science*
47 (1957): 561–69; Paul W. Tappan, *Delinquent Girls in Court;* Francis
A. Allen, *The Borderland of Criminal Justice;* Joel Handler, "The Juvenile
Court and the Adversary System: Problems of Function and Form," 1965
Wisconsin Law Review, pp. 7–51; Lewis Yablonsky, "The Role of Law and
Social Science in the Juvenile Court," *Columbia Law Review* 67 (1967):
281–341; Marlene Arnold, "Juvenile Justice in Transition," *UCLA Law
Review* 14 (1967): 1144–58; Monrad G. Paulsen, "Fairness to the Juvenile
Offender," *Minnesota Law Review* 41 (1957): 547–76; George C. New-
man, ed., *Children in the Courts: The Question of Representation.*

74. "The Juvenile Court Movement from a Lawyer's Standpoint," *Annals
of the American Academy of Political and Social Science* (1914), p. 145.

position was later echoed by Paul Tappan, who suggested that the *parens patriae* argument is an *ex post facto* fiction designed to reconcile reform legislation with traditional legal dogma. Juvenile courts, as Tappan observed, are in fact more akin in spirit and in method to contemporary administrative agencies than to early equity.[75] Many critics consider that the tendency to conceive of the juvenile court as either a "clinic" or "welfare agency," to the exclusion of its other considerable functions, contributes neither to understanding the institution nor to its rational use in serving the public interest.[76]

In support of their criticism of the administration of juvenile justice, the constitutionalists have drawn upon a variety of social science studies. The evidence from these studies suggests that the publicized goals of the juvenile court are rarely achieved. Informal procedures and confidentiality in juvenile court do not necessarily guard juveniles against "degradation ceremonies."[77] The juvenile court, despite any intentions to sympathize with juvenile problems, is structurally organized to make judgments about positive and negative social behavior. Juvenile justice is administered by a politically constituted authority which addresses juvenile misconduct through the threat of coercion. Judicial sanctions can be imposed in the case of either contrary conduct or contrary attitudes, for the juvenile court is authorized to demand certain forms of moral propriety and atti-

---

75. Paul W. Tappan, *Juvenile Delinquency*, p. 169.

76. Allen, *The Borderland of Criminal Justice*, p. 61. "Whatever one's motivation, however elevated one's objectives, if the measures taken result in the compulsory loss of the child's liberty, the involuntary separation of a child from his family or even the supervision of a child's activities by a probation worker, the impact on the affected individual is essentially a punitive one. Good intentions and a flexible vocabulary do not alter this reality. This is particularly so when, as is often the case, the institution to which the child is committed is, in fact, a peno-custodial establishment. We shall escape much confusion here if we are willing to give candid recognition to the fact that the business of the juvenile court inevitably consists, to a considerable degree, in dispensing punishment. If this is true, we can no more avoid the problems of unjust punishment in the juvenile court than in the criminal court" (*ibid.*, p. 18).

77. Harold Garfinkel, "Successful Degradation Ceremonies," *American Journal of Sociology* 61 (1956): 420–24.

tudinal responses, even without the presence of a social victim who is visible and suffering.[78]

Despite attempts to purge "juvenile delinquency" of pejorative implications, it has come to have as much dramatic significance for community disapproval as the label of "criminal" which it replaced. The informal system of communication between school, social agency, and parents operates to disseminate the stigma throughout the adolescent's social world, thus identifying him as "delinquent," "troublemaker," and "problem child." The benevolent philosophy of the juvenile court often disguises the fact that the offender is regarded as a "non-person" who is immature, unworldly, and incapable of making effective decisions with regard to his own welfare and future. Genuine attention is rarely paid to how the offender feels and experiences his predicament; according to Elliot Studt, the present structural arrangement of the juvenile court is likely to invite regression and diminish self-respect in its "clients."[79] David Matza alludes to the "sense of injustice" which is experienced by many adolescents when they are treated with condescension, inconsistency, hypocrisy, favoritism, or whimsy.[80] Other writers have confirmed that authoritarian professionalism and pious intimacy in a courtroom setting are not conductive to trusting and cooperative relationships.[81] Finally, the constitutionalists argue that juvenile institutions are no better and in some cases worse than adult prisons. On purely utilitarian grounds, reformatories are a dismal failure in deterring future criminal behavior."[82]

To summarize, the essence of the constitutionalist argument is that the juvenile court system violates constitutional guarantees of due process and stigmatizes adolescents as "delinquents," thereby

78. For the theoretical and policy implications of "victimless crimes," see Edwin M. Schur, *Crimes Without Victims*.

79. "The Client's Image of the Juvenile Court," in Margaret K. Rosenheim, ed., *Justice for the Child*, pp. 200–16.

80. *Delinquency and Drift*. p. 136.

81. Handler, "The Juvenile Court and the Adversary System," pp. 20–21.

82. Henry D. McKay, "Report on the Criminal Careers of Male Delinquents in Chicago," in Task Force Report, *Juvenile Delinquency and Youth Crime*, pp. 107–13.

performing functions similar to those of the criminal courts. In recent years, this perspective has gained in authority and many states passed new juvenile court acts which attempt to safeguard individual rights.[83] The United States Supreme Court recognized the constitutional argument in 1967 when it delivered its first opinion on the juvenile court.[84] The court added clear procedural guidelines to its earlier statement in the *Kent Case* that the "admonition to function in a 'parental' relationship is not an invitation to procedural arbitrariness."[85] Speaking for the majority in the *Gault Case,* Justice Fortas said that juveniles are entitled to (1) timely notice of the specific charges against them; (2) notification of the right to be represented by counsel in proceedings which "may result in commitment to an institution in which the juvenile's freedom is curtailed";[86] (3) the right to confront and cross-examine complainants and other witnesses; and (4) adequate warning of the privilege against self-incrimination and the right to remain silent.

Justice Fortas cited the constitutionalist argument to indicate that "however euphemistic the title, a 'receiving home' or an 'industrial school' for juveniles is an institution of confinement in which the child is incarcerated. . . . Under our Constitution, the condition of being a boy does not justify a kangaroo court."[87] The right to counsel was the fundamental issue in *Gault* because exercise of the right assures procedural regularity and the implementation of related principles:

A proceeding where the issue is whether the child will be found to be "delinquent" and subjected to the loss of his liberty for years is comparable in seriousness to a felony prosecution. The juvenile needs the

83. For a discussion of one such effort, see Joel Goldfarb and Paul Little, "1961 California Juvenile Court Law: Effective Uniform Standards for Juvenile Court Procedure?" *California Law Review* 51 (1963): 421.

84. *In Re Gault,* 387 U.S. 1 (1967).

85. "There is evidence, in fact, that there may be grounds for concern that the child receives the worst of both worlds: that he gets neither the protections accorded to adults nor the solicitous care and regenerative treatment postulated for children" (*Kent v. United States,* 383, U.S. 541, 555 [1966]).

86. *In Re Gault,* 41.

87. *Ibid.,* 27–28.

assistance of counsel to cope with problems of law, to make skilled inquiry into the facts, to insist upon regularity of the proceedings, and to ascertain whether he has a defense and to prepare and submit it.[88]

The *Gault* decision came shortly after the President's Commission on Law Enforcement and Administration of Justice had made even stronger recommendations concerning the right to counsel:

... counsel must be appointed where it can be shown that failure to do so would prejudice the rights of the person involved. . . . Nor does reason appear for the argument that counsel should be provided in some situations but not in others; in delinquency proceedings, for example, but not in neglect. *Wherever coercive action is a possibility, the presence of counsel is imperative.* . . . [W]hat is urgent and imperative is that counsel be provided in the juvenile courts at once and as a regular matter for all who cannot afford to retain their own. . . . *Counsel should be appointed . . . without requiring any affirmative choice by child or parent.*[89]

There have been other recent suggestions concerning structural changes in juvenile court. The President's Crime Commission recommended that the court's power over noncriminal conduct should be restricted to neglect cases alone because "wide-ranging jurisdiction . . . has often become an anachronism serving to facilitate gratuitous coercive intrusions into the lives of children and families."[90] Margaret Rosenheim and Sanford Kadish, in their reports to the President's Commission, suggested that many juvenile cases can be handled administratively and informally by "consent decree negotiations" so as to avoid the stigma of adjudication.[91] Similarly, Joel Handler has proposed the introduction of adversary procedures

88. *Ibid.*, 36.
89. *Juvenile Delinquency and Youth Crime,* pp. 31, 33, 35; President's Commission on Law Enforcement and Administration of Justice, *The Challenge of Crime in a Free Society,* p. 87 (Washington: U.S. Government Printing Office, 1967).
90. President's Commission, *The Challenge of Crime in a Free Society,* p. 84.
91. *Ibid.*

for adjudication at the administrative level, with provisions for judicial supervision and control.[92] "Pre-court regulation can be improved," write Handler and Rosenheim in a joint article, "to mitigate the harshness of formal proceedings and at the same time protect the individual."[93]

Although the *New York Times* greeted *Gault* as a landmark decision requiring "radical changes," it seems unlikely that the decision will generate anything more than a few modest alterations in the total juvenile court system.[94] Important structural changes will depend ultimately on legislative reform, which does not appear to be forthcoming. In the early 1960's, New York, California, and Illinois passed new juvenile court acts which, according to juvenile court administrators from these states, anticipated the Supreme Court decision. Commenting on *Gault,* judges in New York said that the "ruling would not affect juvenile cases, since it already is the law."[95] Similar pronouncements were made in San Francisco and Chicago. New York introduced legal counsel to family court through the "law guardians" system in 1962, and the Public Defender's Office in Chicago assigned a full-time lawyer to juvenile court in early 1966. The *Gault* opinion was no surprise to juvenile court administrators in these cities.

IN DEFENSE OF YOUTH

Not much is yet known about how the new "legalized" juvenile courts are working, but some information is available concerning

92. Handler, "The Juvenile Court and the Adversary System," pp. 20–21.
93. Joel F. Handler and Margaret K. Rosenheim, "Privacy in Welfare: Public Assistance and Juvenile Justice," *Law and Contemporary Problems* 31 (1966): 377–412. See also Edwin Lemert's comments on "judicious nonintervention" in "Juvenile Justice—Quest and Reality," *Trans-Action* 4 (July, 1967): 30–40.
94. *New York Times,* May 16, 1967.
95. *Ibid.*

the role of the lawyer in juvenile court. Because much of the constitutionalist argument relies on the effectiveness of legal representation, it is worthwhile to examine the impact of counsel in juvenile
court. Before the enactment of the New York Family Court Act in
1962, a study discovered that 92 percent of juvenile respondents
in New York were not represented by counsel.[96] A similar inquiry in
California found that "in most counties attorneys are present in 1%
or less of the juvenile court cases."[97] Another study, based on a national survey of juvenile court judges in 1964, found that "in most
courts lawyers represent children in less than 5% of the cases which
go to hearing."[98]

Edwin Lemert recently studied the effects of the 1961 California
Juvenile Court Act and found that the percentage of cases in which
counsel appeared more than trebled in four years, the median rising
from 3 to 10 percent.[99] "The evidence is impressive," writes Lemert,
"that representation by counsel more often secures a favorable outcome of the case than where there is no counsel. Proportionally, dismissals were ordered nearly three times as frequently in attorney
as in non-attorney cases."[100] Close analysis of the data, however,
shows that attorneys were mostly successful in neglect cases and had
almost no impact on delinquency cases. In fact, in one county
studied, juveniles without attorneys were less likely to be detained
while awaiting trial.[101]

The appropriate role of the lawyer in juvenile court has been
given considerable attention in the literature. Jacob Isaacs, in a recent
study of the New York Family Court, proposed that the juvenile
court lawyer perform the functions of advocate, guardian, and officer
of the court. As advocate, he "must stand as the ardent defender of

96. Charles Schinitsky, "The Role of the Lawyer in Children's Court,"
The Record of N.Y.C.B.A. 17 (1962): 10–26.
97. *Juvenile Delinquency and Youth Crime,* p. 32.
98. Daniel L. Skoler and Charles W. Tenney, "Attorney Representation
in Juvenile Court," *Journal of Family Law* 4 (1964): 77–98.
99. Edwin M. Lemert, "Legislating Change in the Juvenile Court," 1967
Wisconsin Law Review, pp. 421–48.
100. *Ibid.,* p. 442.
101. *Ibid.,* p. 443.

his client's constitutional and legal rights"; as guardian, he is required to have regard for the "general welfare of the minor"; and as officer of the court, he "must assume the duty of interpreting the court and its objectives to both child and parent, of preventing misrepresentation and perjury in the presentation of facts, [and] of disclosing to the court all facts in his possession which bear upon a proper disposition of the matter. . . ."[102] Isaacs' tripartite characterization represents an ideal aim rather than current realities. Lemert, in an empirical study of California juvenile courts, found that adversary tactics are marginal in relation to "the attorney's function as a negotiator and interpreter between judge and family."[103] The public defender, even more than a private lawyer, is likely to become "co-opted into the organization of the court, even becoming its superficial appendage. Factors encouraging this are the low priority public defenders give to juvenile work and the growth of interdepartmental or informal reciprocity with probation officers."[104]

There is strong ideological and organizational pressure from legislatures, judges, and legal commentators to repress adversary tactics in juvenile court. The Florida legislature, for example, has responded to *Gault* with a provision for legal representation through the state division of youth services.[105] This provision reinforces the traditional policy of benign paternalism by assuming that state officials will act in the best interests of young persons charged with crimes. Most juvenile court judges deny the importance of adversary trials and "see the lawyer's chief value as lying in the areas of interpretation of the court's approach and securing cooperation in the court's disposition rather than more traditional roles of fact elicitation and preservation of legal rights."[106] Thomas Welch, writing from the constitutionalist perspective, perceives the attorney as interpreter rather than advocate, because

102. Jacob Isaacs, "The Role of the Lawyer in Representing Minors in the New York Family Court," *Buffalo Law Review* 12 (1963): 501–21.
103. Lemert, "Juvenile Justice—Quest and Reality," p. 40.
104. Lemert, "Legislating Change in the Juvenile Court," p. 431.
105. S. 1506, Florida Legislature, June 2, 1967.
106. Skoler and Tenney, "Attorney Representation in Juvenile Court," p. 97.

he is better situated than anyone to explain the nature and objectives of the juvenile courts. He should explain that the juvenile is not being tried as a criminal, the court is not going to punish him, and criminal court tactics of resistance are not appropriate in juvenile court. . . . Above all, the attorney in a delinquency hearing should discard any personal interest in winning cases. Where punishment has truly been eliminated, real "victory" is realized when a delinquent has been rehabilitated. The real "defeat" lies in obstructing the legitimate operation of the rehabilitation mechanism.[107]

Recent studies of the work of lawyers in Chicago's juvenile court provide some insight into the impact of the *Gault* decision.[108] Less than 3 percent of the city's 13,605 listed attorneys filed appearances in the year following the passage of Illinois' juvenile court act in 1965. Lawyers in the upper echelons of their profession came into contact with juvenile court by accident only. Juvenile cases are given even lower priority than traffic or misdemeanor cases. Prior to governmental funding of legal programs to the poor through the Office of Economic Opportunity, some lawyers from influential firms donated time and money on a voluntary basis. Now, however, most of these lawyers come into contact with juvenile court only as a favor to a friend or an influential client. With the expansion of public defender and legal aid programs, members of large and medium-size firms have less and less to do with the problems of poor people.

Private lawyers in juvenile court are typically "small-fee" practitioners who have solo practices and do predominantly trial work.[109] Like most small-fee work, juvenile cases are rarely profitable, and the effort they require often seems out of proportion to the serious-

107. Thomas A. Welch, "Delinquency Proceedings—Fundamental Fairness for the Accused in a Quasi-Criminal Forum," *Minnesota Law Review* 50 (1966): 681–82.

108. Anthony Platt and Ruth Friedman, "The Limits of Advocacy: Occupational Hazards in Juvenile Court," *Pennsylvania Law Review* 7 (1968): 1156–84; Anthony Platt, Howard Schechter, and Phyllis Tiffany, "In Defense of Youth: A Case Study of the Public Defender in Juvenile Court," *Indiana Law Journal* 43 (1968): 619–40.

109. A more complete description of the "small-fee" lawyer is provided by Jerome E. Carlin, *Lawyers on Their Own,* and Arthur Lewis Wood, *Criminal Lawyer.*

ness of the case, the fee, and the good that can be accomplished. Furthermore, lawyers are only sporadically given priority on the hearing of cases and are not accorded special respect by court functionaries. Under these circumstances, it is understandable why the small-fee lawyer feels uncomfortable in a system which does not acknowledge the informal practices characteristic of his work in other courts. Lawyers who are forced to sit about the court building soon become sensitive to its depressing surroundings and the rows of poor people waiting for officialdom to intervene in their lives. The hypocrisy of private hearings becomes apparent as juveniles are led in handcuffs through the public corridors. The consensus among lawyers is that juvenile court is a dreary and discouraging place.

Small-fee lawyers do not generally regard juvenile court as a punitive organization. They are well aware that the court lacks the formal procedures available in other courts, but find this limitation unobjectionable in practice. The views of lawyers about the rights of children differ quite fundamentally from those expressed by the Supreme Court and academics. Lawyers apply different standards to juvenile clients because they are children, not necessarily because lawyers have been constrained by the court's welfare orientation. A lawyer typically has conscientious reservations about helping a juvenile to "beat a case" and, if a case is won on a technicality, he feels obliged to personally warn his client against the dangers of future misconduct.

Lawyers see it as part of their duty as adults and public officials to sit down and talk with juveniles "on their own level," to impress them with the importance of telling the truth, to deter them from committing similar acts in the future, and to "reinforce to the child what the judge has said." The client is in turn expected to show penitence and gratitude—human qualities which are similarly appreciated by juvenile court judges. Any attempt at defense tactics is complicated by the unpredictability of juvenile clients who "have poor memories," "don't remember," "don't have the social and intellectual maturity of an adult," are likely to "blurt out and convict themselves," and easily "spill the beans." A lawyer is hesitant to put on the witness stand a client who is likely to "crack on cross-examination" or "clam up" and convict himself through silence.

A juvenile client poses further special problems of defense because his whole family is involved in the legal proceeding. Although a lawyer appears on behalf of a juvenile, he is usually hired by and therefore responsible to the juvenile's parents. A client is consulted for factual and biographical information, and instructed how to dress and behave in court, but others decide what should be done to him. Lawyers from influential firms who represent children from a background similar to their own find that juvenile court is a "reasonable place to do business" because all parties to the case share a parental pessimism about "troublesome" youth.

The *Gault* decision encouraged legal aid and public defender offices to send lawyers into juvenile court. In Chicago, the juvenile court public defender maintains two seemingly conflicting definitions of his job. As an "officer of the court," whose prevailing ethic is child saving, he sees himself as a social worker with a law degree. As a social worker, he must acknowledge that juveniles are naturally dependent and require supervision by mature adults. At the same time, however, he is a defense attorney who takes pride in the craft of advocacy.

The public defender resolves this dilemma by doing "what is best for a kid." If he considers his client a "good kid," he will do everything to have the charge dismissed or will plead guilty in return for a warning or light sentence, such as probation. "Bad kids" are given up on. The public defender assumes, along with all juvenile court functionaries, that little can be done to "help" these clients. He pleads them guilty and cooperates to process them into reformatories. They have long records, they are charged with "serious" offenses, and they are likely to antagonize judges with their poor school record. The public defender does not waste his time or credit on "bad kids" because a serious effort on their behalf would only jeopardize his chances with more "worthy" defendants.

The determination of whether a client is "good" or "bad" is crucial to the public defender's consideration of a case. How does he decide to apply these judgmental labels? To a great extent, he looks for criteria which positively indicate moral and social propriety. "Badness" is a residual category[110] applied to clients who do not meet these wholesome criteria. His decision relies primarily upon the demeanor of his client and secondarily upon the demeanor of his client's parents.[111] Race, class, and economic status play a minimal role in this decision because most of his clients are poor and non-white. He is concerned, however, with how his client speaks, the amount of respect he is shown, the way the client dresses, and such highly subjective factors as "charm," "personality," and how "cute" or "pretty" or "handsome" the client might be. If the client is a "clean kid," said a former juvenile court public defender, "you go out of your way to help him." Whether the client is in school or has a job, as opposed to being a "dropout" or unemployed, are meaningful criteria of worthiness. Parents who are employed and show "proper" concern for their child are considered by the public defender to be positive assets. The previous arrest record is also of great importance in making this "determination." It is quite possible for a boy with a substantial record to be seen as "good" if he scores high, so to speak, on the above criteria. However, it is a negative factor in the overall determination. Conversely, any client who has no previous record at all is automatically defined as "good."

Although the public defender enjoys the contest of a trial, advocacy is nevertheless a limited commodity in Chicago's juvenile court. Appeals are rare and impractical, jury trials are not allowed, police testimony is rarely challenged, and witnesses are often unreliable when faced with cross-examination. Also, the public defender is more than a personal social worker or lawyer for individual clients. He is an "officer of the court" and an employee of a system in which he must operate from day to day. As Abraham Blumberg has observed, "accused persons come and go in the court system scheme, but the structure and its occupational incumbents remain to carry

110. The idea of "residual category" is taken from Egon Bittner, "Police Discretion in Emergency Apprehension of Mentally Ill Persons," *Social Problems* 14 (1967): 278–92.

111. For an analogous account of the importance of demeanor in the interaction of juveniles with police, see Irving Piliavin and Scott Briar, "Police Encounters with Juveniles," *American Journal of Sociology* 70 (1964): 206–14.

on their respective careers, occupational and organizational enterprise. . . ."[112] The public defender is "in the system" in a number of ways. First, he is a member of a political community, though in a much less significant sense than judges or state's attorneys.[113] Secondly, the public defender is a county employee and is paid out of the same budget that supports all court personnel. Finally, he is a court employee and, like his counterparts in the state's attorney's office, subject to the authority and discretionary powers of individual judges.

His performance is judged by his superiors in a variety of ways. Thus, he is concerned with his "batting average"—that is, the percentage of won and lost cases—and "doing a good job." He is expected to be properly prepared in court, not to ask for an unreasonable number of continuances, not to unnecessarily antagonize the state's witnesses, and not to offend judges by requesting a change of venue on the grounds of prejudice. The public defender knows that assessments of his competence by judges will ultimately reach his boss.

The public defender has informal, friendly relationships with judges, prosecutors, and bailiffs in juvenile court. A former public defender said that he was "on a first name basis with everybody in court." One prosecutor was a personal friend of his and it was not uncommon for the public defender to go out to lunch with a group of judges and prosecutors. Being "in the system" provides the public defender with tactical advantages, because he quickly learns the personal idiosyncrasies of judges and prosecutors. For example, "I know Judge D. is prosecution-minded, but I've had a lot of good dismissals from him." Also, the public defender is attuned to politically sensitive issues and wants to avoid confrontations which will discredit his membership in the court community. "The judges don't like to hear about police brutality," said a former juvenile court pub-

112. Abraham S. Blumberg, "The Practice of Law as a Confidence Game: Organizational Cooptation of a Profession," *Law and Society Review* 1 (June, 1967): 20.

113. Political sponsorship is not a necessary requirement for an aspiring public defender. The office is politically vulnerable but does not advance the political careers of its members.

lic defender. "I'd rather not handle this type of case because I get a lot of police officers to testify for me. I've won cases that way. They wouldn't want to do that for a guy who was trying to cut their throats at every opportunity on police brutality."

Although the public defender accepts the child-saving ethic which pervades the juvenile court, he is also faced with the problem of handling huge caseloads in a manner which is expedient[114] and, he hopes, just. Like almost all situations where people work together, informal ties affect the performance of the objective task at hand.[115] This is no less true in the "halls of justice" than it is in a factory, or store, or other work location. The public defender often sits in a judge's chambers, not discussing the next case but the next vacation, not pondering the problems of gang behavior but the relative merits of the city's night clubs. It is not unreasonable then that we find a state's attorney on occasion dropping a charge for no other reason than that it is a favor of convenience for his friend, the public defender. It is not unreasonable also that a judge can say to a public defender: "I wouldn't have dismissed this case unless you were handling it." The converse situation is also true. The public defender will take a particular course of action as a gesture of friendship to other court personnel. According to Blumberg, "the accused's lawyer has far greater professional, economic, intellectual and other ties to the various elements of the court system than he does to his own clients. In short, the court is a closed community."[116]

Aside from the role that cooperation plays in facilitating the processing of large caseloads, it also makes the entire process more

114. On expediency and efficiency in processing court cases, see Jerome H. Skolnick, "Social Control in the Adversary System," *Journal of Conflict Resolution* 11 (1967): 52–70.

115. For discussions of the crucial role the "informal" organization plays in shaping the goals of the formal structure, see Philip Selznick, "An Approach to a Theory of Bureaucracy," *American Sociological Review* 8 (1943): 47–54, and Peter M. Blau, *Bureaucracy in Modern Society,* pp. 45–67. For empirical work which has validated this process, see Peter M. Blau, *The Dynamics of Bureaucracy;* Alvin Gouldner, *Patterns of Industrial Bureaucracy;* Philip Selznick, *T.V.A. and the Grass Roots;* and Julius A. Roth, "Hired Hand Research," *American Sociologist* 1 (August, 1966): 190–96.

116. Blumberg, "The Practice of Law as a Confidence Game," p. 21.

personally tolerable for everyone involved. Court interaction is intensely focused upon deciding the fate of others' lives and this responsibility is made impossible if conflict is the norm underlying the task at hand.[117] The court functionaries see themselves as colleagues rather than adversaries, for "the probability of continued future relations and interaction must be preserved at all costs."[118]

SUMMARY

The juvenile court system "personalized" the administration of justice by removing many aspects of due process and approaching "troublesome" youth in medical-therapeutic terms. Juvenile court functionaries were given the power to reach more juveniles and to commit them in increasing numbers to penal institutions. The flexibility and informality of these proceedings came under attack from moralists and constitutionalists; the former were concerned that permissiveness and judicial informality would encourage disrespect for law and negate the ceremonial functions of public trials; the latter claimed that juvenile court inflicted punishment without regard to due process or individual rights.

The constitutionalist perspective prevailed and directed attention to the distinctions between the rhetoric and objective reality of juvenile justice. The circumstances under which children are detained in Illinois has not changed significantly over the last sixty years; criticism of overcrowding, poor staffing, discriminatory practices, brutality, and inefficiency is as applicable now as it was then. The *Gault* opinion recognized these conditions and proposed the "legalization" of juvenile court practice in order to protect juveniles against arbitrary and basically punitive procedures. The practical result of *Gault* was the introduction of lawyers into juvenile court.

117. "Closely knit groups in which there exists a high frequency of interaction and high personality involvement of the members have a tendency to suppress conflict" (Lewis Coser, *The Functions of Social Conflict,* p. 151).
118. Blumberg, "The Practice of Law as a Confidence Game," p. 20.

Private lawyers who work in juvenile court are typically small-fee practitioners who make their living from minor criminal and civil matters. In the ideal lawyer-client relationship, the client brings a fee, trust, dependence, and gratitude to the contract, whereas the laywer is required to predict the probable outcome of a case, to perform esoteric services competently, to reinforce the bargaining strength of a defendant, and to accomplish results which would not otherwise be achieved without his presence.[119] But there are a variety of novel occupational hazards in juvenile court: juvenile clients usually bring modest and undependable fees; informal bargaining and negotiated pleas have little significance; fringe benefits, such as accessibility to court personnel or priority over defendants without lawyers, are usually denied or erratically tolerated; a lawyer may often be faced with a conflict of interest between a client and his parents; trial is to be avoided because the chances of victory are slight; and the vagueness of delinquency laws, the unpredictability of juveniles as witnesses, and the difficulty of discrediting the testimony of adult officials make an adversary posture inadvisable.

Few private lawyers take cases in juvenile court, and members of leading law firms handle juvenile matters only by accident or as a personal favor. It seems likely that the public defender model of representation will become widely operative in urban juvenile courts and that court-appointed lawyers will be charged with the task of implementing reforms suggested by the Supreme Court. According to a study of the Chicago juvenile court, the public defender subscribes to the juvenile court's rehabilitative ethic and similarly looks for personal and social cues (demeanor, school record, "home situation," etc.) which indicate whether or not a client is salvageable. The public defender cooperates with other court personnel in order to make his job more personally tolerable and to maximize his efficiency in processing clients. This cooperation is not antithetical to his role as defense lawyer, because he shares a common perspective of "doing what is best for the kids."

This analysis does not imply that the public defender has been

119. The "personal-service occupation" is analyzed by Erving Goffman, *Asylums,* pp. 323–86.

"coopted"[120] into a juvenile court superstructure. It is inaccurate to regard the public defender as a "fallen" lawyer who sells out his clients in return for personal security or bureaucratic expediency. Rather, the public defender brings to his job common sense notions about adolescence and "troublesome" behavior. His views on youth and delinquency are really no different from other adult officials (teachers, social workers, youth officers, etc.) who are charged with regulating youthful behavior. Juveniles get the same kind of treatment in juvenile court that they get in school or at home or on the streets, and lawyers accept this as one of the inevitable and appropriate consequences of adolescence.

It is unlikely that lawyers will appreciably affect the subjective experience of defendants in juvenile court. The structural demands under which a lawyer operates make it very apparent to clients that he is not "their" advocate dedicated to an adversary defense.[121] The relationship is generally one of passivity and dependence.[122] It is not surprising that among juveniles the public defender is characterized as a person of dubious loyalty to his clients:

You always got to have a lawyer. I would never take one of those public defenders because they work for the city. . . . They sit down with the

120. This term is especially used by Blumberg and by Lemert.

121. "When we got to court, the lawyer was already there. He spoke to Dad, and Dad yes-sirred him all over the place, kept looking kind of scared, and tried to make the man think he knew what he was talking about. When the lawyer came over to me and said, 'Hello Claude, how are you?' and shook my hand and smiled, I had the feeling that God had been kicked right out of heaven and the meek were lost. And when he started talking to me—not really talking to me, just saying the stupid things that white people say to little colored boys with a smile on their faces, and the little colored boys are supposed to smile too—nothing in the world could have made me believe that cat was on our side. We weren't even people to him, so how the hell was he going to fight our fight? I wanted to ask Dad why he went and got this guy, but I knew why. He thought all Jews were smart. I could have gotten all that shit out of his head. Anybody could see that this cat wasn't so smart. No, he was just lucky—lucky that the world had dumb niggers like Dad in it" (Claude Brown, *Manchild in the Promised Land*, p. 93).

122. Richard Korn, "The Private Citizen, the Social Expert, and the Social Problem: An Excursion through an Unacknowledged Utopia," in Bernard Rosenberg, Israel Gerver, and F. William Howton, eds., *Mass Society in Crisis*, pp. 576–93.

judge and they got this piece of paper and they talk it over and decide what this nigger's gonna get, whether he's gonna get six months or less. The cat don't talk to you till you come in. They bring you in from the bullpen and you're standing in front of the judge and he kind of puts his hand up over his mouth and whispers sideways to you, "What happened? How do you plead?" And you tell him in three minutes and then he goes on and you get busted. So I would never take no public defender, because those ofays down there in court just want to put you away.[123]

Perhaps the most degrading aspect of the juvenile court process is the general lack of credibility invested in the defendant by court functionaries. The public defender is only one of many court employees who tries to justify the "appearance of justice" and uphold the court's authority, despite any personal reservations. Juvenile clients are regarded even by their lawyers as subordinates and "non-persons" who have little competence to appreciate their own behavior or determine where their best interests lie. The *Gault* decision will not in itself enhance the bargaining power or autonomy of young offenders. The participation of lawyers in juvenile court is likely to make the system more efficient and orderly, but not substantially more fair or benevolent.

123. Interview with sixteen-year-old black youth after his trial in Chicago's juvenile court. This interview is taken from an action research project on legal services to youth.

Chapter 7: *A Concluding Note*

This study has attempted to revise popular conceptions about the origins and benign character of the child-saving movement. The child savers should in no sense be considered libertarians or humanists: (1) Their reforms did not herald a new system of justice but rather expedited traditional policies which had been informally developing during the nineteenth century. (2) They implicitly assumed the "natural" dependence of adolescents and created a special court to impose sanctions on premature independence and behavior unbecoming to youth. (3) Their attitudes toward "delinquent" youth were largely paternalistic and romantic, but their commands were backed up by force. They trusted in the benevolence of government and similarly assumed a harmony of interest between "delinquents" and agencies of social control. (4) They promoted correctional programs requiring longer terms of imprisonment, long hours of labor and militaristic discipline, and the inculcation of middle-class values and lower-class skills.

The child-saving movement was not so much a break with the past as an affirmation of faith in certain aspects of the past. Parental authority, home education, domesticity, and rural values were emphasized because they were in decline as institutions at this time. The normative premises of the child savers, as C. Wright Mills observed of a later generation of "social pathologists," were primarily rural and Jeffersonian in orientation.[1] The participation of politically conservative, socially prominent, middle-class women in the child-saving movement further served to reinforce a code of moral values which was seemingly threatened by urban life, industrialism, and the influx of immigrant cultures. In a rapidly changing and increasingly complex urban society, the child-saving philosophy represented a defense against "foreign" ideologies and a proclamation of cherished values.

Despite the regressive and nostalgic thrust of the child-saving movement, it generated new social and professional roles, especially for women. The new job of social worker combined elements of an old and partly fictitious role—stalwart of family life—with elements of a new role—emancipated career woman and social servant. At the same time, child saving was further legitimized by the rising influence of a professional class of correctional administrators who developed medical-therapeutic strategies for controlling and reforming "delinquent" youth.

The child-saving movement had its most direct consequences on the children of the urban poor. The fact that "troublesome" adolescents were depicted as "sick" or "pathological," were imprisoned "for their own good," and were addressed in a paternalistic vocabulary, and exempted from criminal law processes, did not alter the subjective experiences of control, restraint, and punishment. As Philippe Ariès observed in his historical study of European family life, it is ironic that the obsessive solicitude of family, church, moralists, and administrators for child welfare served to deprive children of the freedoms that they had previously shared with adults and to deny their capacity for initiative, responsibility, and autonomy.[2] The "invention" of delinquency consolidated the inferior social status and dependency of lower-class youth.

The child-saving ethic still motivates contemporary programs of

1. C. Wright Mills, "The Professional Ideology of Social Pathologists," in Bernard Rosenberg, Israel Gerver, and F. William Howton, eds., *Mass Society in Crisis*, pp. 92–111.
2. Philippe Ariès, *Centuries of Childhood: A Social History of Family Life*, passim.

delinquency control, though its application is far more tough-minded and unsentimental than it was sixty years ago. The *Gault* decision may curb some of the more blatant improprieties in juvenile court, but it will have little impact on police handling of juveniles, the increasing flow of cases into court, the penal character of juvenile institutions, and the mechanical expediency of lower-court justice. The new juvenile court acts do not address the problem of police mishandling of adolescents nor do they provide practical remedies for the humiliating invasion of privacy suffered by "pre-delinquent" youth.[3] The introduction of lawyers into juvenile court runs the risk of improving procedural efficiency and reinforcing the child-saving ethic. Local governments do not consider it in their best interests to encourage neighborhood legal programs which champion organized efforts against local institutions such as the police, schools, or welfare authorities. As Joel Handler has observed, "the development of sound social policy and the proper implementation of that policy are beyond the competence of most lawyers. . . . The crucial battle-grounds of social direction and control of the urban scene will not be individual suits against bureaucrats or other court cases." The activity generated by most law schools and legal programs is often peripheral and irrelevant "as the vast public programs take shape and begin to involve the city populations."[4]

The growing concern with youth crime and urban violence has

3. Joel F. Handler and Margaret K. Rosenheim, "Privacy in Welfare: Public Assistance and Juvenile Justice," *Law and Contemporary Problems* 31 (1966): 377–412. According to Irving Piliavin and Scott Briar, "the discretion practiced by juvenile officers is simply an extension of the juvenile court philosophy, which holds that in making legal decisions regarding juveniles, more weight should be given to the juvenile's character and life-situation than to his actual offending behavior. . . . The problem is that such clinical-type decisions are not restrained by mechanisms comparable to the principles of due process and the rules of procedure governing police decisions regarding adult offenders. Consequently, prejudicial practices by police officers can escape notice more easily in their dealings with juveniles than with adults" ("Police Encounters with Juveniles," *American Journal of Sociology* 70 (1964): 213–14.
4. Joel F. Handler, *The Role of Legal Research and Legal Education in Social Welfare*, p. 9.

prompted a variety of anti-delinquency programs: job training, summer outings and sports, tutoring for dropouts, civic pride projects, etc. Most of these programs are seasonal, employing recreational-therapeutic strategies to "keep a cool summer" and to coopt militant black youth leaders. The goal of salvation has been replaced by a more pragmatic and hardheaded concern for controlling violence and youth rebellions. The social worker and youth worker are no longer greeted with passive servility by their "clients" in the urban ghettoes. They have become society's "dirty workers" who are "increasingly caught between the silent middle-class, which wants them to do the dirty work and keep quiet about it, and the objects of that dirty work, who refuse to continue to take it lying down." Lee Rainwater compares the helping professions with "civilian colonial armies" who "find their right to respect from their charges challenged at every turn, and often they must carry out their daily duties with fear for their physical safety."[5]

With the rise of black militancy in recent years, there has been a corresponding hardening of official anti-delinquency programs. Intelligence units are supplementing and sometimes replacing youth officers, and the police have developed counterinsurgency techniques to manage gangs.[6] Self-help efforts by urban youth are generally discredited, and "youth programs" rarely involve young people in

5. Lee Rainwater, "The Revolt of the Dirty-Workers," *Trans-action* 5 (November, 1967): 2.

6. ". . . the police have sought to aid juveniles to avoid clashes with the law through setting up recreation programs, 'big brother' assignments, systems of referral to welfare agencies, informal probation, and even police social work. But such undertakings have declined in recent years and tend to be looked upon as divergent from essential police functions such as apprehension of criminals, recovery of property, and maintenance of public order. This may also point to growing police disillusionment with more generalized or community delinquency prevention programs. Police in some cities sharply disagree with community organizers of such projects over the issue of maintaining the autonomy of neighborhood gangs. They take a jaundiced view of attempts to divert such groups into more compliant pursuits, preferring rather to break them up" (Edwin M. Lemert, "Juvenile Justice—Quest and Reality," *Trans-action* 4 [July, 1967]: 32).

the decision-making process.[7] Rather than increasing opportunities for the exercise of legitimate power by adolescents, public agencies have opted for closer supervision as a means of decreasing opportunities for the exercise of illegitimate power.[8] Since urban youth have few legitimate means of rejecting or changing the institutions which govern their lives, it is not surprising that there has been collective violence in the form of "riots" or "uprisings." What is surprising is that there has not been more collective violence from the most powerless and oppressed group in American society—those who are young, black, and poor. As the gap between social deviance and political marginality narrows, it becomes increasingly necessary to explore how public officials and government agencies contribute to the maintenance of the subordinate social status of powerless groups.

There is an urgent need for academics and policymakers to appreciate that "delinquency," aside from its psychological and subcultural motivation, is the product of social judgment and "procedural definition"[9] by public officials. There is still a reluctance on the part of researchers to investigate how the label of "delinquent" is distributed and enforced through the youth culture. This neglect is due in large part to the positivistic influence and scholar-technician tradition in the study of social problems. The rise of the "multiversity"[10]

7. The opposition of the local police force to the autonomy and potential political power of the Blackstone Rangers gang in Chicago led to a Senate investigation of the misuse of federal "poverty" funds in June, 1968. The harrassment of the Blackstone Rangers by the police is documented by Robert A. Levin, "Gang-Busting in Chicago," *The New Republic,* June 1, 1968, pp. 16–18.

8. Gerald Marwell, "Adolescent Powerlessness and Delinquent Behavior," *Social Problems* 14 (1966): 35–47.

9. The notion of "procedural definition" is developed by David Sudnow, *Passing On: The Social Organization of Dying.* See also, John I. Kitsuse and Aaron V. Cicourel, "A Note on the Uses of Official Statistics," *Social Problems* 11 (1963): 131–39.

10. Clark Kerr, *The Uses of the University.* The lack of competent research in these areas is also due to the unavailability of funds when compared, for example, with research done on defense and national security. Approximately 15 percent of the Defense Department's annual budget is allocated to research, compared with 1 percent of the total federal expenditure for crime

and "agency-determined" research has given further respectability to "methods engineering" approaches, especially in the field of corrections.[11] Accordingly, much of what passes as scholarly "research" tends to avoid issues that might be critical of responsible officials and management, and instead caters to facilitating the efficient and smooth operation of established systems.

---

control (President's Commission on Law Enforcement and Administration of Justice, *The Challenge of Crime in a Free Society*, p. 273).

11. Herbert Blumer, "Threats from Agency-Determined Research: The Case of Camelot," in Irving Louis Horowitz, ed., *The Rise and Fall of Project Camelot*, pp. 153–74.

Appendix

THE CRIMINAL RESPONSIBILITY
OF CHILDREN

A general impression has been created in the literature of juvenile justice that prior to the reforms of the child-saving movement, children were treated by the criminal courts as though they were adults.[1] The creation of the juvenile court is often characterized as a significant victory for enlightenment over the forces of oppression and ignorance.[2] The popularity of this myth can be attributed to the lack of empirical scholarship on the history of American criminal law and to the tendency of many writers to view judicial and penal history from an evolutionary perspective. The modern view of the juvenile court suffers from a sentimental interpretation of history to suit progressive explanations of how social problems are "civilized."

1. Herbert H. Lou, *Juvenile Courts in the United States, passim;* Timothy D. Hurley, *Origin of the Illinois Juvenile Court Law, passim;* Katherine Louise Boole, *The Juvenile Court: Its Origin, History and Procedure,* chap. 1; Julian W. Mack, "The Juvenile Court," *Harvard Law Review* 23 (1909): 104–22; and almost every textbook on criminology. Critiques of this position are very scarce, but see Wiley B. Sanders, "Some Early Beginnings of the Children's Court Movement in England," *National Probation Association Yearbook* 39 (1945): 58–70, and B. E. F. Knell, "Capital Punishment: Its Administration in Relation to Juvenile Offenders in the Nineteenth Century and its Possible Administration in the Eighteenth," *British Journal of Delinquency* 5 (1965): 198–207.

2. "With the dawn of the twentieth century, the juvenile court idea moves forward on the principle that man may dare to remove the blindfold of justice so that the parties may be seen as human beings with their individualized strengths and frailties, personalizing justice" (Gustave L. Schramm, "The Juvenile Court Idea," *Federal Probation* 13 [September, 1949]: 19–20).

The child savers, however, felt that the juvenile court was consistent with traditional legal values and even argued that it was a
logical development of the courts' equity jurisdiction, thus legitimizing their reforms by reference to established doctrines.[3] If the juvenile court was as "radical" as some writers have suggested, it is
unlikely that the child savers would have been able to recruit the
political and professional support of state and local bar associations.
It seems more accurate to describe the juvenile court as a specialized
institution which executed traditional legal policies with more efficiency and flexibility.

The following case materials throw some light on how children
were handled by the criminal courts in the nineteenth century. The
evidence tends to refute some of the more sensational accounts of
judicial oppression. Modern popular histories of crime and the criminal law in England have described with graphic detail the infliction
of brutal punishments on young children.[4] Many writers have cited
well-known nineteenth-century cases of the execution of children
under the age of fourteen years. Arthur Koestler reported that in
1801 Andrew Branning, aged thirteen, was publicly hanged for
breaking into a house and stealing a spoon. He also noted that, in
1808, Michael Hammond, aged eleven, and his sister, aged seven,
were publicly hanged at Lynn.[5] Moreover, Leon Radzinowicz has
further documented the fact that, in 1814, "five children, the young-
est eight and the oldest twelve years of age, were sentenced to death
at the Old Bailey. . . . [I]n some instances sentences of death passed
on children were actually executed; thus a boy of fourteen was
hanged at Newport for stealing."[6] According to Koestler, a boy of
nine was publicly hanged at Chelmsford in 1831 for having set fire
to a house, and another, aged thirteen, was executed at Maidstone.[7]
Finally, Radzinowicz states that in 1833 a boy of nine was sentenced

3. Paul W. Tappan, *Juvenile Delinquency*, p. 169.
4. See, for example, Christopher Hibbert, *The Roots of Evil*, which is
typical of popular histories of crime.
5. Arthur Koestler, *Reflections on Hanging*, p. 21.
6. Leon Radzinowicz, *A History of English Criminal Law and its Administration from 1750: The Movement for Reform 1750–1833*, p. 14.
7. Koestler, *Reflections on Hanging*, p. 15.

to hang for pushing a stick through a cracked shop-window and pulling out printer's color to the value of two pence.[8] According to one leading authority, "prior to the Victorian era the execution of a child was by no means unusual."[9]

The five cases usually cited in books and journals are given in Table 1. B. E. F. Knell recently examined the evidence which sug-

TABLE 1

Supposed Cases of Execution of Children in England

CASE	AGE	OFFENCE	YEAR	SENTENCE
1. Andrew Branning	13	Breaking and Entering: stealing spoon	1801	Death
2. Michael Hammond	11	Felony	1808	Death
3. Hammond's sister	7	Felony	1808	Death
4. A boy	9	Arson	1831	Death
5. John Bell	13	Felony	1831	Death

SOURCE: B. E. F. Knell, "Capital Punishment," *British Journal of Delinquency* 5 (1965): 200.

gests that these five children were executed. In the first place, he discovered that Andrew Branning was not executed but instead transported to New South Wales for the rest of his life. Defendants (2) and (3) were certainly not executed in the nineteenth century and may not have been executed in the eighteenth century when they were in fact tried. The proper date of their trial was 1708, not 1808, and there exists no firm evidence to prove that the death sentence was carried out. Knell found the following account in a nineteenth-century history of the town of Lynn: "In 1708, according to one of our Ms. accounts of the time, two children were hanged

8. Radzinowicz, *History of English Criminal Law*, p. 14. See also, Gerald Gardiner, "The Judicial Attitude to Penal Reform," *Law Quarterly Review* 65 (1949): 196.
9. James B. Christoph, *Capital Punishment and British Politics* 15 (London: George Allen and Unwin Ltd., 1962).

here for felony, one eleven, and the other but seven years of age; which, *if true,* must indicate very early and shocking depravity in the sufferers, as well as unusual and excessive rigour on the part of the magistrates in the infliction of capital punishment." As for case (4), no report of such an execution was found in the newspapers of that period. "On a stronger note," writes Knell, "had this execution taken place, there should have been a record of it in *The Criminal Register* for the county of Essex. In this register for the year in question only two cases of arson are recorded. In one of these cases no prosecution was brought, and as for the other, the incendiary was an adult. In view of these facts, it seems unlikely that a boy of nine was hanged at Chelmsford in 1831."

Of the five cases, it was only in the case of John Andy Bird Bell that the death sentence was definitely carried out. Knell found reports of the execution in *The Times* and *The Kent and Essex Mercury,* both dated August 2, 1831. Bell was tried for the murder of a young boy whom he had robbed and killed in a wood. A few weeks later he confessed to the murder, was tried and condemned to death despite a recommendation of mercy by the jury. On the Monday following the trial, he was led to the gallows: "After the rope was adjusted round his neck, he exclaimed in a firm and loud tone of voice, 'Lord have mercy upon us. Pray good Lord have mercy upon us. All people before me take warning by me.' " The execution "took place over the turnkey's lodge," and, owing to the "tender age of the culprit, for he was not yet fourteen," and "the circumstances under which the crime was perpetrated," there assembled "an immense concourse of people to witness the sad spectacle."[10]

Although English criminal law of the nineteenth century contains accounts of children under fourteen being executed for felonies, there is no evidence to suggest that this was a regular practice. On the contrary, it appears that the severity of the law was mitigated by (1) bringing minor charges against children, (2) refusing to prosecute children, and (3) refusing to convict a child in cases where there was a possibility of the death penalty. Also, the King's pardon was often used to save children from death when all other measures had

10. Knell, "Capital Punishment," pp. 200–201.

failed.[11] Knell examined the court records of the Old Bailey and found that between the years 1801 and 1836, 103 children were sentenced to death. "Of these 103, not one was executed. In practically every case the offense was that of theft. None was convicted of murder. The law, therefore, in the case of children where stealing was concerned, was for all intents and purposes a dead letter."[12]

TABLE 2

Number and Age of Juvenile Offenders Sentenced to Death Between the Years 1801 and 1836 With Their Respective Offences

AGE	BREAK-ING & ENTER-ING	STEAL-ING IN HOUSE	SHOP-LIFT-ING	ROB-BERY BY FORCE	HORSE-STEAL-ING	UTTER-ING FALSE COIN	TOTAL
7	0	0	0	0	0	0	0
8	1	0	0	0	0	0	1
9	2	0	2	0	0	0	4
10	2	0	2	1	0	0	5
11	7	4	1	0	0	0	12
12	14	7	2	1	3	0	27
13	27	20	2	2	1	2	54
TOTAL	53	31	9	4	4	2	103

SOURCE: B. E. F. Knell, "Capital Punishment," *British Journal of Delinquency* 5 (1965): 206.

By the beginning of the nineteenth century, the rules of criminal responsibility for children were clearly established. According to Chitty's *Criminal Law* and Russell's *Treatise on Crimes and Mis-*

11. Radzinowicz, *History of English Law,* pp. 83–164.
12. Knell, "Capital Punishment," p. 199. Children were regularly *sentenced* to death for the most trivial offenses. For example, in 1833, Nicholas White was indicted for "feloniously breaking and entering the dwelling-house of Thomas Batchelor . . . and stealing therein, fifteen pieces of paint, value 2d." The death sentence was commuted to a whipping and transportation for seven years (*ibid.,* p. 198). Knell claims that the practice of sentencing children to death in England stopped with the case of John Smaills in 1836 (*ibid.,* p. 202).

demeanors, children under the age of seven were presumed incapable of committing a crime, whereas "on the attainment of fourteen years of age, the criminal actions of infants are subject to the same modes of construction as those of the rest of society." Children between the ages of seven and fourteen were also presumed to be "destitute of criminal design," a presumption which could be rebutted by the prosecution if "guilty knowledge" was clearly and unambiguously demonstrated.[13] The burden of proof was on the prosecution and any doubt had to operate in favor of the defendant. Thus, in the case of *R. v. Owen,* 1830, a child of ten years was acquitted of a charge of stealing coals. In his summing up to the jury, Judge Littledale held that:

In this case there are two questions, first, did the prisoner take these coals; and secondly, if she did, had she at the time a guilty knowledge that she was doing wrong. The prisoner, as we have heard, is only ten years of age; and unless you are satisfied by the evidence that in committing this offense she knew that she was doing wrong, you ought to acquit her. Whenever a person committing a felony is under fourteen years of age, the presumption of law is that he or she has not sufficient capacity to know it is wrong; and such a person ought not to be convicted, unless there be evidence to satisfy the jury that the party, at the time of the offense, had a guilty knowledge that he or she was doing wrong.[14]

The responsibility of children in the United States during the nineteenth century was formulated according to traditional common law principles. Many of the earliest commentaries on the criminal law, such as *The American Justice* and *The Crown Circuit Companion,* were merely abridgments of works by such English jurists as Coke, Hale, Hawkins, and Blackstone.[15] William Blackstone's

13. E. Chitty, *A Practical Treatise on the Criminal Law,* 3: 724; William Oldnall Russell, *A Treatise on Crime and Misdemeanors,* 1: 3.

14. *R. v. Owen,* 4 C. & P. 236 (1830). Also, in *R. v. Smith* (1 Cox 260, 1845), a boy of ten years was acquitted on a charge of arson. The jury found that he did not have "guilty knowledge that he was committing a crime."

15. Burn's *Abridgment or the American Justice,* p. 248; *The Crown Circuit Companion,* p. 288 (New York: R. M. Dermut and D. D. Arden, 1816). See also, Joel Prentiss Bishop, *Commentaries on the Criminal Law,* chap. 13, and Irving Browne, *The Elements of Criminal Law,* p. 5.

Commentaries (1796) contain a systematic treatment of the criminal law and his summary of the criminal incapacity of children was, in effect, incorporated into American law. The *Commentaries* served as a model for contemporary jurists; judges also cited his theoretical statements to justify specific decisions:

By the law, as it now stands, and has stood at least ever since the time of Edward the Third, the capacity of doing ill, or contracting guilt, is not so much measured by years and days, as by the strength of the delinquent's understanding and judgment. For one lad of eleven years old may have as much cunning as another of fourteen; and in these cases our maxim is that "malitia supplet aetatem." Under seven years of age indeed an infant cannot be guilty of felony; for then a felonious discretion is almost an impossibility in nature: but at eight years old he may be guilty of felony. Also, under fourteen, though an infant shall be *prima facie* adjudged to be *doli capax;* yet if it appear to the court and jury that he was *doli capax,* and could discern between good and evil, he may be convicted and suffer death. Thus a girl of 13 has burnt for killing her mistress; and one boy of 10, and another of 9 years old, who had killed their companions have been sentenced to death, and he of 10 years actually hanged; because it appeared upon their trials, that the one hid himself, and the other hid the body he had killed; which hiding manifested a consciousness of guilt, and a discretion to discern between good and evil. And there was an instance in the last century, where a boy of 8 years old was tried at Abingdon for firing two barns; and, it appearing that he had malice, revenge, and cunning, he was found guilty, condemned and hanged accordingly. Thus also, in very modern times, a boy of ten years old was convicted on his own confession of murdering his bedfellow; there appearing in his whole behavior plain tokens of mischievous discretion; and as the sparing this boy merely on account of his tender years might be of dangerous consequence to the public, by propagating a notion that children might commit such atrocious crimes with impunity, it was unanimously agreed by all the judges that he was a proper subject of capital punishment.[16]

American case law on the criminal responsibility of children was more elaborate and sophisticated than its English counterpart. Ad-

16. William Blackstone, 4 *Commentaries on the Laws of England* 23–24 (Oxford: Clarendon Press, 1796).

ditionally, some of the same cases developed rules of evidence for the protection of young offenders.

In *State v. Doherty* (1806),[17] a young girl between 12 and 13 was indicted for the murder of her father. When challenged by the court she remained mute, and a plea of "not guilty" was entered on her behalf. During the trial, "the defendant stood up erect in the bar several hours, her countenance was ghastly pale, without the least expression, or indication of understanding."[18] On the question of responsibility, Judge White instructed the jury that:

> Their inquiry was, whether the prisoner was the person who took the life of the deceased, and, if they were of that opinion to inquire whether it were done with malice aforethought. If a person of fourteen years of age does an act, such as stated in this indictment, the presumption of law is that the person is "doli capax." If under fourteen and not less than seven, the presumption of law is that the person cannot discern between right and wrong. But this presumption is removed, if from the circumstances it appears that the person discovered a consciousness of wrong.[19]

The jury returned a verdict of not guilty.

In *State v. Aaron* (1818),[20] a young Negro slave of 11 years was accused of murdering another young child. Although there was circumstantial evidence that the defendant had known the victim as a playmate and had been working in the field where the murder took place, he at first denied the crime. Following the inquest, "he was taken apart by one or more of the jurors and told that he had better confess the whole truth, and he did then confess that he had thrown the child into the well, in which the body had been found, and from which he had seen it taken. . . ."[21] At the trial he again denied the crime but was convicted and sentenced to death. On appeal to the Supreme Court of New Jersey, counsel for the defendant claimed that the prosecution had failed to rebut the presumption that a child of 11 years is incapable of committing a crime. Chief Justice Kirk-

17. 2 Tenn. 79 (1806).
18. *Ibid.,* 82.
19. *Ibid.,* 87.
20. 4 N.J.L. 263 (1818).
21. *Ibid.,* 272–73.

patrick ordered a new trial on the grounds that the defendant had been convicted by a mere naked confession, uncorroborated, and obtained by pressure, which should not have been admitted as evidence. (The trial judge had justified the extortion of the confession on the grounds that "it was the anxiety only of a moral and religious community, seeking to discover the perpetrator, that it might be purged from the guilt of shedding blood.[22]) The Chief Justice held that the presumption of innocence on the part of the defendant could only be rebutted "by *strong* and *irresistible* evidence that he had sufficient discernment to distinguish good from evil." Were it demonstrated that the defendant could "comprehend the nature and consequences of his act, he may be convicted and have judgment of death. . . . With respect to confessions in general," the judge continued, "and especially with respect to the confessions of infants, it is necessary to be exceedingly guarded."[23] Confessions obtained "by the flattery of hope or by the impression of fear, *however slightly the emotion may be implanted,* [are] not admissible evidence."[24]

22. *Ibid.,* 278. The trial judge subsequently restated the rules of responsibility for children: "The great subject of inquiry in all cases, ought to be, the legal capacity of the prisoner; and this is found in some, much earlier than others. The real value of the distinctions is to fix the party upon whom the proof of this capacity lies. There is indeed an age so tender that the nature and consequences of acts cannot be comprehended, and every uncorrupted feeling of the heart, as well as every moral and legal principle, forbids punishment. But after we pass this age and progress towards maturity, there have been periods settled, which ascertain the presumption of law, as to the existence of this capacity. If under fourteen, especially under twelve years, the law presumes that it does not exist and if the state seek to punish, it must conclusively establish it. If above the age of fourteen, the law presumes its existence, and if the accused would seek to avoid punishment, he must overcome that presumption by sufficient evidence. But wherever the capacity is established, either by this presumption of law or the testimony of witnesses, punishment always follows the infraction of the law. If the intelligence to apprehend the consequences of acts; to reason upon duty; to distinguish between right and wrong; if the consciousness of guilt and innocence be clearly manifested, then this capacity is shown: in the language of the books, the accused is 'capax doli,' and as a rational and moral agent, must abide the results of his own conduct" (*ibid.,* 279).
23. *Ibid.,* 271.
24. *Ibid.,* 272 (emphasis in the original).

In *State v. Bostick* (1845),[25] the defendant, a white girl of twelve years, was indicted for arson. Mary Bostick had been a servant of Mrs. Ann Fisher who described her as a "very shrewd, artful girl; not intelligent, or very capable of learning; but smart to work, and shrewd in mischief." The defendant had confessed to her mistress that she had set fire to the house on purpose. Two young children who had been in the charge of the defendant had been burnt to death, and the prosecution sought to establish the malicious motivation of Mary Bostick. The defendant appealed on the ground that the confession had been improperly obtained, "as being brought about by promises, or inducements of favor. " A majority of the court agreed and ruled out the confession and acquitted the defendant.

One or two unavailing attempts had been made, to induce her to confess. Afterwards her mistress took her into another room, and questioned her whether she did the act. The child at first denied it. Her mistress then told her, "that she was suspected of the offence, and if she confessed it, the suspicion would not be stronger; that she (the mistress) did not expect to do anything with her, but was going to send her home." The prisoner then confessed, that when she went upstairs in the evening, she placed the candle under the clothes which hung from the bed. Here then is an inducement to confess; a promise of favor held out by a person in authority, and a hope raised in the mind of the child, that she would be sent to her home. Hence, a doubt and uncertainty arise, whether the confession was not made, more under the influence of hope, than from a consciousness of guilt.[26]

In *Walker's Case* (1820),[27] a young boy just over seven years was indicted for petit larceny. The boy's mother said that "his senses were impaired," and the prosecutor offered no evidence to demonstrate his mental capacity to commit a criminal act. The defense submitted that:

... as a child of seven was held incapable of crime, and between that age and fourteen it was necessary to show his capacity; and that, in proportion

25. 4 Del. (4 Harr.) 563 (1845).
26. *Ibid.,* 565.
27. 5 *City-Hall Recorder* (New York City) 137 (1820).

as he approached to seven, the inference in his favour was the greater, and as he approached to fourteen the less, that there was not sufficient evidence in this case to support the prosecution, especially as strong evidence of incapacity had been produced on his part.[28]

Upon this principle, the Mayor charged the jury, who immediately acquitted the defendant.

Stage's Case (1820)[29] involved a group of children, between the ages of seven and fourteen, who were indicted for grand larceny. George Stage, who was eight years old, was arrested while trying to escape from a private house with a stolen bear skin. In convicting and sentencing the defendant to three years in the state prison, the court held:

... with regard to an infant, between the age of seven and fourteen, the Jury should be satisfied that he had a capacity of knowing good from evil. And proof of this may be given either by extrinsic testimony, or it may arise from the circumstances of the case. In this case, the fact of concealment, and of an attempt to escape appear; and it will rest with the Jury to determine whether this boy did not know, at the time he stole this property, that he was doing wrong.[30]

In *People v. Davis* (1823,)[31] William Davis, fifteen, and James McBride, thirteen, were indicted and pleaded "not guilty" to a charge of grand larceny. The recorder instructed the jury that:

... the presumption of law was in favor of an infant under fourteen years of age, that under seven the law supposed the infant incapable to commit a crime. He is supposed to want discretion to judge between right and wrong; but from that age to fourteen, the law still supposed him innocent, and in order to show his liability for crimes, it was necessary to prove his capacity, that it was the province of the jury to say, from all the evidence before them, whether James McBride was guilty or not guilty; that he was present, and assisted in felony, was satisfactorily proved, but whether liable on account of his tender years, was the point for them to decide, no proof of his capacity or incapacity had yet been given; the presumption

28. *Ibid.,* 138.
29. *Ibid.,* 177.
30. *Ibid.,* 178.
31. 1 *Wheeler Criminal Law Cases* 230 (1823).

was therefore in his favor up to the period the law supposed he has attained his capacity.[32]

The jury rendered a verdict of guilty against Davis, and not guilty for McBride.

In *People v. Teller* (1823),[33] Jason Teller, thirteen, and William Teller, who was over fourteen, were indicted for petit larceny after the stolen property had been found in their possession and both had confessed to the crime. The evidence of Jason's capacity was unsatisfactory; some of the police officers, who knew the boy, thought him active, shrewd, and intelligent, while others had a different opinion of his capacity. The jury returned a verdict of guilty against William Teller and of not guilty for Jason Teller. In a note to this case, the reporter reviewed English and American law on the subject of the criminal responsibilty of children. He quoted Hale, Hawkins, and Blackstone, noting that their "principles have long been established in Great Britain and have been adopted in this country. Their decisions, therefore, upon this subject are good authority here." The reporter then summarized the principles of capacity:

Infancy is a satisfactory excuse for the commission of any crime up to the period of seven years, and may or may not extend to fourteen. But upon the attainment of that age, the person of an infant is placed precisely upon the same footing as the rest of mankind, as it respects their accountability for crimes; for at and after this period, the law supposes the party has attained a judgment capable, and a conscience willing to decide between right and wrong.[34]

If the circumstances under which a felony is committed by an infant between 7 and 14 years of age, indicate that he was doing wrong while stealing, this is tantamount to evidence of his capacity.[35]

In *State v. Guild* (1828),[36] a Negro slave, aged twelve, was ac-

32. *Ibid.*, 230–31.
33. *Ibid.*, 231.
34. *Ibid.*, 231–32.
35. *Ibid.*, 233–34. In *Commonwealth v. Elliott*, 4 Law Rep. 329 (1842), a boy of twelve years was acquitted of a charge of murder: "The defense . . . rests mainly on the entire want of any adequate motives for so malignant an act; on the youth and inexperience of the prisoner. . . ."
36. 10 N.J.L. 163 (1828).

cused of beating to death an old woman. The defendant confessed to the crime but the question of his capacity to form intent was disputed. The prosecutor sought to establish that the defendant was "a cunning smart boy," "full of mischief," "smarter than common black boys of his age," and "ingenious," and "acute in many things."[37] A witness for the defense admitted that "he knows the difference between good and evil" and had "intelligence enough to know when he did wrong [and] capacity enough to distinguish between right and wrong."[38]

In the trial court, Judge Drake instructed the jury as to the presumption in favor of persons between seven and fourteen, and told them that, to find the defendant guilty, they must realize that

". . . at the age of this defendant, sufficient capacity is generally possessed in our state of society, by children of ordinary understanding, and having the usual advantages of moral and religious instruction. You will call to mind the evidence on this subject; and if you are satisfied that he was able, in a good degree, to distinguish between right and wrong; to know the nature of the crime with which he is charged . . . his infancy will furnish no obstacle, in the sense of incapacity, to his conviction."[39]

On appeal, the Supreme Court of New Jersey upheld the verdict of the lower court and, apparently, ignored the principles relating to confessions established in *State v. Aaron*.[40] The court approved Blackstone's opinion that "mischievous discretion" was sufficient proof of criminal capacity and held that the defendant was a rational and moral agent who should be judged by his act and motives.[41] The

37. *Ibid.*, 170.
38. *Ibid.*
39. *Ibid.*, 174.
40. The court, in *Guild,* said that "although an original confession may have been obtained by improper means, subsequent confessions of the same or of like facts may be admitted, if the court believes from the length of time intervening, from proper warning of the consequences of confession, or from other circumstances, that the delusive hopes or fears under the influence of which the original confession was obtained, were entirely dispelled" (*ibid.,* 180–81).
41. The Chief Justice approved the following statement from Leach's edition of Hawkins: ". . . from this supposed imbecility of mind, the protective humanity of the law will not, without anxious circumspection, permit an

defendant was subsequently sentenced to death and executed.

In *Godfrey v. State* (1858),[42] a young Negro slave about eleven, was indicted for the murder of a four-year-old child, who had been in his charge. The defendant claimed that "an Indian had done it; that they hunted for Indians, but could not find any." Several witnesses for the prosecution testified that "the [dead] child was on the floor, all bloody; that he was cut on the face and head, three cuts, and a bruise as if with the head of a hatchett; . . . his brain was projecting from his skull." There was further evidence against the defendant that he had been covered by blood and had been wet; the hatchet had been found in a bucket of water. One witness testified that Godfrey had said on the evening of the killing that he had killed Lawrence because he had broken his kite, and he would do it again if they did not hang him. There was conflicting evidence as to the character and intelligence of the defendant: One neighbor observed that he is "a smart, intelligent boy, heap smarter than boys of twelve years generally are," another described him as "kind and gentle" and probably not yet eleven years old.

The jury was informed of the presumption in favor of the defendant because of his age and further instructed that:

. . . they must take into consideration his condition as a negro and a slave, with all the evidence in the case; and that unless [they were satisfied from the evidence] . . . that he was fully aware of the nature and consequences of the act which he had committed, and had plainly shown intelligent malice in the manner of executing the act, they should render a verdict of not guilty. . . .[43]

The jury returned a verdict of guilty but the presiding judge, doubting the propriety of passing sentence under the circumstances of the case, reserved the question for the decision of the appellate court. On appeal, the Supreme Court of Alabama affirmed the judgment,

---

infant to be convicted on his own confession. Yet if it appear, by strong and pregnant evidence and circumstances; that he was perfectly conscious of the nature and malignity of the crime, the verdict of a jury may find him guilty and judgment of death be given against him" (*ibid.*, 189).

42. 31 Ala. 323 (1858).
43. *Ibid.*, 326–27.

citing *State v. Guild*[44] in which "a negro slave, of less than twelve years was convicted of murder and executed," and approving the 'good and evil test, as stated in *State v. Aaron*.[45]

In *State v. Learnard* (1869),[46] the defendant, a male adult, was charged with a burglary and larceny which had been effected by his two children, a boy of about sixteen and a girl of about thirteen. The boy had been prosecuted in a prior term and, on his plea of guilty, was sentenced to the reform school. The defendant pleaded that he was not a principal to the offense because "a girl thirteen or fourteen years old, of good size and ordinarily intelligent, who was capable of working away from home for wages, and who had done so, is of sufficient discretion to be responsible for what crimes she commits."[47] For the defendant, one witness testified concerning the girl's capacity to commit a crime: "She worked for me; I think she earned one dollar per week; she appeared to have intelligence; think she could distinguish between right and wrong. Don't think she ever attended sabbath school; don't think her morals very good."[48] The jury returned a verdict of guilty, stating that the daughter "was under the age of discretion and had not sufficient discretion to be responsible for this act, that she entered the store, and took the goods, by direction of the respondent, that the respondent by said threats compelled his daughter to enter the store and take the goods, and that she committed the act through fear of loss of her life. . . ."[49]

On appeal, the defendant claimed there was sufficient evidence to demonstrate that the girl "could distinguish right from wrong" and therefore had "sufficient degree of discretion" to render her guilty of a crime. In dismissing the appeal, it was held that any doubt should operate in favor of a young child in "the dubious stage of discretion"; the law "has never undertaken to say that any defined

44. 10 N.J.L. 163 (1828).
45. 4 N.J.L. 263 (1818).
46. 41 Vt. 585 (1869).
47. *Ibid.*
48. *Ibid.*
49. *Ibid.*, 587.

TABLE 3

Leading Cases on the Criminal Responsibility of Children in American Law, 1806–82

CASE	DATE	OFFENSE	AGE OF OFFENDER	VERDICT	SENTENCE	OUTCOME
1. Doherty: Tennessee	1806	Murder	12	Not guilty	Acquittal	
2. Aaron (slave): New Jersey	1818	Murder	11	Not guilty; reversed by Supreme Court	Acquittal	
3. Walker: New York	1820	Petit larceny	7	Not guilty	Acquittal	
4. Stage: New York	1820	Grand larceny	8	Guilty	Prison	Three years in state prison
5. Davis: Federal Case	1823	Grand larceny	13	Not guilty	Acquittal	
6. Teller: Federal Case	1823	Petit larceny	13	Not guilty	Acquittal	
7. Guild (slave): New Jersey	1828	Murder	12	Guilty	Death	Executed
8. Elliott: Federal Case	1834	Murder	12	Not guilty	Acquittal	
9. Bostick: Delaware	1845	Arson and murder	12	Not guilty; reversed by Supreme Court	Acquittal	
10. Godfrey (slave): Alabama	1858	Murder	11	Guilty	Death	Executed

11. Learnard: Vermont	1869	Burglary and larceny	13	Not guilty	Acquittal	
12. Angelo: Illinois	1880	Manslaughter	11	Not guilty; reversed by Supreme Court	Acquittal	
13. Toney: South Carolina	1881	Malicious trespass	12	Guilty	Not specified	Not specified
14. Adams: Missouri	1882	Murder	12	Not guilty; reversed by Supreme Court	Acquittal	

physical dimensions or strength, and being 'ordinarily intelligent, and working away from home for wages,' constitute the capacity for crime, or the criterion of such capacity."[50]

In *Angelo v. People* (1880),[51] Theodore Angelo, eleven, was charged with homicide. He was convicted of manslaughter and the jury sentenced him to the penitentiary for six years. A motion for a new trial was overruled by the court, and he was re-sentenced to the reform school for four years. On appeal to the Supreme Court of Illinois, the defendant said that his capacity and malice had not been proved "beyond a reasonable doubt." In Illinois, a child under ten years was legally incapable of committing a crime, and between the ages of ten and fourteen he was prima facie incapable and deemed *doli incapax.*

In a highly sophisticated and compassionate opinion by Justice Walker,[52] the court reversed the decision of the trial court on the grounds that there was no evidence as to the defendant's capacity.

... the rule required evidence strong and clear beyond all doubt and con-tradiction, that he was capable of discerning between good and evil; and the legal presumption being that he was incapable of committing the crime, for want of such knowledge, it devolved on the People to make the strong and clear proof of capacity, before they could be entitled to a con-viction. This record may be searched in vain to find any such proof. There was no witness examined on that question, nor did any one refer to it. There is simply evidence as to his age. For aught that appears, he may have been dull, weak, and wholly incapable of knowing good from evil. It does not appear, from even the circumstances in evidence, that he may not have been mentally weak for his age, or that he may not have even approached idiocy.[53]

50. *Ibid.,* 589.

51. 96 Ill. 209 (1880).

52. Justice Walker criticized the prosecution counsel for proposing to the jury that the defendant's refusal to take the witness stand should be taken as evidence of his guilt. "We can not conceive that any member of the bar could deliberately seek by such means to wrongfully procure a conviction and the execution of a fellow being, when his highest professional duty to his client only requires him to see that there is a fair trial according to the law and evidence" (*ibid.,* 213).

53. *Ibid.,* 212–13.

Appendix

201

In *State v. Toney* (1881),[54] Lawrence Toney, about twelve, and others were charged with malicious trespass. The jury determined that the defendant, "a well-grown boy, apparently at least over twelve years," was guilty because "he was conscious that his act was wrongful" and "he could discern between right and wrong." On appeal, the Supreme Court of South Carolina affirmed: The "evidence of malice was strong and clear, beyond all doubt and contradiction."[55]

In *State v. Adams* (1882),[56] a Negro boy of twelve was indicted for murder in the first degree, having killed another youth, aged seventeen, by stabbing him in the heart with a pocket knife. Witnesses for the prosecution testified that the two boys were often fighting and that the defendant killed the deceased when he was attacked with a pitchfork. The jury found the defendant guilty of first degree murder. The Morgan Circuit Court of Missouri reversed the judgment; the higher court held that a lesser degree of homicide would have been more appropriate, aside from the fact "no effort seems to have been made at the trial to show the defendant possessed criminal capacity."[57]

The criminal responsibility of children in the United States during the nineteenth century was determined according to traditional principles of English law and by the elaboration of rules of procedure and evidence, which leaned toward the protection and benefit of the defendant. There seems to be no justification for the propo-

54. 15 S.C. 409 (1881).
55. Chief Justice Simpson held that: "Out of tenderness to infants—the ease with which they may be misled—their want of foresight and their wayward disposition, no doubt, the evidence of malice, which is to supply age, should be strong and clear beyond all doubt and contradiction; . . . but we find no authority for the position that this evidence must be outside of the facts of the offence itself . . ." (*ibid.*, 414).
56. 76 Mo. 355 (1882).
57. *Ibid.*, 358. "But we are very clearly of opinion that the court erred in its view of the law touching the age of defendant. We refer to the third and seventh instructions given at the instance of the State. These instructions virtually told the jury that the defendant's age should not affect the conclusion at which they should arrive, any more than if he had been of mature years. This is not the law" (*ibid.*, 358).

sition that children were regularly executed; on the contrary, the courts were extremely hesitant to sentence a child under fourteen to death and, where such a case arose, it was either appealed by the defense counsel or certified by the trial judge to the state supreme court. According to contemporary judicial records and legal textbooks, it appears that only two children under fourteen were judicially executed between the years 1806 and 1882.[58] In both cases, the defendants were Negro slaves and, in one case, the victim was the son of a white property owner.[59]

In fourteen leading cases on the criminal responsibility of children in the United States between 1806 and 1882, seven children were indicted for homicide, one for manslaughter, five for various degrees of larceny, and one for malicious trespass. In ten instances, the jury returned a verdict of "not guilty"; one child was found "guilty" of trespass but the sentence was not reported; two children, aged eleven and twelve respectively, were executed, and the remaining child, aged eight, was sentenced to three years in a state prison. Granted that these cases were unusual and involved appeal court decisions, they nevertheless suggest that the criminal law recognized that children under fourteen years old were not to be held as responsible for their actions as adults. Black children apparently were not granted the same immunities as white children and it seems unlikely that Guild and Godfrey would have been executed if they had been white.

58. *Godfrey v. State,* 31 Ala. 323 (1858); *State v. Guild,* 10 N.J.L. 163 (1828). See Table 3.
59. There is a possibility that in the other case, *State v. Guild,* the victim was also white.

Bibliography

Chapter 1. Introduction

This study relies extensively on the theoretical contributions to the sociology of deviance by Francis Allen *(The Borderland of Criminal Justice)*, How-ard Becker *(Outsiders)*, Kai Erikson *(Wayward Puritans)*, Joseph Gusfield *(Symbolic Crusade)*, David Matza *(Delinquency and Drift)*, and Paul Tappan *(Delinquent Girls in Court)*.

Books:

Allen, Francis A. *The Borderland of Criminal Justice: Essays in Law and Criminology.* Chicago: University of Chicago Press, 1964.
Becker, Howard S. *Outsiders: Studies in the Sociology of Deviance.* New York: Free Press Paperback, 1966.
Boole, Katherine L. *The Juvenile Court: Its Origin, History and Procedure.* Ph.D. dissertation, University of California, 1928.
Brown, Claude. *Manchild in the Promised Land.* New York: Macmillan, 1965.
Cloward, Richard A. and Ohlin, Lloyd E. *Delinquency and Opportunity.* New York: Free Press, 1960.
Cohen, Albert K. *Delinquent Boys.* New York: Fress Press, 1955.
Durkheim, Emile. *Rules of Sociological Method.* Glencoe: Free Press, 1950.
Erikson, Kai T. *Wayward Puritans: A Study in the Sociology of Deviance.* New York: John Wiley, 1966.
Gusfield, Joseph R. *Symbolic Crusade: Status Politics and the American Temperance Movement.* Urbana: University of Illinois Press, 1963.
Lou, Herbert H. *Juvenile Courts in the United States.* Chapel Hill: University of North Carolina Press, 1927.
Matza, David. *Delinquency and Drift.* New York: John Wiley, 1964.
Merton, Robert K. *Social Theory and Social Structure.* New York: Free Press, 1963.
Mills, C. Wright, ed. *Images of Man.* New York: George Braziller, 1960.

Nyquist, Ola. *Juvenile Justice.* London: Macmillan, 1960.
Parsons, Talcott. *Social Structure and Personality.* New York: Fress Press, 1965.
Ranulf, Svend. *Moral Indignation and Middle Class Psychology.* Copenhagen: Levin and Munksgaard, 1938.
Shaw, Clifford R. and McKay, Henry D. *Juvenile Delinquency and Urban Areas.* Chicago: University of Chicago Press, 1942.
Tappan, Paul W. *Delinquent Girls in Court.* New York: Columbia University Press, 1947.
Teeters, Negley K. and Reinneman, John Otto. *The Challenge of Delinquency.* New York: Prentice-Hall, 1950.
Wolfgang, Marvin E.; Savitz, Leonard; and Johnston, Norman, eds. *The Sociology of Crime and Delinquency.* New York: John Wiley, 1962.

Articles:

Bates, Helen Page. "Digest of Statutes Relating to Juvenile Courts and Probation Systems." *Charities* 13 (January, 1905): 329–36.
Bloch, Herbert. "Juvenile Delinquency: Myth or Threat?" *Journal of Criminal Law, Criminology and Police Science* 49 (1958): 303–9.
Chute, Charles L. "Fifty Years of the Juvenile Court." 1949 *National Probation and Parole Association Yearbook:* 1–20.
———. "The Juvenile Court in Retrospect." *Federal Probation* 13 (September, 1949): 3–8.
Dexter, Lewis A. "On the Politics and Sociology of Stupidity in our Society." In *The Other Side: Perspectives on Deviance,* edited by Howard S. Becker. New York: Free Press, 1964.
Dobbs, Harrison A. "In Defense of Juvenile Courts." *Federal Probation* 13 (September, 1949): 24–29.
Handler, Joel F. "The Juvenile Court and the Adversary System: Problems of Function and Form." 1965 *Wisconsin Law Review:* 7–51.
Jeffrey, Clarence Ray. "The Historical Development of Criminology." In *Pioneers in Criminology,* edited by Hermann Mannheim. London: Stevens and Sons, 1960.
Kadish, Sanford H. "The Crisis of Over-criminalization." *Annals* 374 (November, 1967): 157–70.
Kitsuse, John I. and Cicourel, Aaron V. "A Note on the Uses of Official Statistics." *Social Problems* 11 (1963): 131–39.
Matza, David. "Subterranean Traditions of Youth." *Annals* 338 (1961): 102–18.
———. "Positions and Behavior Patterns of Youth." In *Handbook of Modern Sociology,* edited by Robert E. L. Farris. Chicago: Rand McNally, 1964.

Miller, Walter B. "Lower Class Culture as a Generating Milieu of Gang Delinquency." *Journal of Social Issues* 4 (1958): 5–19.
Packer, Herbert L. "Copping Out." *New York Review of Books* 9 (October 12, 1962): 17–20.
Seeley, John R. "The Making and Taking of Problems: Toward an Ethical Stance." *Social Problems* 14 (1967): 382–89.
Smith, Roger. "Status Politics and the Image of the Addict." *Issues in Criminology* 2 (1966): 157–75.
Sykes, Gresham M. and Matza, David. "Techniques of Neutralization: A Theory of Delinquency." *American Sociological Review* 22 (1957): 664–70.
Tappan, Paul W. "Who Is the Criminal?" *American Sociological Review* 12 (1947): 96–102.

Chapter 2. Images of Crime, 1870–1900

The *Proceedings of the National Conference of Charities and Correction (PNCCC)* from 1876 to 1900 provide the main source of documentation. (Before 1880 the conference had a shorter name and this publication was entitled *Proceedings of the Annual Conference of Charities [PACC]*). The publisher of all the conference volumes was George H. Ellis, Boston. Other significant primary sources include Charles Cooley ("'Nature v. Nurture' in the Making of Social Careers"), Arthur MacDonald *(Criminology and Abnormal Man)*, and William Douglas Morrison *(Juvenile Offenders)*. The following secondary sources were also relied upon: Arthur Fink *(Causes of Crime)* and Richard Hofstadter *(The Age of Reform and Social Darwinism in American Thought)*.

Books:

Barnes, Harry Elmer and Teeters, Negley K. *New Horizons in Criminology.* Englewood Cliffs, N.J.: Prentice-Hall, 1963.
Cooley, Charles. *Social Process.* New York: Charles Scribner's Sons, 1918.
Dugdale, Richard L. *The Jukes: A Study in Crime, Pauperism, Disease, and Heredity.* New York: G. P. Putnam's Sons, 1877.
Ellis, Havelock. *The Criminal.* London: Walter Scott, 1890.
Fink, Arthur E. *Causes of Crime: Biological Theories in the United States, 1800–1915.* New York: A. S. Barnes, 1962.
Fletcher, Robert. *The New School of Criminal Anthropology.* Washington: Judd and Detweiler, 1891.
Ginger, Ray. *Altgeld's America: The Lincoln Ideal versus Changing Realities.* Chicago: Quadrangle Paperbacks, 1965.

Goffman, Erving. *Stigma: Notes on the Management of Spoiled Identity.*
Englewood Cliffs, N.J.: Prentice-Hall, 1965.

Handlin, Oscar, ed. *Children of the Uprooted.* New York: George Braziller,
1966.

Heath, James, ed. *Eighteenth Century Penal Theory.* London: Oxford University Press, 1963.

Higham, John. *Strangers in the Land.* New York: Atheneum, 1965.

Hofstadter, Richard. *The Age of Reform.* New York: Vintage Books, 1955.

————. *Social Darwinism in American Thought.* Boston: Beacon Press,
1965.

Hooton, Ernest. *Crime and the Man.* Cambridge: Harvard University Press,
1939.

Lasch, Christopher. *The New Radicalism in America, 1889–1963: The Intellectual as a Social Type.* New York: Knopf, 1965.

Lubove, Roy. *The Professional Altruist: The Emergence of Social Work as a
Career, 1880–1930.* Cambridge: Harvard University Press, 1965.

MacDonald, Arthur. *Criminology.* New York: Funk and Wagnalls, 1893.

————. *Abnormal Man.* Washington: Government Printing Office, 1893.

Mercier, Charles. *Criminal Responsibility.* New York: Physicians and Sur-
geons Book Co., 1929.

Morrison, William Douglas. *Juvenile Offenders.* New York: D. Appleton,
1897.

Pierce, Bessie Louise. *A History of Chicago,* vol. 3. New York: Knopf, 1957.

Steffens, Lincoln. *The Shame of the Cities.* New York: McClure, Phillips,
1904.

Strauss, Anselm. *Images of the American City.* New York: Free Press of
Glencoe, 1961.

Radzinowicz, Leon. *Ideology and Crime.* London: Heinemann Educational
Books, 1966.

Ray, Isaac. *A Treatise on the Medical Jurisprudence of Insanity.* Boston:
Little, Brown, 1953.

Szasz, Thomas. *Psychiatric Justice.* New York: Macmillan, 1965.

Vold, George B. *Theoretical Criminology.* New York: Oxford University
Press, 1958.

Wines, Enoch C. *The State of Prisons and of Child-Saving Institutions in the
Civilized World.* Cambridge: Harvard University Press, 1880.

Articles:

Allen, Nathan. "Prevention of Crime and Pauperism." In *PACC, Cincinnati,
1878:* 111–24.

Bittner, Egon and Platt, Anthony. "The Meaning of Punishment." *Issues in Criminology* 2 (1966): 79–99.

Brace, Charles Loring. "The 'Placing Out' Plan for Homeless and Vagrant Children." In *PACC, Saratoga, 1876:* 135–45.

Bremner, Robert. "The Historical Background of Modern Welfare: Shifting Attitudes." In *Social Welfare Institutions: A Sociological Reader,* edited by Mayer N. Zald. New York: John Wiley, 1965.

Caldwell, Peter. "The Duty of the State to Delinquent Children." In *PNCCC, New York, 1898:* 404–10.

Cooley, Charles H. " 'Nature v. Nurture' in the Making of Social Careers." In *PNCCC, Grand Rapids, 1896:* 399–405.

Cooper, Sarah B. "The Kindergarten as Child-Saving Work." In *PNCCC, Madison, 1883:* 130–38.

Dugdale, Richard L. "Heredity Pauperism, as Illustrated in the 'Juke' Family." In *PACC, Saratoga, 1877:* 81–99.

Faulkner, Charles E. "Twentieth Century Alignments for the Promotion of Social Order." In *PNCCC, Topeka, Kan., 1900:* 1–9.

Fishback, W. P. "Address of Welcome." In *PNCCC, Indianapolis, 1891:* 4–7.

Giddings, Franklin H. "Is the Term 'Social Classes' a Scientific Category?" In *PNCCC, New Haven, 1895:* 110–16.

Gould, E. R. L. "The Statistical Study of Hereditary Criminality." In *PNCCC, New Haven, 1895:* 134–43.

Halleck, Seymour. "American Psychiatry and the Criminal: A Historical Review." *American Journal of Psychiatry* 121, no. 9 (March, 1965): i–xxi.

Henderson, Charles R. "Relation of Philanthropy to Social Order and Progress." In *PNCCC, Cincinnati, 1899:* 1–15.

Hill, R. W. " 'The Children of Shinbone Alley.' " In *PNCCC, Omaha, 1887:* 229–35.

Kerlin, I. N. "The Moral Imbecile." In *PNCCC, Baltimore, 1890:* 244–50.

Lathrop, Julia. "Development of the Probation System in a Large City." *Charities* 13 (January, 1905): 344–49.

Leonard, Clara T. "Family Homes for Pauper and Dependent Children." In *PACC, Chicago, 1879:* 170–78.

Letchworth, William P. "Children of the State." In *PNCCC, St. Paul, 1886:* 138–57.

Matza, David. "Poverty and Disrepute." In *Contemporary Social Problems,* edited by Robert K. Merton and Robert A. Nisbet. New York: Harcourt, Brace & World, 1966.

McCulloch, Oscar C. "The Tribe of Ishmael: A Study in Social Degradation." In *PNCCC, Buffalo, 1888:* 154–59.

Newton, R. Heber. "The Bearing of the Kindergarten on the Prevention of Crime." In *PNCCC, St. Paul, 1886:* 53–58.

Platt, Anthony and Diamond, Bernard L. "The Origins of the 'Right and
    Wrong' Test of Criminal Responsibility and its Subsequent Development
    in the United States: An Historical Survey." *California Law Review* 54
    (1966): 1227–60.
Radzinowicz, Leon and Turner, J. C. W. "A Study of Punishment." *Canadian
    Bar Review* 21 (1943): 91–97.
Reeve, Charles H. "Dependent Children." In *Proceedings of the Annual Con-
    gress of the National Prison Association, Boston, 1888:* 101–13.
Sarbin, Theodore R. "The Dangerous Individual: An Outcome of Social
    Identity Transformations." *British Journal of Criminology* 7 (1967):
    285–95.
Scouller, J. D. "Can We Save the Boys?" In *PNCCC, St. Louis, 1884:* 102–
    14.
Wardner, Louise Rockford. "Girls in Reformatories." In *PACC, Chicago,
    1879:* 185–89.
Warner, Beverley. "Child Saving." In *Proceedings of the Annual Congress
    of the National Prison Association, Indianapolis, 1898:* 377–78.
Wey, Hamilton D. "A Plea for Physical Training of Youthful Criminals."
    In *Proceedings of the Annual Congress of the National Prison Association,
    Boston, 1888:* 181–93.
Whyte, William Foote. "Social Disorganization in the Slums." *American
    Sociological Review* 8 (1943): 34–39.
Wines, Frederick H. "Report of Committee on Causes of Pauperism and
    Crime." In *PNCCC, St. Paul, 1886:* 207–14.
———. "The Healing Touch." In *PNCCC, Topeka, 1900:* 10–26.
Wolfgang, Marvin E. "Cesare Lombroso." In *Pioneers in Criminology*, edited
    by Hermann Mannheim. London: Stevens & Sons, 1960.

Chapter 3. The New Penology

Most of the primary source data are taken from the *Proceedings of the Na-
tional Conference of Charities and Correction (PNCCC)*, published by
George H. Ellis, Boston, and initially entitled *Proceedings of the Annual
Conference of Charities (PACC)*, and from the *Proceedings of the National
Prison Association* from 1874 to 1900. Other significant primary sources
include Zebulon Brockway *(Fifty Years of Prison Service)* and Enoch
Wines *(The State of Prisons and of Child-Saving Institutions in the Civi-
lized World)*. The following secondary sources were useful: Lawrence
Cremin *(The Transformation of the School)*, Ray Ginger *(American So-
cial Thought)*, and Max Grünhut *(Penal Reform)*.

Books:

Addams, Jane, ed. *The Child, the Clinic and the Court.* New York: New Republic, 1925.
Barnes, Harry Elmer and Teeters, Negley K. *New Horizons in Criminology.* Englewood Cliffs, N.J.: Prentice-Hall, 1963.
Brace, Charles Loring. *The Dangerous Classes of New York and Twenty Years' Work Among Them.* New York: Wynkoop and Hallenbeck, 1872.
Brockway, Zebulon R. *Fifty Years of Prison Service.* New York: Charities Publication Committee, 1912.
Cremin, Lawrence A. *The Transformation of the School: Progressivism in American Education, 1876–1957.* New York: Vintage Books, 1961.
Ginger, Ray, ed. *American Social Thought.* New York: Hill and Wang, 1961.
Grünhut, Max. *Penal Reform.* Oxford: Clarendon Press, 1948.
Henderson, Charles R., ed. *Penal and Reformatory Institutions.* New York: Charities Publication Committee, 1910.
Hofstadter, Richard. *Anti-intellectualism in American Life.* New York: Knopf, 1963.
Lewis, O. F. *The Development of American Prisons and Prison Customs, 1776–1845.* Albany, N.Y.: Prison Association of New York, 1922.
Lewis, W. David. *From Newgate to Dannemora.* Ithaca, N.Y.: Cornell University Press, 1965.
MacDonald, Arthur. *Abnormal Man.* Washington: Government Printing Office, 1893.
Mannheim, Hermann. *The Dilemma of Penal Reform.* London: George Allen & Unwin, 1939.
Morrison, William Douglas. *Juvenile Offenders.* New York: D. Appleton, 1897.
Spencer, Herbert. *Education: Intellectual, Moral and Physical.* New York: D. Appleton, 1896.
Teeters, Negley K. *Deliberations of the International Penal and Penitentiary Congresses, 1872–1935.* Philadelphia: Temple University Book Store, 1949.
Wines, Enoch C. *The State of Prisons and of Child-Saving Institutions in the Civilized World.* Cambridge: Harvard University Press, 1880.

Articles:

Allison, James. "Juvenile Delinquents: Their Classification, Education, Moral and Industrial Training." In *PNCCC, New York, 1898.*

Brockway, Zebulon R. "Prison Discipline in General." In *PACC, Cincinnati, 1878:* 106–11.

Buckner, R. C. "Child Saving." In *Proceedings of the Annual Congress of the National Prison Association, Indianapolis, 1898:* 278–81.

Caldwell, Peter. "The Reform School Problem." In *PNCCC, St. Paul, 1886:* 71–76.

Carey, James and Platt, Anthony. "The Nalline Clinic: Game or Chemical Superego?" *Issues in Criminology* 2 (Fall, 1966): 223–44.

Carpenter, Mary. "Suggestions on Reformatory Schools and Prison Discipline, Founded on Observation Made During a Visit to the United States." In *Proceedings of the National Prison Reform Congress, St. Louis, 1874:* 157–73.

————. "What Should be Done for the Neglected and Criminal Children of the United States?" In *PACC, Detroit, 1875:* 66–84.

Chapin, Henry Dwight. "Anthropological Study in Children's Institutions." In *PNCCC, New York, 1898:* 424–25.

Charlton, T. J. "Report of the Committee on Juvenile Delinquents." In *PNCCC, Baltimore, 1890:* 214–30.

Elmore, A. E. "Report of the Committee on Reformatories and Houses of Refuge." In *PNCCC, St. Louis, 1884:* 84–91.

Folks, Homer. "The Care of Delinquent Children." In *PNCCC, Indianapolis, 1891:* 136–50.

Fulton, Levi S. "Education as a Factor in Reformation." In *PNCCC, St. Paul, 1886:* 65–71.

Hite, J. C. "Moral Elevation in Reformatories: What Is Required to Produce It." In *PNCCC, St. Paul, 1886:* 59–65.

Howe, G. E. "The Family System." In *PNCCC, Cleveland, 1880:* 209–26.

Laverty, P. H. "The Management of Reformatories." In *PNCCC, St. Louis, 1884:* 87–91.

Letchworth, William P. "Children of the State." In *PNCCC, St. Paul, 1886:* 138–57.

Lynde, W. P. "Prevention in Some of Its Aspects." In *PACC, Chicago, 1879:* 162–70.

Martinson, Robert. "The Age of Treatment: Some Implications of the Custody-Treatment Dimension." *Issues in Criminology* 2 (Fall, 1966): 275–93.

Neff, William Howard. "Reformatories for Juvenile Delinquents." In *PNCCC, Baltimore, 1890:* 230–34.

Newton, R. Heber. "The Bearing of the Kindergarten on the Prevention of Crime." In *PNCCC, St. Paul, 1886:* 23–28.

Nibecker, F. H. "The Influence of Children in their Homes after Institution Life." In *PNCCC, New Haven, 1895:* 216–29.

Bibliography

Otterson, Ira D. "General Features of Reform School Work." In *PNCCC, Denver, 1892:* 166–74.
Powelson, Harvey and Bendix, Reinhard. "Psychiatry in Prison." In *Mental Health and Mental Disorder,* edited by Arnold M. Rose. New York: W. W. Norton, 1955.
Rainwater, Lee. "The Revolt of the Dirty-Workers." *Trans-action* 5 (November, 1967): 2, 64.
Reeder, R. R. "To Cottage and Country." *Charities* 13 (January, 1905): 364–67.
Wey, Hamilton D. "A Plea for Physical Training of Youthful Offenders." In *Proceedings of the Annual Congress of the National Prison Association, Boston, 1888:* 181–93.
Wines, Frederick H. "Reformation as an End in Prison Discipline." In *PNCCC, Buffalo, 1888:* 193–98.
Wohl, R. Richard. "'The Rags to Riches Story': An Episode of Secular Idealism." In *Class, Status and Power: A Reader in Social Stratification,* edited by Reinhard Bendix and Seymour Martin Lipset. Free Press of Glencoe, 1953.

Chapter 4. Maternal Justice

The child savers were prolific writers and much of the data in this chapter are taken from the autobiographical writings of Jane Addams, Louise de Koven Bowen, and Julia Lathrop, together with the club records of various feminist organizations. Most of Louise Bowen's writing are collected by Mary Humphrey *(Speeches, Addresses, and Letters of Louise de Koven Bowen).* The most valuable secondary sources on this topic are the recent studies of Joseph Gusfield *(Symbolic Crusade)* and Christopher Lasch *(The New Radicalism in America, 1889–1963).*

Books:

Addams, Jane, ed. *Hull-House Maps and Papers.* New York: Thomas Y. Crowell, 1930.
———. *The Spirit of Youth and City Streets.* New York: Macmillan, 1930.
———. *My Friend, Julia Lathrop.* New York: Macmillan, 1935.
———. *Twenty Years at Hull-House.* New York: Signet Classic, 1961.
Beaumont, Gustave de and Tocqueville, Alexis de. *On the Penitentiary System in the United States.* Carbondale, Ill.: Southern Illinois University Press, 1964.
Bowen, Louise de Koven. *Our Most Popular Recreation Controlled by the*

Liquor Interests: A Study of Public Dance Halls. Chicago: Juvenile Protective Association, 1912.

————. *The Colored People of Chicago.* Chicago: Juvenile Protective Association, 1913.

————. *Safeguards for City Youth at Work and at Play.* New York: Macmillan, 1914.

————. *The Straight Girl on the Crooked Path: A True Story.* Chicago: Juvenile Protective Association, 1916.

————. *The Road to Destruction Made Easy in Chicago.* Chicago: Juvenile Protective Association, 1916.

————. *Growing Up With a City.* New York: Macmillan, 1926.

————. *Open Windows.* Chicago: Ralph Fletcher Seymour, 1946.

Brim, Orville G. *Education for Child Rearing.* New York: Free Press, 1965.

Conroy, Frank. *Stop-Time.* New York: Viking Press, 1965.

Frank, Henriette Greenbaum and Jerome, Amalie Hofer. *Annals of the Chicago Woman's Club for the First Forty Years of its Organization, 1876–1916.* Chicago: Chicago Woman's Club, 1916.

Gorer, Geoffrey. *The American People: A Study in National Character.* New York: W. W. Norton, 1948.

Grimes, Alan P. *The Puritan Ethic and Woman Suffrage.* New York: Oxford University Press, 1967.

Gusfield, Joseph R. *Symbolic Crusade: Politics and the American Temperance Movement.* Urbana: University of Illinois Press, 1963.

Hofstadter, Richard. *The Age of Reform.* New York: Vintage Books, 1955.

Humphrey, Mary E., ed. *Speeches, Addresses, and Letters of Louise de Koven Bowen,* 2 vols. Ann Arbor, Mich.: Edward Brothers, 1937.

Lasch, Christopher. *The New Radicalism in America, 1889–1963: The Intellectual as a Social Type.* New York: Knopf, 1965.

Parsons, Talcott and Bales, Robert F. *Family, Socialization and Interaction Process.* Glencoe, Ill.: Free Press, 1955.

Powers, Dorothy Edwards. *The Chicago Woman's Club.* Master's thesis, University of Chicago, 1939.

Vice Commission of Chicago. *The Social Evil in Chicago.* Chicago: Gunthrop-Warren Printing Co., 1911.

Articles:

Horowitz, Irving Louis and Liebowitz, Martin. "Social Deviance and Political Marginality: Toward a Redefinition of the Relation Between Sociology and Politics." *Social Problems* 15 (1968): 280–96.

Howe, G. E. "The Family System." In *Proceedings of the National Conference of Charities and Correction (PNCCC), Cleveland, 1880:* 209–26.

Leonard, Clara T. "Family Homes for Pauper and Dependent Children." In *Proceedings of the Annual Conference of Charities (PACC), Chicago, 1879:* 170–78.

Lynde, W. P. "Prevention in Some of Its Aspects." In *PACC, Chicago, 1879:* 162–70.

Otterson, Ira D. "General Features of Reform School Work." In *PNCCC, Denver, 1892:* 166–74.

Randall, C. D. "Child-Saving Work." In *PNCCC, St. Louis, 1884:* 115–22.

Richardson, Anne B. "The Cooperation of Woman in Philanthropy." In *PNCCC, Denver, 1892:* 216–22.

Sickels, Lucy M. "Woman's Influence in Juvenile Reformatories." In *PNCCC, Nashville, 1894:* 164–67.

Sunley, Robert. "Early Nineteenth-Century American Literature on Child Rearing." In *Childhood in Contemporary Cultures,* edited by Margaret Mead and Martha Wolfenstein. Chicago: University of Chicago Press, 1955.

Chapter 5. The Child-Saving Movement in Illinois

The following public and private documents were extensively consulted for this chapter: *Biennial Reports of the Board of State Commissioners of Public Charities of the State of Illinois* from 1871 to 1893, *Proceedings of the National Prison Association* from 1874 to 1900, *Proceedings of the Illinois Conference of Charities* from 1898 to 1901, and archives of the Chicago Bar Association. For the years 1890 to 1900, the writer also examined newspaper accounts of child saving in the *Chicago Inter Ocean* and *Chicago Tribune.* Other historical documents and collections were made available by the Illinois State Historical Library and Chicago Historical Society.

Books:

Abbot, Edith and Breckenridge, Sophonisba P. *The Delinquent Child and the Home.* New York: Survey Associates, 1916.

Addams, Jane. *My Frield, Julia Lathrop.* New York: Macmillan, 1935.

Altgeld, John P. *Our Penal Machinery and Its Victims.* Chicago: Jansen, McClurg, 1884.

Bowen, Louise. *Growing Up With a City.* New York: Macmillan, 1926.

Brown, James. *The History of Public Assistance in Chicago, 1833–1893.* Chicago: University of Chicago Press, 1941.

Cranston, Leslie A. *Early Criminal Codes of Illinois and their Relation to the Common Law of England*. Illinois: Cranston, 1930.
Farwell, Harriet S. *Lucy Louise Flower, 1837–1920: Her Contribution to Education and Child Welfare in Chicago*. Chicago: privately printed, 1924.
Frank, Henriette Greenbaum and Jerome, Amalie Hofer. *Annals of the Chicago Woman's Club for the First Forty Years of its Organization, 1876–1916*. Chicago: Chicago Woman's Club, 1916.
Ginger, Ray. *Altgeld's America: The Lincoln Ideal versus Changing Realities*. Chicago: Quadrangle Paperbacks, 1965.
Hirsch, Elizabeth Francis. *A Study of the Chicago and Cook County School for Boys*. Master's thesis, University of Chicago, 1926.
Hurley, Timothy D. *Origin of the Illinois Juvenile Court Law*. Chicago: The Visitation and Aid Society, 1907.
Jeter, Helen Rankin. *The Chicago Juvenile Court*. Washington: United States Children's Bureau Publication no. 104, 1922.
Johnson, Arlien. *Public Policy and Private Charities: A Study of Legislation in the United States and of Administration in Illinois*. Chicago: University of Chicago Press, 1931.
Lou, Herbert H. *Juvenile Courts in the United States*. Chapel Hill: University of North Carolina Press, 1927.
Randall, Evelyn Harriet. *The St. Charles School for Delinquent Boys*. Master's thesis, University of Chicago, 1927.
Rosenheim, Margaret Kenney, ed. *Justice for the Child*. New York: Free Press of Glencoe, 1962.

Articles:

Beveridge, Helen L. "Reformatory and Preventive Work in Illinois." In *Proceedings of the National Conference of Charities and Correction, Boston, 1881:* 276–78.
Bruce, Andrew A. "One Hundred Years of Criminological Development in Illinois." *Journal of Criminal Law and Criminology* 24 (1933): 11–49.
Dudley, Oscar L. "The Illinois Industrial Training School for Boys." In *Proceedings of the National Conference of Charities and Correction, Indianapolis, 1891:* 145–50.
Fulcomer, Daniel. "Instruction in Sociology in Institutions of Learning." In *Proceedings of the National Conference of Charities and Correction, Nashville, 1894:* 67–85.
Sanders, Wiley B. "Some Early Beginnings of the Children's Court Movement in England." *National Probation Association Yearbook* 39 (1945): 58–70.

Wardner, Louise Rockwood. "Girls in Reformatories." In *Proceedings of the Annual Conference of Charities, Chicago, 1879:* 185–89.

Chapter 6. The Fate of the Juvenile Court

This chapter draws upon a variety of historical and contemporary sources relating to the juvenile court system. The following journals provide most of the earlier data: *Survey, Charities,* and *Journal of Criminal Law, Criminology and Police Science.* The most original critiques of the juvenile court include studies by Francis Allen *(The Borderland of Criminal Justice),* Edwin Lemert ("Legislating Change in the Juvenile Court"), David Matza *(Delinquency and Drift),* and Paul Tappan *(Delinquent Girls in Court).*

Books:

Addams, Jane, ed. *The Child, the Clinic and the Court.* New York: New Republic, 1925.

Allen, Francis A. *The Borderland of Criminal Justice: Essays in Law and Criminology.* Chicago: University of Chicago Press, 1964.

Barrows, Samuel J., ed. *Children's Courts in the United States: Their Origin, Development and Results.* Washington: Government Printing Office, 1904.

Blau, Peter M. *The Dynamics of Bureaucracy.* Chicago: University of Chicago Press, 1955.

———. *Bureaucracy in Modern Society.* New York: Random House, 1956.

Brown, Claude. *Manchild in the Promised Land.* New York: Macmillan, 1965.

Carlin, Jerome E. *Lawyers on Their Own.* New Brunswick, N.J.: Rutgers University Press, 1962.

Chicago Bar Association. *Juvenile Court Committee Report.* October 28, 1899.

Comfort, Alex. *Authority and Delinquency in the Modern State.* London: Routledge and Kegan Paul, 1950.

Coser, Lewis. *The Functions of Social Conflict.* Glencoe, Ill.: Fress Press, 1956.

Devlin, Patrick. *The Enforcement of Morals.* London: Oxford University Press, 1959.

Giles, F. T. *Children and the Law.* London: Penguin Books, 1959.

Goffman, Erving. *Asylums.* New York: Anchor Books, 1961.

Goodhart, A. L. *English Law and the Moral Law.* London: Stevens and Sons, 1953.

Goodspeed, Weston A. and Healey, Daniel D. *History of Cook County, Illinois.* 2 vols. Chicago: The Goodspeed Historical Association, 1909.

Gouldner, Alvin. *Patterns of Industrial Bureaucracy.* Glencoe, Ill.: Free Press, 1955.

Halmos, Paul. *The Faith of the Counsellors.* New York: Schocken Books, 1966.

Hart, H. L. A. *Law, Liberty and Morality.* Stanford, Calif.: Stanford University Press, 1963.

Heath, James. *Eighteenth Century Penal Theory.* London: Oxford University Press, 1963.

Hirsh, Elizabeth Francis. *A Study of the Chicago and Cook County School for Boys.* Master's thesis, University of Chicago, 1926.

Holmes, Oliver Wendell. *The Common Law.* Boston: Little, Brown, 1881.

Matza, David. *Delinquency and Drift.* New York: John Wiley, 1964.

Newman, George G., ed. *Children in the Courts: The Question of Representation.* Ann Arbor, Mich.: Institute of Continuing Legal Education, University of Michigan, 1967.

Parsons, Talcott. *The Social System.* Glencoe, Ill.: The Free Press, 1951.

President's Commission on Law Enforcement and Administration of Justice. *The Challenge of Crime in a Free Society.* Washington: U.S. Government Printing Office, 1967.

Randall, Evelyn Harriet. *The St. Charles School for Delinquent Boys.* Master's thesis, University of Chicago, 1927.

Rosenheim, Margaret K., ed. *Justice for the Child.* New York: Free Press, 1962.

Schur, Edwin M. *Crimes Without Victims.* Englewood Cliffs, N.J.: Prentice-Hall, 1965.

Selznick, Philip. *T.V.A. and the Grass Roots.* Berkeley: University of California Press, 1949.

Stephen, James Fitzjames. *History of the Criminal Law in England,* 3 vols. London: Macmillan, 1883.

Tappan, Paul W. *Delinquent Girls in Court.* New York: Columbia University Press, 1947.

———. *Juvenile Delinquency.* New York: McGraw-Hill, 1949.

Werthman, Carl. *Delinquency and Authority.* Master's thesis, University of California, Berkeley, 1964.

Wigmore, John H., ed. *The Illinois Crime Survey.* Chicago: Blakely Printing, 1929.

Wood, Arthur L. *Criminal Lawyer.* New Haven: College and University Press, 1967.

Articles:

Arnold, Marlene. "Juvenile Justice in Transition." *UCLA Law Review* 14 (1957): 1144–58.

Baker, Harvey H. "Procedure of the Boston Juvenile Court," *Survey* 23 (February, 1910): 643–52.

Balint, Michael. "On Punishing Offenders." In *Psychoanalysis and Culture,* edited by George B. Wilbur and Warner Muensterberger. New York: International Universities Press, 1951.

Beemsterboer, Matthew J. "The Juvenile Court—Benevolence in the Star Chamber." *Journal of Criminal Law, Criminology and Police Science* 50 (1960): 464–75.

Bittner, Egon. "Police Discretion in Emergency Apprehension of Mentally Ill Persons." *Social Problems* 14 (1967): 278–92.

Bittner, Egon and Platt, Anthony. "The Meaning of Punishment." *Issues in Criminology* 2 (1966): 79–99.

Blumberg, Abraham S. "The Practice of Law as a Confidence Game: Organizational Cooptation of a Profession." *Law and Society Review* 1 (June, 1967): 15–39.

Caldwell, Robert G. "The Juvenile Court: Its Development and Some Major Problems." *Journal of Criminal Law, Criminology and Police Science* 51 (1961): 493–511.

Diana, Lewis. "The Rights of Juvenile Delinquents: An Appraisal of Court Procedures." *Journal of Criminal Law, Criminology and Police Science* 47 (1957): 561–69.

Flexner, Bernard. "The Juvenile Court as a Social Institution." *Survey* 23 (February, 1910): 607–38.

Folks, Homer. "Juvenile Probation in New York." *Survey* 23 (February, 1910): 667–73.

Garfinkel, Harold. "Successful Degradation Ceremonies." *American Journal of Sociology* 61 (1956): 420–24.

Goldfarb, Joel and Little, Paul. "1961 California Juvenile Court Law: Effective Uniform Standards for Juvenile Court Procedure?" *California Law Review* 51 (1963): 421–47.

Handler, Joel. "The Juvenile Court and the Adversary System: Problems of Function and Form." 1965 *Wisconsin Law Review:* 7–51.

Handler, Joel F. and Rosenheim, Margaret K. "Privacy in Welfare: Public Assistance and Juvenile Justice." *Law and Contemporary Problems* 31 (1966): 377–412.

Henderson, Charles R. "Juvenile Courts: Problems of Administration." *Charities* 13 (January, 1905): 340–43.

Hermann, Stephen M. "Scope and Purposes of Juvenile Court Jurisdiction." *Journal of Criminal Law, Criminology and Police Science* 48 (1958): 590–607.

Isaacs, Jacob. "The Role of the Lawyer in Representing Minors in the New York Family Court." *Buffalo Law Review* 12 (1963): 501–21.

Korn, Richard. "The Private Citizen, the Social Expert, and the Social Problem: An Excursion through an Unacknowledged Utopia." In *Mass Society in Crisis,* edited by Bernard Rosenberg, Israel Gerver, and F. William Howton. New York: Macmillan, 1964.

Lathrop, Julia C. "The Development of the Probation System in a Large City." *Charities* 13 (January, 1905): 344–49.

Lemert, Edwin M. "Juvenile Justice—Quest and Reality." *Trans-action* 4 (July, 1967): 30–40.

———. "Legislating Change in the Juvenile Court." 1967 *Wisconsin Law Review:* 421–48.

Lindsey, Ben B. "The Boy and the Court." *Charities* 13 (January, 1905): 350–57.

Lindsey, Edward. "The Juvenile Court Movement from a Lawyer's Standpoint." *Annals* (1914): 140–58.

Ludwig, F. L. "Considerations Basic to Reform of Juvenile Offenders." *St. John's Law Review* 29 (1955): 226–37.

Mack, Julian W. "The Law and the Child." *Survey* 23 (February, 1910): 638–43.

McKay, Henry D. "Report on the Criminal Careers of Male Delinquents in Chicago." In Task Force Report, *Juvenile Delinquency and Youth Crime:* 107–13. Washington: U.S. Government Printing Office, 1967.

Mead, George H. "The Psychology of Punitive Justice." *American Journal of Sociology* 23 (1918): 577–602.

Nunberg, Henry. "Problems in the Structure of the Juvenile Court." *Journal of Criminal Law, Criminology and Police Science* 48 (1958): 500–516.

Paulsen, Monrad G. "Fairness to the Juvenile Offender." *Minnesota Law Review* 41 (1957): 547–67.

———. "Rights and Rehabilitation in the Juvenile Courts." *Columbia Law Review* 67 (1967): 281–341.

Piliavin, Irving and Briar, Scott. "Police Encounters with Juveniles." *American Journal of Sociology* 70 (1964): 206–14.

Platt, Anthony and Friedman, Ruth. "The Limits of Advocacy: Occupational Hazards in Juvenile Court." *Pennsylvania Law Review* 7 (1968): 1156–84.

Platt, Anthony; Schechter, Howard; and Tiffany, Phyllis. "In Defense of Youth: A Case Study of the Public Defender in Juvenile Court." *Indiana Law Journal* 43 (1968): 619–40.

Roth, Julius A. "Hired Hand Research." *American Sociologist* 1 (August, 1966): 190–96.

Rubin, Sol. "Protecting the Child in the Juvenile Court." *Journal of Criminal Law, Criminology and Police Science* 43 (1952): 425–40.

Schinitsky, Charles. "The Role of the Lawyer in Children's Court." *The Record of New York City Bar Association* 17 (1962): 10–26.

Schramm, Gustav L. "The Juvenile Court Idea." *Federal Probation* 13 (September, 1949): 19–23.

Selznick, Philip. "An Approach to a Theory of Bureaucracy." *American Sociological Review* 8 (1943): 47–54.

Skoler, Daniel L. and Tenney, Charles W. "Attorney Representation in Juvenile Court." *Journal of Family Law* 4 (1964): 77–98.

Skolnick, Jerome H. "Social Control in the Adversary System." *Journal of Conflict Resolution* 11 (1967): 52–70.

Thurston, Henry W. "Ten Years of the Juvenile Court of Chicago." *Survey* 23 (February, 1910): 656–66.

Tuthill, Richard S. "The Chicago Juvenile Court." In *Proceedings of the Annual Congress of the National Prison Association, Philadelphia, 1902:* 115–24.

Van Waters, Miriam. "The Socialization of Juvenile Court Procedure." *Journal of Criminal Law and Criminology* 12 (1922): 61–69.

Welch, Thomas A. "Delinquency Proceedings—Fundamental Fairness for the Accused in a Quasi-Criminal Forum." *Minnesota Law Review* 50 (1966): 653–96.

Wigmore, John H. "Juvenile Court vs. Criminal Court." *Illinois Law Review* 21 (1926): 375–77.

Yablonsky, Lewis. "The Role of Law and Social Science in the Juvenile Court." *Columbia Law Review* 67 (1967): 281–341.

Chapter 7. A Concluding Note

Books:

Ariès, Philippe. *Centuries of Childhood: A Social History of Family Life.* New York: Vintage Books, 1965.

Handler, Joel F. *The Role of Legal Research and Legal Education in Social Welfare.* Institute for Research on Poverty, University of Wisconsin: unpublished paper, 1967.

Horowitz, Irving Louis, ed. *The Rise and Fall of Project Camelot.* Massachusetts: M.I.T. Press, 1967.

Kerr, Clark. *The Uses of the University.* New York: Anchor Books, 1961.

President's Commission on Law Enforcement and Administration of Justice. *The Challenge of Crime in a Free Society.* Washington: Government Printing Office, 1967.
Sudnow, David. *Passing On: The Social Organization of Dying.* Englewood Cliffs, N.J.: Prentice-Hall, 1967.

Articles:

Handler, Joel F. and Rosenheim, Margaret K. "Privacy in Welfare: Public Assistance and Juvenile Justice." *Law and Contemporary Problems* 31 (1966): 377–412.
Kitsuse, John I. and Cicourel, Aaron V. "A Note on the Uses of Official Statistics." *Social Problems* 11 (1963): 131–39.
Lemert, Edwin M. "Juvenile Justice—Quest and Reality." *Trans-action* 4 (July, 1967): 30–40.
Levin, Robert A. "Gang-Busting in Chicago." *The New Republic,* June 1, 1968: 16–18.
Marwell, Gerald. "Adolescent Powerlessness and Delinquent Behavior." *Social Problems* 14 (1966): 35–47.
Mills, C. Wright. "The Professional Ideology of Social Pathologists." In *Mass Society in Crisis,* edited by Bernard Rosenberg, Israel Gerver, and F. William Howton. New York: Macmillan, 1964.
Piliavin, Irving and Briar, Scott. "Police Encounters with Juveniles." *American Journal of Sociology* 70 (1964): 206–14.
Rainwater, Lee. "The Revolt of the Dirty-Workers." *Trans-action* 5 (November, 1967): 2, 64.

Appendix

There are very few useful secondary sources on nineteenth-century criminal law in the United States. There is nothing comparable to Leon Radzinowicz's *History of English Criminal Law and its Administration from 1750* or B. E. F. Knell's paper on "Capital Punishment." This chapter relies almost exclusively on primary case materials.

Books:

Bishop, Joel Prentiss. *Commentaries on the Criminal Law.* Boston: Little, Brown, 1856.
Blackstone, William. *Commentaries on the Laws of England.* Oxford: Clarendon Press, 1796.

Bibliography 221

Boole, Katherine Louise. *The Juvenile Court: Its Origin, History and Procedure.* Ph.D. thesis, University of California, Berkeley, 1928.
Browne, Irving. *The Elements of Criminal Law.* Boston: Boston Book Co., 1892.
Burn's *Abridgement or the American Justice.* Dover, N.H.: 1792.
Chitty, D. *A Practical Treatise on the Criminal Law.* London: A. J. Calpy, 1816.
Christoph, James B. *Capital Punishment and British Politics.* London: George Allen and Unwin, 1962.
Hibbert, Christopher. *The Roots of Evil.* New York: Little, Brown, 1955.
Hurley, Timothy D. *Origin of the Illinois Juvenile Court Law.* Chicago: The Visitation and Aid Society, 1907.
Koestler, Arthur. *Reflections on Hanging.* London: Victor Gollancz, 1955.
Lou, Herbert H. *Juvenile Courts in the United States.* Chapel Hill: University of North Carolina Press, 1927.
Radzinowicz, Leon. *A History of English Criminal Law and Its Administration from 1750: The Movement for Reform 1750–1833.* New York: Macmillan, 1948.
Russell, William Oldnall. *A Treatise on Crime and Misdemeanors,* 2 vols. London: Joseph Butterworth, 1819.
Tappan, Paul W. *Juvenile Delinquency.* New York: McGraw-Hill, 1949.

Articles:

Knell, B. E. F. "Capital Punishment: Its Administration in Relation to Juvenile Offenders in the Nineteenth Century and Its Possible Administration in the Eighteenth." *British Journal of Delinquency* 5 (1965): 198–207.
Mack, Julian W. "The Juvenile Court." *Harvard Law Review* 23 (1909): 104–22.
Sanders, Wiley B. "Some Early Beginnings of the Children's Court Movement in England." *National Probation Association Yearbook* 39 (1945): 58–70.
Schramm, Gustav L. "The Juvenile Court Idea." *Federal Probation* 13 (September, 1949): 19–23.

Cases:

Angelo v. People, 96 Ill. 209 (1880).
Commonwealth v. Elliot, 4 Law Rep. 329 (1842).
Godfrey v. State, 31 Ala. 323 (1858).
People v. Davis, 1 *Wheeler Criminal Law Cases* 230 (1823).
People v. Teller, 1 *Wheeler Criminal Law Cases* 231 (1823).

R. v. Owen, 4 C. & P. 236 (1830).

R. v. Smith, 1 Cox 260 (1845).

Stage's Case, 5 *City-Hall Recorder* (New York City) 177 (1820).

State v. Aaron, 4 N.J.L. 263 (1818).

State v. Adams, 76 Mo. 355 (1882).

State v. Bostick, 4 Del. 563 (1845).

State v. Doherty, 2 Tenn. 79 (1806).

State v. Guild, 10 N.J.L. 163 (1828).

State v. Learnard, 41 Vt. 585 (1869).

State v. Toney, 15 S.C. 409 (1881).

Walker's Case, 5 *City-Hall Recorder* (New York City) 137 (1820).

Index